HONOR BY FIRE

HONOR

BY

FIRE

JAPANESE AMERICANS
AT WAR IN EUROPE
AND THE PACIFIC

LYN CROST

★

PRESIDIO

Published by Presidio Press
505 B San Marin Dr., Suite 300
Novato, CA 94945-1340

Library of Congress Cataloging-in-Publication Data

Crost, Lyn.
    Honor by fire : Japanese Americans at war in Europe and the
Pacific / Lyn Crost.
        p.   cm.
    Includes bibliographical references and index.
    ISBN 0-89141-521-1
    1. World War, 1939–1945—Japanese Americans. 2. World War,
1939–1945—Campaigns. 3. Japanese Americans—History—20th
century.
    I. Title.
    D753.8.C76 1994
    940.54'04—dc20   94-16319
                                     CIP

Maps of the European theater are from *The Story of the 442nd Combat Team,*
compiled by members of the 442nd Combat Team and published in 1945 by
Information-Education Section, Mediterranean Theater of Operations, USA
(MTOUSA). The map of Burma is from *Stilwell's Command Problems,* published by the Center of Military History, U.S. Army, Washington, D.C.

Typography by ProImage

Printed in the United States of America

To my grandmother,
Elizabeth Barry Welch
(1867–1947)

CONTENTS

ACKNOWLEDGMENTS

In assembling this record of Japanese-American military service during World War II, I must first acknowledge that its completion is due to the help of three men:

Tom Kawaguchi, veteran of the 442nd Regimental Combat Team and a founder of the National Japanese American Historical Society, who realized from the beginning the necessity of compiling the worldwide record of the Nisei during that war.

Ted Tsukiyama, veteran of the Military Intelligence Service (MIS), without whose encouragement this history might never have been written.

Thomas Whital Stern, my husband, whose wise counsel, encouragement, and patience kept me going during the months of research through correspondence, long-distance phone calls, and interviews.

While gathering information, I found that books by men who served in the 100th/442nd Regimental Combat Team or the Military Intelligence Service provided the most graphic accounts of Nisei activities during the war. *Bridge of Love,* by my friend of many years, John Tsukano, conveys the feelings and reaction of the Nisei under fire in a well-documented history of the 100th/442nd Regimental Combat Team.

Chester Tanaka's *Go For Broke* made many battles come alive with pictures and graphic accounts. I am also indebted to Chet for providing the title for this book: *Honor By Fire.*

Tom Ige's *Boy from Kahaluu* provided a personal glimpse of the feelings and anguish of a Nisei serving with an army invading the country of his ancestors, Okinawa.

Paul Bannai, on behalf of the MIS Club of Southern California, gave me permission to use excerpts from the book edited by Tad Ichinokuchi: *John Aiso and the M. I. S.*

Even before censorship was lifted in 1972 on activities of the MIS Nisei, the late Richard Oguro began compiling a history of their service for his book *Senpai Gumi.* It has been an invaluable guide throughout my work, and I am deeply grateful to his widow, Doris Oguro, for permission to use its material.

Dr. Clifford Uyeda, president of the National Japanese American Historical Society, and Harry Fukuhara, president of the MIS Association of Northern California, have permitted me to draw on information from *The Pacific War and Peace,* which was edited by both organizations and contains information not found in other references. Dr. Uyeda has also been the patient recipient of my long-distance phone calls searching for clarification and information about specific Nisei wartime service.

From the founding of the Military Intelligence Service Language School five weeks before Pearl Harbor was bombed until his retirement more than three decades later from the Defense Language Institute, Shigeha Kihara was a guiding light of the MIS Nisei and has always been ready to answer questions about their history for which nobody else had answers.

I deeply appreciate the permission given by Sheila Harrington to use material from *Yankee Samurai,* written by her father, the late Joseph D. Harrington.

Richard Sakakida took time to write for me an account of his undercover work in the Philippines during World War II and patiently answered my many letters and phone calls.

Minoru Hara was kind enough to meet with me in New York to review scenes of MIS activities, which his diary so graphically describes.

Grant Hirabayashi guided me through the Burma jungle fighting of Merrill's Marauders and was always ready at the other end of a telephone line to answer questions about MIS activities.

Two friends who have passed away provided information about the 100th Battalion that is not found in books. Donald Kuwaye, longtime editor of the 100th's magazine, *Puka Puka Parade,* gathered many firsthand war accounts for his publication. And Mitsuyoshi Fukuda's explanations of the 100th's battles at Cassino and elsewhere were an invaluable guide during my writing.

Dr. John Alfred Burden, the man who first called America's attention to the value of using Nisei linguists on front lines of the Pacific War, provided information about that early struggle when the Nisei were desperately trying to prove their loyalty to the United States while others were still skeptical about them.

Dr. Edward J. Drea, chief of the Research and Analysis Division, U.S. Army Center of Military History, took time from a busy schedule to advise me about military technicalities.

Hoichi Kubo was a constant inspiration: his admiration for Hawaii's Original 100th Infantry Battalion matches my own, although he was compelled to leave it and serve in the MIS because of his linguistic ability.

Over the years, Hideo Nakamine has provided information about the 522nd Field Artillery Battalion.

Other men who have patiently helped me in my search for information either in letters, telephone calls, or interviews are:

Homer Hachiya (brother of MIS Silver Star winner Frank Hachiya), Yokio Kawamoto, Larry (Shorty) Kasumura, Hirano (Mike) Kiyoshi, Mike Kreskosky, James Maeda, Stanley Nakamoto, Charles Nishimura, Sagie Nishioka, Mamoru Noji, Ben Tamashiro, Walter Tanaka, Billy Taylor, Mike Tokunaga, Roy Uyehata, and Taro Yoshihashi.

My guide through all this has been Joan Griffin, senior editor of Presidio Press, who patiently edited my manuscript, bringing it through the minefields of repetition and other fallacies, and Dale Wilson, executive editor of Presidio Press, who, along with publisher Bob Kane, believed that the history of Japanese Americans in both Europe and the Pacific throughout World War II should be told.

In such a broad account I have concentrated on the most important military engagements and may be guilty of errors or of neglecting battles that should have been included. I also may have inadvertently omitted names that belong here. For that I apologize. I talked to hundreds of Japanese Americans who served in the 100th/442nd Regimental Combat Team during World War II. Few are mentioned here, but the memory of their spirit and loyalty has been the inspiration for this book. I wanted to combine their history and that of Japanese Americans who served with the MIS in order to provide at least a glimpse of the global activities of the Nisei during World War II.

PREFACE

They have been my friends for the past half century. If I were hurt or in desperate need, they would be there still—I know that. For they are among the most faithful, the most caring, and yet the most modest in light of what they have done. They are the Japanese-American soldiers who fought in World War II. I met hundreds of them on the battlefields of Europe and in the big hospitals of Italy where they lay wounded, hurting, yet still cheerful, calling out to a general—this time Brig. Gen. Ralph C. Tobin: "Hey, General! I'll be back on the line in ten days."

I know this because General Tobin told me so as he recounted stories about them. He and Lt. Gen. Alexander M. Patch, commander of the U.S. Seventh Army, and Lt. Gen. Mark W. Clark, commander of the U.S. Fifth Army, and Maj. Gen. Charles W. Ryder, commander of the great 34th Division from the Midwest heartland of America—all wanted the Japanese-American soldiers in their commands, and each general had his treasured recollections about their indomitable courage.

That was long ago. Now, in the 1990s, I fear for them and their children because these Americans have Japanese faces. They survived the wounds of war, but now they are vulnerable to the prejudice that still exists in America, decades after the war in which they fought for this country. I cannot let this happen without trying to tell you about these Japanese-American soldiers of World War II.

It could be my friends of the Japanese-American 522nd Field Artillery Battalion, who fed prisoners from the Nazi death camp at Dachau.

It could be my friend who was in the University of Hawaii ROTC unit that helped guard Hawaii on that terrible night of December 7, 1941, when the Islands expected to be invaded by Japan. It could by my friend Dan Inouye, who wanted to be a doctor but lost his right arm fighting Germans in Italy. The names flash on and on through memory and pain.

I must tell you about these men: of the 100th Infantry Battalion, whose wounds and deaths at Monte Cassino in Italy earned the outfit the sobriquet "Purple Heart Battalion"; of the 442nd Regimental Combat Team, which followed the 100th onto European battlefields. For its size and length of service, the 100th/442nd Regimental Combat Team was the most decorated military unit in American history. The men fought together through the cold, winter-shrouded Vosges Mountains of France to rescue an enemy-surrounded battalion of Texans.

I want to tell you about the six thousand Japanese-American linguists of the Military Intelligence Service, who were on every embattled island of the Pacific, fought with Merrill's Marauders through the jungles of Burma, assisted the opposing forces of Mao Tse-tung and Chiang Kai-shek in China, worked in Pentagon offices to track changes in Japan's naval and army forces, and interpreted top-secret decoded messages between Germany and Japan. The U.S. government pledged these Japanese Americans of the Military Intelligence Service to secrecy, which endured for more than a quarter century after World War II ended, so that few know of their contributions.

I can tell you what I saw in Europe and what I have since been able to find out from men who fought in other war theaters—men who are proud of their battles for the United States of America but who are so modest that you must drag the stories out of them, or hear the accounts from others.

The story must be told. Americans do not know how hard these men fought in a war to keep democracy alive. Too few remember, or have ever known, that Americans of many colors and races fought during World War II to keep alive our freedom, our way of life. There were also segregated black units such the Tuskegee Airmen, whose courage and fighting in Europe were second to none, and the 92nd Division, which fought on Italy's Ligurian coast. Few remember them now, but they were there when they were needed. I can tell you only about the Japanese Americans because I lived and worked among them, and they became my friends.

As you walk along America's streets, do not forget that the next man or woman or child you meet whose color is different from yours may be the child or grandchild of a soldier who fought for the freedom you now enjoy. He may have been black, tan, yellow, or white. But he was, first of all, an American.

CHAPTER 1

PU'ULOA BECOMES PEARL HARBOR

For me the beginning was Hawaii, before Pearl Harbor, home to races from around the world. I had wanted to go to Ireland when I graduated from Brown University because that was the childhood home of my beloved maternal grandmother, who brought me up. But where could I get a job in a country so poor it had few jobs for its own people? So I revised my plans and headed for Hawaii to visit a Dutch aunt, my father's eldest sister, who had lived there since the turn of the century, first on the island of Molokai and later in Honolulu, on the island of Oahu. My about-face wasn't as strange as it seems. As far back as I could remember, my aunt had written to me from that faraway place. With almost every letter came pictures of streets bordered by palm trees, mountains shadowed in clouds, a house in Honolulu. If I couldn't go to Ireland, why not Hawaii? It was the gateway to the Orient. Perhaps that would be next on my agenda—maybe in a job on an English-language newspaper.

If you're "fresh off the boat" in Hawaii, you don't stand much chance of getting a job. But I was lucky. A Brown University economics professor doing a survey there for the U.S. Bureau of Labor Statistics hired me as an assistant, at a salary slightly above starvation level. So I visited sugar and pineapple plantations and the big ranches and began to learn about these Islands where East meets West, where descendants of many races had come together. After that, I got a temporary job on the *Honolulu Star-Bulletin;* then I finally found my real working home on *The Honolulu Advertiser.* Our city editor was Robert Trumbull, who later became one of the most distinguished *New York Times* foreign correspondents.

1

Short staffed, he assigned me to a bit of everything—from scrounging Waikiki for interviews with visiting celebrities to covering the Territorial Legislature.

It was a time when Japanese navy training ships were sailing the Pacific and crowds lined Hawaii's docks to see them. We didn't know that President Roosevelt had ordered the FBI to note anybody fraternizing with the crews so that they could be incarcerated if war broke out.[1] We never thought that the Islands would be Japan's target in a war. But, in usurping the independence of the Kingdom of Hawaii, the United States had paved the way for disaster.

An 1887 treaty negotiated by American businessmen in Hawaii gave the United States the exclusive right to enter the harbor of Pearl River on the island of Oahu, to establish a coaling and repair station for American vessels and to improve the entrance of the harbor. Old Hawaiians called the area, now known as Pearl Harbor, Pu'uloa (Long Hill). When news of the agreement with the United States reached Hawaiians, they took to the streets in protest. But it was futile. Pu'uloa no longer belonged to them.

At that time King Kalakaua was trying to distance his country from the United States because of increasing domination of Hawaii by American business interests, and in fact had sought to forge a relationship with Japan. In 1881, during his trip around the world, the king stopped in Japan. In private conversations with Emperor Meiji, Kalakaua proposed the formation of a federation of Asiatic nations. Nothing came of this idea, but Kalakaua was successful in another proposal, which stemmed from two of the king's worries: Hawaii needed cheap labor for its sugar plantations; and the native population, which had been ravaged by diseases brought by the white man, needed to be rejuvenated. He also believed that there was a genetic relationship between Polynesians and Japanese. As a result of these conversations between Kalakaua and Japanese officials, almost a thousand Japanese laborers immigrated to Hawaii in 1885.

The final blow to Hawaii's independence came in 1898 when the U.S. Congress accepted, by joint resolution, annexation of Hawaii as a territory. For this, American business interests, with the help of U.S. armed forces, had overthrown the legally constituted Hawaiian monarchy and made Hawaii's ruler, Queen Liliuokalani, a prisoner in her own palace. When the American flag was raised over Iolani Palace old Hawaiians wept, and their chieftains predicted that their Islands would become a target for America's enemies.

As 1941 began, no one even dreamed that Japan would be bold enough to attack Hawaii, which was called "the Gibraltar of the Pacific." It was considered impregnable. It was the guardian of America's West Coast. And it was still the playground of the Pacific. Movie moguls and their stars, the titled and untitled of Europe, the wealthy and those who had scrimped for a once-in-a-lifetime vacation, flocked to the shores of Waikiki. I used to see them as I collected news for *The Honolulu Advertiser* column "Beachcombings." I also observed that Hawaiian natives and longtime residents didn't welcome the thousands of workers who were flocking from the U.S. mainland to the Islands to build more army and navy installations. "Carpetbaggers" was what they called the newcomers, borrowing a term from the post–Civil War South.

Talk of a Japanese strike somewhere in the Pacific was increasing. Maybe it would be the Panama Canal or the Philippines. Certainly the Japanese would go into Southeast Asia. Never Hawaii! Shipping lanes between the Islands and the U.S. mainland might be affected, however, curtailing food imports. The Territory sent an emergency request to Washington, D.C., for $3.5 million so the Islands could lay in a six-months' supply of food. The request was turned down.

At the opening of the Territorial Legislature's session in Iolani Palace that spring of 1941, hula dancers put on a brilliant performance. The music was gay and loud; wine and *okolehao* flowed freely. Famous and near-famous visitors occupied front seats in the gallery. The most important legislation up for consideration was the Hawaii Defense Act, referred to locally as the "M-Day Bill," which would establish civilian agencies to deal with any Island emergency. But the legislature concentrated on more immediate local problems and, by the end of the session, the M-Day Bill remained untouched. There seemed to be no urgency. It wasn't until October that the legislature finally met in special session and passed the bill. The Pearl Harbor bombing was to be the first "emergency."

Against the backdrop of nonchalance, there was increasing concern about Japan's incursions in the Pacific. Agents of the Corps of Intelligence Police (CIP), predecessor of the Counterintelligence Corps (CIC), were searching the Islands for young Japanese-American men with superior knowledge of the Japanese language and culture. These were the descendants of the Japanese laborers brought to Hawaii as a result of Kalakaua's conversations with Japan's emperor, and the migration of Japanese that followed. The Nisei were the first-generation Japanese born in the United States of alien parents, called the Issei. Most of Hawaii's Nisei had grown up on farms, in small wooden shacks on plantations, or in concentrated urban areas, but always with strong family alliances that exposed them to the customs, traditions, language, and religions of Japan. Every day they trudged to Japanese-language school; but they also attended American public schools, where they saluted and pledged allegiance to the American flag, learned about the Pilgrim fathers and the first Thanksgiving, the American Revolution, the Declaration of Independence, and the Constitution.

By late March two CIP recruits, Arthur Komori and Richard Sakakida, were being trained to use codes and ciphers and to recognize persons who had background or information that would enhance American knowledge of Japan, its people, and, above all, its plans for aggression. The two men were told only that they would ultimately be sent to the Philippines, that their assignment would be dangerous, and that nobody except their immediate families should be informed of their mission. In April they sailed on a U.S. transport, working as deckhands in civilian clothes to conceal their involvement with American intelligence.

They landed secretly in the Philippines, where CIP officers briefed them on their assignment: to carry out counterintelligence investigation of the Japanese community in Manila and identify those connected with the Japanese military. Their cover story: they had jumped ship to escape the army draft back home. They were given keys to a post office mailbox, told to check it twice a day for instructions, and advised to register at separate hotels. From these inconspicuous beginnings, Sakakida and Komori would ultimately play highly significant roles in the Pacific struggle against Japan.

Also in that spring of 1941, a Japanese "teacher" arrived in Honolulu from Japan. This was not unusual because of Hawaii's many Japanese-language schools. Noting, however, that the "teacher" traveled on a diplomatic passport, the FBI asked *The Honolulu Advertiser* to try to find out more about him. Ray Coll, Sr., the *Advertiser*'s longtime managing editor, asked me to talk to them. "You've got such an innocent-looking face, they'll never suspect you," he said.

I went to the consulate, where Japanese officials met me with bows and hurried Japanese conversation among themselves; then they scurried off behind closed doors, leaving me in the vestibule waiting for an answer. Finally it came: the consulate didn't know anything about anyone of that description. So sorry. So much for the innocent face!

As 1941 rolled on, it became apparent that the Orient was no longer a gateway to my imagined future, so in the autumn I returned to the U.S. mainland. I was in Washington, D.C., when I heard about Japan's attack on Pearl Harbor. The breathless staccato announcements kept rolling out of my small radio.

It didn't seem real. It couldn't be happening! But the news bulletins kept coming, and I rushed to United Press headquarters to watch throughout the night as information unfolded, worse with every dispatch. As I listened I remembered my trip to the Japanese consulate: this must be what the phony "teacher" had been working on that spring. Nobody would have believed it then. And Webley Edwards, Honolulu Radio KGMB's veteran announcer, had to keep screaming into his microphone, "This is the real McCoy!" before anyone believed it now.

Japan's mission to destroy American military targets had been precisely planned so that it would be completed before Japan declared war on the United States two hours and thirty-five minutes after its first bombs fell on Hawaii. The deceit, as well as the carnage, unified a hitherto isolationist America.

Despite its carefully planned deception in attacking Pearl Harbor, however, Japan had missed its chance to occupy Hawaii and gain a foothold on American soil from which it could easily bomb the U.S. mainland. As Harry Albright points out in his book *Pearl Harbor, Japan's Fatal Blunder,* only Oahu was heavily fortified; the remaining islands of Hawaii were practically defenseless. Landing on them would have been a shoo-in. Harry Albright ought to know. He was a member of the intelligence headquarters of the Hawaiian Department of the U.S. Army, and had previously been a top reporter for the *Honolulu Star-Bulletin.*

The Japanese attack meant that, at last, FBI men could search the Japanese consulate. Honolulu police guarding the consulate spotted Consul General Nagao Kita and Vice Consul Arojiro Okuda burning secret codebooks and uncoded messages; the police grabbed the evidence. The documents spelled out, in detail, signals about movements of the Pearl Harbor fleet, which were to be sent to Japanese subs by a German national, Bernard Julius Otto Kahn.

In the investigation that followed the attack, no Hawaii resident of Japanese ancestry was ever apprehended for spying. Secretary of the Navy Frank Knox, however, leaped to that conclusion. On December 9 he flew to the Islands and was back in Washington six days later for a press conference. There he made a statement most damaging to the Japanese Americans: "I think the most effective Fifth Column work of the war was done in Hawaii, with the possible exception of Norway."

This unfounded accusation would haunt Hawaii's Japanese Americans throughout the war, as they fought Germans in Europe and crawled through Pacific island jungles to interrogate Japanese prisoners.

And so the war began. Shortly before midnight on December 7, a full lunar rainbow arched clear and vivid across Hawaiian skies. To ancient Hawaiians it had been an omen of victory.

To me, the attack on Hawaii was a challenge to get back into newspaper work. I had been working with a bevy of college professors whom President Roosevelt had called in to record the history of American preparations for war. Now men were being called up for the draft or for work in war agencies, and newspapers were beginning to hire women as news writers instead of relegating them to the women's pages. After months of haunting the National Press Club for contacts that might lead to a news job, I got lucky. Early in 1943 the Associated Press hired me to work in its Washington Bureau.

Among my Capitol Hill assignments were the offices of West Coast congressmen and Hawaii's delegate to Congress, Joseph R. Farrington, publisher of the *Honolulu Star-Bulletin.* News from these sources about the fate of Japanese Americans wasn't good: Navy Secretary Knox's accusations of sabotage in Hawaii had set off a firestorm that fanned the flame of hate lighted by Japan's attack on Pearl Harbor and fed by long-standing American suspicions of Asians. It also effectively blocked the struggle for Hawaii's statehood, which Delegate Farrington supported.

In September 1943, when Hawaii's 100th Infantry Battalion landed at Salerno, articles about this Japanese-American unit began appearing in newspapers throughout the United States. They were followed the next year by articles about the Japanese-American 442nd Regimental Combat Team when it joined the 100th Battalion in Europe. I longed to be overseas to write about these soldiers, but that seemed impossible. I was a newcomer at the AP; others, who had been there much longer, received the overseas assignments. So I waited and kept hoping. In December 1944 my dream was unexpectedly realized.

Farrington, appalled by the growing lists of Japanese-American casualties, went to France to talk to men of the 100th/442nd Regimental Combat Team. When he returned to Washington, I arranged to interview him. In the middle of his description of conditions overseas he stopped, looked at me, and said: "We have so many men from Hawaii fighting in Europe that I think my paper should have a correspondent there. Would you like the job?"

Much as I liked the AP, my answer was spontaneous: "Oh yes! I'd love it!"

In early March 1945, I finally crossed the Atlantic Ocean on the *Queen Mary*, landing in Scotland. I journeyed to England, then to Paris, France, where I reported to Supreme Headquarters, Allied Expeditionary Force (SHAEF). I spent more than seven months in Europe, then returned to Washington to become the *Star-Bulletin*'s Washington correspondent and cover the joint congressional hearings on Pearl Harbor.

Most of my time in Europe was spent with the 100th/442nd Regimental Combat Team; I left the unit only to interview men from Hawaii who were serving in other military units or to cover important events. When the war ended, the veterans had time to talk at length, describing battles they had fought, their problems, their hopes for the future.

But for Japanese Americans—for all Americans—the story starts at Pearl Harbor. Japan's attack brought the United States into the war and awakened in Japanese Americans a deep sense of obligation to the country of their birth. They were determined to have a part in defending it.

CHAPTER 2

BIRTH OF THE
LEGENDARY BATTALION

If anybody wondered what Japanese Americans would do if Japan bombed U.S. soil, Hawaii's Nisei could have told them. Hundreds belonged to the Hawaii National Guard's 298th and 299th Regiments, and when radio announcer Webley Edwards's call went out for all those on leave to report to their duty stations, they rushed through throngs of traffic to get there, crowding onto buses or the running boards of automobiles or traveling on foot if they were close enough. Other Nisei, too young or too old for army service, ran to help friends and family members who had been wounded and killed. Seventeen-year-old Daniel Inouye, rushing to help at Lunalilo School's first-aid station, looked up at the enemy planes and shouted: "You dirty Japs!"

Amid confusion and chaos, men scrambled to take up military positions. Hoichi Kubo, a medical technician on duty at Schofield Barracks, heard blasting and airplane noise around Pearl Harbor but didn't know that war had started until demands began pouring in for plasma. As he worked to distribute the needed supplies, Kubo had no way of knowing that he would end up as a linguist for the Military Intelligence Service, or that his actions in the Pacific would be rewarded with a Distinguished Service Cross.

Ted Tsukiyama, a University of Hawaii student who later became a Military Intelligence Service linguist in the China-Burma-India Theater, heard the explosions and saw a sky black with smoke. He thought: They're sure making this maneuver look real! Then he turned on a radio and heard the announcer screaming, "Take cover, get off the streets! This is the real thing!" And then came the radio announcement that all members of the university ROTC must report to their campus units immediately. Tsukiyama, now an attorney in Hawaii, recalls what happened:

> I jumped into my ROTC uniform and rushed up to the university campus. There were reports that Japanese paratroopers had landed. Our orders were to deploy and meet the enemy and delay their advance into the city. With pounding hearts, we moved to the south end of the campus and scanned for the enemy. To put it bluntly, we were scared!
>
> But not for long. As we thought of the sneak attack that morning, a wave of fury and anger swept over us. There was no doubt or decision as we advanced. It was going to be "either them or us."

Everybody who could handle a gun was needed that awful day. The ROTC was converted into the Hawaii Territorial Guard, which had been established under the emergency M-Day Act. Students were issued gas masks and round, pie-shaped helmets of World War I vintage and assigned to guard Iolani Palace and electric, water, telephone, and other utility installations. As Tsukiyama describes it:

> We were assigned to the Iwilei industrial area to guard the waterfront, the port, the fuel tanks, the cannery, the gas storage and vital installations in that area. I can still picture the silhouettes of our boys standing on those gas tanks or peering out over the harbor waters, with only a Springfield '03 in hand. . . . We were proud to be in uniform. We were serving our country in its direct hour of need.

The regular U.S. military was supported by Hawaii's National Guard, with its hundreds of Japanese-American troops, guarding the miles of coastline and what remained of the great military installations. They waited in grief, fear, and anger, but they were ready.

Early on the morning of December 8, Corp. David M. Akui of the Hawaii National Guard captured the first Japanese prisoner of war, Ens. Kazuo Sakamaki, who had commanded a malfunctioning Japanese minisub. As Sakamaki struggled out of the ocean, Nisei who were guarding the shoreline at Bellows Air Force Base surrounded him and took him prisoner. Thomas Kiyoshi Tsubota was one of the guards. He would ultimately be among the fourteen handpicked Nisei Military Intelligence Service linguists to fight with Merrill's Marauders in Burma.

Orders were soon received that changed everything for the Japanese Americans. Ted Tsukiyama remembers what happened to the university ROTC group:

> On January 19, 1942, we were summoned one early morning in the 3 or 4 A.M. darkness, and told by our commander that orders had been received that all guardsmen of Japanese ancestry would be released. . . .
>
> We made the long truck journey back to the university armory and we were honorably discharged. When we parted, our officers cried. Our fellow guardsmen, our classmates and friends for many years, they cried. And, of course, we cried. . . .
>
> To this day, I have difficulty in grasping words in the English language that can adequately and sufficiently describe our feelings that day when we were dismissed from the service of our own country only because our faces and our names resembled that of the enemy. . . . The very bottom had dropped out of our existence!
>
> We had nothing left to do but to go back to school. But nothing made sense. Not when our nation was crying for war manpower and yet we were deemed useless.[1]

By law, the Nisei could not be thrown out of the Hawaii National Guard, so military authorities did the next best thing: they put them in Schofield Barracks ("Boom Town") under armed guard and took away their rifles. There they were confined to their tents except to use the latrine, and even then they were escorted by armed guards. The Nisei endured patiently, without protest, hoping for another chance. After two days they were released to their former commands, but many were shipped to the outlying islands of Hawaii and Maui. It was during this transfer that the first Japanese Americans died. Military histories don't record the incident, but James Maeda, who later fought in Europe with the 100th Infantry Battalion, tells the story of what became known as the "Torpedo Gang," survivors of a Japanese submarine attack.

Early on the morning of January 28, 1942, the *Royal T. Frank* was steaming toward Hawaii from Honolulu in convoy with a destroyer and the motor ship *Kaiae,* which carried ammunition. The *Frank* was towing a barge loaded with ammunition. The little fleet was in the Alenuihaha Channel (one of the world's roughest passages). Shigeru Ushijima, one of the draftees, had spent the previous night on deck at the stern of the ship. . . .

At 6:55 A.M., Captain Edward Sharpe on the *Kaiae* saw the wake of the torpedo heading toward the *Frank*. The destroyer watch saw it, too, and began dropping depth charges. By this time Ushijima and his friends . . . were wide awake. They also saw the torpedo pass by. A few minutes later we heard something scrape the side of the ship. It must have been another torpedo which didn't explode. A third torpedo hit us and blew up the ship.

Ushijima said: "I had time to put on my life jacket before the torpedo hit. The explosion knocked me over on my back. When the ship started to sink we jumped into the water. The draftees who slept in the hold never made it. All of us who survived were on topside."

George Taketa said: "I was saved by a mailbag which I clutched until being picked up."

Yoshio Ogomori had returned to the hold for new clothes since he was wet from the rain that morning. Watching a dice game, he felt the nudge of the second torpedo and while going up on deck the next torpedo exploded and he found himself in the ocean and met Ushijima, who was floating.

Eight of the nine survivors of the *Royal T. Frank* joined the 100th Infantry Battalion. . . . They did not receive any Purple Hearts or other medals for their experience in the cold Hawaiian waters. However, membership in this "Torpedo Gang" is rather unique.[2]

Back in Washington, hysteria gripped the nation's leadership. A major topic of discussion during the president's cabinet meetings was the question of what to do about the Japanese in Hawaii. The president,

Navy Secretary Knox, and War Department officials at first wanted to evict everybody of Japanese descent from the Island of Oahu (where the main military installations were located) and isolate them, possibly on the island of Molokai, site of Father Damien's leper colony, or send them to concentration (internment) camps* on the mainland. Transporting them, however, meant using ships badly needed for war. It would also mean loss of the major workforce in the Islands at a time when every person was needed to rebuild military installations. There were approximately 158,000 people of Japanese descent in Hawaii— more than 35 percent of the population and the Islands' largest ethnic group. General Delos C. Emmons, who had succeeded Gen. Walter Short as commander of the army's Hawaiian Department, rejected the president's idea.

Members of Congress from the West Coast, however, were demanding that all Japanese residents of their states be evacuated. Newspapers backed their congressmen with screaming headlines. Joining the cry were nationally syndicated columnists, including one of the most influential, Westbrook Pegler. His column of February 16, 1942, demanded: "The Japanese in California should be under armed guard to the last man and woman and to hell with habeas corpus until the danger is over."

Congressional tempers were running so high that one California congressman seized a newspaper reporter by the collar and the seat of the pants and threw him into a Capitol corridor. The newsman had argued that evacuating Japanese from their homes and putting them into internment camps would violate the U.S. Constitution.

J. Edgar Hoover, director of the Federal Bureau of Investigation (FBI), called the movement a mixture of politics and hysteria and not an urgent national defense measure. But on February 19, three days after Pegler's column appeared, the president signed Executive Order 9066: 120,000 West Coast residents of Japanese descent were forced from their homes—

---

*Although the term "concentration" camp was used consistently throughout World War II by government officials—including Presidents Roosevelt and Truman, U.S. Supreme Court justices, and members of Congress—we have used the term "internment" camps to differentiate them from the camps established in Europe by Nazi Germany, except where a direct quotation is involved.

whether born in Japan or the United States, whether veterans of World War I, children, newborn babies, handicapped, or disabled. They ended up in ten internment camps surrounded by watchtowers and armed guards. They lived in tar-paper barracks, with as many as five or six people in each small room. Beds were army cots; mattresses were empty gunnysacks, which the newly arrived, bewildered people were ordered to fill with straw. The only running water, showers, and toilets were in communal bathrooms. Only Japanese and their American-born children were thus singled out. Descendants of other nations at war with the United States—Germany, Italy—were accepted as true Americans, even after German spies were caught on American soil.

The roundup in Hawaii was more selective. About fifteen hundred Japanese community leaders—such as Shinto and Buddhist priests, language-school officials, commercial fishermen, and leading business-men—were first incarcerated on Sand Island, a spit of land that lies off Honolulu, then shipped to the mainland to remain in internment camps throughout the war. (None were ever proved guilty of activi-ties injurious to the United States.)

By February 1942 the War Department classified all Japanese-American men of draft age in the United States as 4-C (enemy aliens) and for-bade them to enlist in America's armed forces. But the army had to retain men already drafted because of the antidiscrimination restric-tions of the Draft Act. So Japanese Americans did remain in the Ha-waii National Guard.

The world had gone *kapakahi,* as Hawaiians say. It was lopsided, crazy. War hysteria had resulted in the imprisonment of all Japanese on the West Coast but not in Hawaii, where they were two thousand miles closer to Japan. And the Islands still faced the threat of enemy invasion or, at least, more bombing.

By the end of May 1942 it was thought that another deadly round with the enemy was imminent. Everybody in Hawaii carried gas masks, and the streets were patrolled from sundown to sunrise. Bombers flew in from the mainland, then headed westward toward the far Pacific. Ships were streaming out of Pearl Harbor. Residents around Hono-lulu Harbor were advised to move inland. And these questions were still being asked: Would Japan's soldiers dress in U.S. Army uniforms and pass themselves off as Americans if they invaded? How loyal to America would Nisei soldiers be if the enemy landed? The obvious answer was to not take a chance—to get all Japanese-American members of the Hawaii National Guard off the Islands.

On the night of June 3, as Japan's fleet approached Midway Island, the problem became urgent: something had to be done immediately about Hawaii's Japanese-American soldiers.

On June 5, as the Japanese attack on Midway was being thwarted, Japanese-American soldiers were hurried aboard the Matson liner SS *Maui* to sail for the U.S. mainland. They were called the "Hawaiian Provisional Infantry Battalion," which didn't mean much of anything to anybody. That night 1,432 men sailed from Hawaii, all Japanese Americans except their Caucasian officers. None of the Nisei were allowed to carry guns. When they sailed out of Honolulu Harbor, the men had no idea what was going to happen to them. Few had had time to say good-bye to family or friends, and they wondered if they would ever see their beloved Islands again. They worried about what would happen to their families if the enemy landed. But there was nothing they could do, so they hid their sorrows. They broke out the cards and dice and their ubiquitous ukuleles, and made the best of a bad situation.

On June 6, when the United States announced its victory at Midway, the men on the SS *Maui* cheered. Their islands and families were safe from enemy invasion—at least for the time being. As they sailed along the California coast, after a zigzagging journey across the Pacific to escape enemy subs, they saw—for the first time—white men working the docks. They watched, amazed. At home only Asians and dark-skinned men worked the docks. When they landed at Oakland, their outfit got a new, strange name: 100th Infantry Battalion (Separate). The "separate" meant that it was not attached to any other military organization. Another puzzle: just what were they meant to be?

The West Coast was still in turmoil with the evacuation of its Japanese population to inland camps, and the trains awaiting the Nisei troops took off with all window shades down and headed in different directions. Nobody wanted trouble, and that's what might happen if onlookers caught sight of the trains' passengers, although most white people couldn't tell one Asian from another. In fact, Chinese on the West Coast were wearing badges or other types of identification announcing that they were Chinese so that they wouldn't be mistaken for Japanese and beaten.

The men of the 100th Infantry Battalion still didn't know whether they'd end up in one of those camps. But to keep up their spirits, they started new crap games in which large quantities of cash changed hands, played their ukuleles, and sang Hawaiian songs until the trainmen knew them by heart. At one stop, women handing out refreshments commented on "those nice Chinese boys"; the men listened but didn't respond. No one wanted to start a fight. Along the way they peeked around window shades, watching for the barbed wire of an internment camp. When the trains finally stopped, five days later, they had reached Camp McCoy, the big U.S. Army base near the little town of Sparta, Wisconsin. This was where they would start their training.

En route they had renamed their outfit. The 100th became the "One Puka Puka." *Puka* is the Hawaiian word for "hole," and a zero, certainly, has a hole in the middle. Everywhere they went they would take their smattering of languages: a mixture of Hawaiian, Chinese, Japanese, and a little English—where necessary. No one who was not an Islander could begin to understand it!

So the 100th Infantry Battalion began its second period of training, this time in America's Midwest, which did not share the racial intolerance of the West Coast. People were curious at first about these strange men, then grew to admire them, and invited them to their homes for meals and music and conversation. The Nisei reciprocated with luaus and barbecues. They entertained with hula dances, their "grass skirts" concocted from whatever greenery was at hand and worn over khaki pants. They added guitars to their ukulele band, plus a roster of Stephen Foster songs that they sang with pathos rivaling that of true southerners. With their usual good humor they made the best of a questionable deal—questionable because they still didn't know if the army would ever let them get into the fight.

They were a unique bunch of soldiers. More than 90 percent were sons of immigrant parents; about one-third were also citizens of Japan. Only by going through a tedious process could they rid themselves of this unwanted alliance. On intelligence tests, the battalion averaged a mere few points below the 110 demanded for officer candidate school. Their height averaged five feet four inches, well below army norms. Throughout the war they were one big headache for the Quartermaster Corps, which had to scrounge—often without success—to find clothes and boots small enough for them. Their top officers were all white men, former members of the Hawaii National Guard. Some of the officers were Island born; others had lived there so long that they were accepted as kamaainas—Island-born or old-time residents. Even officers with multiple college degrees could speak pidgin as well as privates. And—most important—everybody was "on trial" together.

Hawaii-born Lt. Col. Farrant L. Turner, the battalion commander, had been in World War I. They called him the "Old Man." He fought the army brass for fair treatment of his men and even dressed down a general for referring to them as "Japs."

Undoubtedly it was Maj. Jim Lovell, the battalion's executive officer, who knew the men best from his teaching days in Honolulu schools. Everybody in the outfit eventually had a nickname. Lovell's was simply "The Major." When his life was in danger during the war, men risked their own lives to save him. When he was wounded and hospitalized, they worried that he might never return to the battalion. And when he did return, word spread quickly throughout the battalion, via "coconut wireless": "The Major is back."

Captain Katsumi Kometani, a dentist who had sponsored an Island baseball team and a swimming team, was assigned as morale officer. He was to become confidant—father, mother, a whole family—to the men. When they were lonely or worried about families back home, they confided their troubles to Kometani. And, all too often, his was the last face they saw before they died.

One Japanese-American officer was destined to become known throughout the United States. Like many in the outfit, Spark Matsunaga had come up the hard way. His father was a plantation worker and his mother sold tofu to supplement the family income. When he won a thousand-dollar prize in a newspaper subscription contest, he left six hundred dollars of it with his parents and, with the remaining four hundred dollars, entered the University of Hawaii. During his college years he worked at a myriad of jobs to earn money: chopping wood, feeding white mice used in university nutrition experiments, training with the ROTC. He was to become a U.S. senator from the state of Hawaii and one of the most respected members of Congress.

Lieutenant Mitsuyoshi "Mits" Fukuda would ultimately be promoted to major and become the first Japanese American to command an army battalion. Like Matsunaga, Fukuda came from a poor family. His immigrant father went to work on Waialua Plantation as a carpenter. His mother, who came to Hawaii a year later, was a picture bride. When the Great Strike of 1920 was called among plantation laborers, his family hitchhiked to Honolulu, where his father got a job in a lumber mill. Fukuda would always remember walking the long, hot, dusty roads to Honolulu when he was just a toddler.

Eventually, twelve additional lieutenants were needed. Among those sent for Turner's inspection was 2d Lt. Young Oak Kim, a graduate of officers' training school. Kim was of Korean descent; knowing the historic enmity between Japan and Korea, Turner offered Kim a transfer. But Kim wanted to remain with the 100th. In time, he would become the most decorated member of the battalion, and the most popular. When Kim wore a beanie instead of a regulation cap, others copied him until Turner put a stop to it.

In between tough workouts, the battalion's baseball team took on all comers. With "Turtle" Omiya playing, they won most of the time. And, of course, these Islanders wanted to see as much as possible of the mainland. A few even got to the East Coast, where people thought they were Native American. On a trip to Washington, D.C., Mike Tokunaga found two taxi drivers debating which tribe he belonged to. When he told them he was a Japanese American, they didn't believe him, but one gave him a free ride to the next monument he wanted to visit.

The 100th Battalion probably had more unique personalities than most military units, among them the "old men"—Cyclone and Elmo. In June 1941 Cyclone (Edward T. Hirokawa) was five months short of his thirty-sixth birthday when, by some bizarre mistake, he was inducted into the U.S. Army. At that time men age twenty-seven or more were not being inducted. When the army realized its mistake, Cyclone was released and placed on reserve status. But when Pearl Harbor was bombed, Cyclone reported back for service even though, by law, he was not required to do so. He was dubbed "Cyclone" when men of Able Company learned about his boxing prowess as a contender in the Hawaii amateur bantamweight division. By the time he was evacuated from Italy, after being wounded during a Stuka dive-bomber raid, he wore a chestful of decorations.[3]

Then there was Elmo Okido, two days older than Cyclone and the oldest enlisted man in the battalion. At age twenty-one he joined the Hawaii National Guard, was released from active duty in 1940 because he was overage, but reported back for duty the day Pearl Harbor was bombed.[4]

At Camp McCoy, the 100th men didn't let Washington's suspicions of their loyalty defeat their efforts to become part of America's battle line. And their determination did not dull their sense of humor. Take their nicknames: Peep Sight had small, narrow eyes. Wah Wah was a very talkative guy. Sea Dog had been a merchant marine before entering the service. Tak Tak was anyone whose first name or surname began with "Tak." Pa-paa was an old man. Buck Teeth and Baldy need no explanation.[5]

One matter, however, had troubled the men for a long time. They didn't like being hyphenated Americans. Instead of being called "Japanese Americans" they decided they should be called Americans of Japanese Ancestry, or AJAs. If you *had* to call them Japanese Americans, they preferred it without a hyphen. They reserved the term "Japs" for the enemy. Anybody who called them that was in for a fight.

It didn't take long for the gregarious 100th men to become known in the Midwest. They were in demand for community events sponsoring war bond purchases. They marched in Wisconsin's capital, Madison. They were favored guests on the University of Wisconsin campus. And they were frequent guests, en masse, in Chicago, where they were dined, feted with receptions, and taken on sight-seeing tours. Wherever they went they made friends, but they would have to wait a long time before they got the chance to prove to the rest of the country that they were truly Americans.

Another cadre of Japanese Americans, however, was already facing the enemy in the Aleutian Islands, which Japan had invaded, and in the South Pacific.

CHAPTER 3

NISEI OF THE MIS

B y the time the 100th Infantry Battalion reached the U.S. mainland in June 1942 to train at Wisconsin's Camp McCoy, Japanese Americans of the Military Intelligence Service (MIS) had begun spreading through the Pacific to fight with a special skill of crucial importance: knowledge of the Japanese language. Hundreds were termed Kibei—American-born Japanese who received their education in Japan but returned to the United States. Most of these men were also Nisei—the first generation of Japanese born in the United States. They would be the eyes and ears of Allied forces around the world.

Those who claimed that Japanese Americans would never fight "their own people" had never heard about the MISers, as they called themselves. Japan never guessed they existed, and they remained an American weapon of utmost secrecy.

The Japanese Americans of the MIS were attached, in teams of ten, to 150 units, including the Alaska Defense Command, Dutch Harbor, Alaska; Central Pacific Command, Pearl Harbor, Hawaii; Southwest Pacific Command, Brisbane, Australia; European Command, Paris, France; CONUS (Continental U.S. Command); and PACMIRS (Pacific Military Intelligence Research Section). The Japanese Americans of the MIS served with military forces of the United States, Great Britain, Canada, Australia, New Zealand, India, and China. And they served in every major campaign and in every major battle in the Pacific.

They were at the front interrogating captives for immediate information, and in the rear interpreting captured documents. They parachuted into inaccessible areas with the troops. In radio intelligence squadrons, they monitored communications between Japanese fighter planes and towers at Japanese airfields.

Because Japan thought its language was so complicated that foreigners could never cope with it, many Japanese military communications were not coded. As a result, Nisei linguists could translate them, along with thousands of Japanese soldiers' diaries and other captured documents, to give Allied commands information about enemy plans, movements, the condition of troops, and technical descriptions of weapons. The Nisei presence at the front was also vital to learn from captured soldiers details of enemy plans that could be put to immediate use in winning battles. So they were shot at, wounded, and killed, along with other GIs.

Even before the Japanese attack on Pearl Harbor, some U.S. Army officers recognized that few Americans knew the Japanese language. With the increasing possibility of war with Japan, they set out to do something about it. The idea of a school to train Japanese-American linguists for wartime use was first conceived by Col. Carlisle C. Dusenbury and Col. Wallace Moore, backed by Col. Moses W. Pettigrew, executive officer, Intelligence Branch, G-2. Dusenbury was a former Japanese-language student; Moore's family had been missionaries in Japan. Together they planned the organization of a language school, which was approved by Col. Rufus S. Bratton, chief of the Far Eastern Section of G-2, who collaborated with Lt. Gen. Clarence R. Huebner in the final planning of the school.

To inaugurate the new school, Lt. Col. (later Lt. Gen.) John Weckerling, a linguist and a former assistant military attaché in Tokyo, was recalled from duty in Panama. His assistant was Capt. (later Col.) Kai E. Rasmussen, a West Point graduate who had also been an assistant military attaché in Tokyo. The natural place for such a school, they figured, was on the West Coast, where there were many Japanese Americans, so they headed for the Presidio of San Francisco. They managed to obtain for their use a decrepit abandoned hangar at Crissy Field. The facility was called the Fourth Army Intelligence School. Through the decades to follow it would have new locations and new names, until it became the present Defense Language Institute at the Presidio of Monterey, California, one of the most outstanding language training centers in the world, with an enrollment of three thousand students and a faculty of more than a thousand native-speaking instructors teaching twenty-five languages. But in those days before Pearl Harbor, Weckerling and Rasmussen sought only Japanese-speaking Americans for linguistic training.

To start the school was an almost insurmountable task. First, Weckerling and Rasmussen had to line up their students. In a survey of nearly four thousand Nisei, they found few advanced linguists. The Nisei had become too Americanized. There was another difficulty: Nisei who were capable of speaking conversational Japanese had no training in Japanese military vocabulary and special forms of Japanese writing.

On one of their screening tours of Nisei in military service, they found a man superbly trained in the Japanese language: John Fujio Aiso. He was a graduate cum laude of Brown University and a doctor in jurisprudence from Harvard, and had studied legal Japanese at Chuo University while working as an attorney for British businesses in Japan. The U.S. Army had been using him as an enlisted mechanic in a motor maintenance battalion, though he knew little about mechanics. Weckerling and Rasmussen chose Aiso as their director of academic training. He became the heart and soul of the new school, bringing with his language skills an understanding of the personal difficulties of the Nisei in a country at war with their ancestral land.

Weckerling and Rasmussen also discovered three highly qualified Japanese-American civilians eager to help by donating their libraries and language skills to the proposed school: Akira Oshida, Tetsuo Imagawa, and Shigeya Kihara. Kihara had a master's degree in international relations from the University of California at Berkeley. He was to serve for more than three decades as an enduring force in the development of the school into the Defense Language Institute. With these four men, Weckerling and Rasmussen began preparing a course of instruction.

The school, however, lacked everything else. The abandoned hangar was totally empty: no seats, no tables, no sleeping quarters. Textbooks were limited to the few books Weckerling and Rasmussen had brought back from Japan, and the personal collections donated by Oshida and Kihara. How were they to clean up the old hangar, furnish it, get enough textbooks, pay salaries, and provide food and beds for students on the two thousand dollars that the War Department had allowed Weckerling for his school? The answer: a lot of hard work.

They walked the streets of San Francisco seeking the lowest bids from printers to duplicate their teaching materials. They foraged bookstores and university libraries for Japanese-language texts. Using Japanese and U.S. Army manuals as references, they compiled texts on Japanese military terminology. Assisted by early arriving Nisei students, they hauled abandoned orange crates and boxes to the hangar for use as chairs and desks. Wooden partitions were built up to separate classrooms from offices and sleeping quarters. Beds were three-tiered bunks. They borrowed typewriters and other supplies. Finally, on November 1, 1941, the Fourth Army Intelligence School welcomed its first sixty students: two Caucasians who wanted to brush up on their Japanese-language skills, and fifty-eight Nisei, of whom fifteen were soon dropped because they failed to meet requirements. The first class was scheduled to graduate in one year.

Thirty-six days after classes began, Pearl Harbor was bombed; the War Department issued orders that no Nisei would be allowed to serve overseas. This policy would have eliminated the use of Japanese-American linguists to assist the U.S. Army, Navy, and Marine Corps commands in the Pacific, thereby hampering field intelligence agencies. Knowledgeable War Department officers, including Colonel Pettigrew, fought back. As a result, the order was rescinded, and the new school was allowed to proceed with its plans.

Pressure for Japanese linguists soon began, and the school pushed its courses at top speed. Even before the first commencement, rescheduled for May 1942, teams of Nisei had left for the Pacific. Yoshio Hotta led a five-man Nisei linguist team to the Aleutian Islands. Captain John Alfred Burden, a doctor from Hawaii who had been raised in Japan and was one of the school's two Caucasian graduates, led two Nisei to Fiji. The other Caucasian graduate, Maj. E. David Swift, the son of missionary parents in Japan, was rushed to Australia with a group of Nisei; they would become the first team to work in the Allied Translator and Interpreter Section (ATIS), which Swift helped form. Sergeant Mac Nagata was sent to New Caledonia to work with the Americal Division, commanded by Maj. Gen. Alexander M. Patch. Some American military officers unaccustomed to Nisei linguists among their troops didn't know what to do with them. Masanori Minamoto reported to Tonga in April 1942, only to be assigned as a truck driver; Tateshi Miyasaki followed him there and was made a general's jeep driver. Eventually, graduates from subsequent classes would be sent all over the world.

When the West Coast military commander, Lt. Gen. John L. DeWitt, complying with President Roosevelt's Executive Order 9066, issued commands removing everyone of Japanese ancestry from the West Coast, the language school students found themselves in an awkward position. If they ventured onto San Francisco's streets, they risked being attacked. So they remained within the sanctuary of the Presidio, preparing to defend the very people who would have threatened them.

Weckerling was soon recalled to Washington to serve in the army's Intelligence Section, and Rasmussen remained in charge of the school. Meanwhile, the army was seeking new quarters for its language school because of increasing attendance and the hostility toward Japanese Americans on the West Coast. Except for Governor Harold Stassen of Minnesota, western state governors rejected the transfer of Japanese to their areas. So the Fourth Army Intelligence School moved to Camp Savage in Minnesota, the "Gopher State." The site had been a Civilian Conservation Corps center and, later, a shelter for homeless men. The War Department assumed control of the institution and renamed it the Military Intelligence Service Language School (MISLS). One of its students, Chris Ishii, a former Disney Studio artist, designed a logo in honor of Minnesota's state animal: a snarling gopher ready to fight. (Before war's end, the school would move to Fort Snelling, Minnesota, to accommodate its increasing enrollment.)

Thanks to continued recruitment, the school had two hundred students and fifteen instructors when it moved to Camp Savage. By then, U.S. military units were begging for the graduates, who were becoming an unheralded but indispensable part of Allied fighting forces. The pressure was on; the demands were increasing. The army found more linguists in a detachment of enlisted Japanese Americans who had been transferred from the West Coast to Midwest army centers and listed as a separate unit, the Detached Enlisted Men's List (DEML). These men had been distributed among army camps and given nonmilitary duties. Walter Tanaka, for example, was tending furnaces at Fort Custer, Michigan, when MIS recruiters found him. On the night of the attack on Pearl Harbor, he had been at Fort Ord in California, loading ammunition into machine-gun belts. He later served as an interpreter in the Fifth Air Force in Australia, New Guinea, and the Philippines, assisting Caucasian Army Air Forces officers and the Australian Naval Air Force in the interrogation of Japanese air prisoners of war.

Two of the early Nisei recruits to the Counterintelligence Police were working in the Philippines when war broke out. The Filipino Constabulary placed all Japanese in the Philippines in an evacuation center. Thus began one of the most compelling stories of World War II—that of Richard Sakakida.

Instructed to monitor activities of the detained Japanese, Sakakida also went to the evacuation center. His duty was to observe the Japanese and report back to G-2. Under an arrangement with constabulary officials, however, he was free to leave at any time. While on a shopping trip for the evacuation center, he was arrested by a constabulary agent unfamiliar with him and accused of being a spy. Fortunately, he was soon identified as a member of the U.S. Army Counterintelligence Corps and turned over to G-2.

Now wearing his U.S. Army uniform, he was ordered to Bataan. There he helped counter Japanese propaganda by broadcasting messages urging the Japanese to surrender. Having no planes to drop leaflets to the enemy, U.S. forces used lengths of old half-inch galvanized pipe to catapult messages prepared by Sakakida. Needing assistance to translate Japanese documents, Sakakida asked for Clarence Yamagata, a Nisei attorney who had been attached to the Japanese consulate in Manila.

A month before Bataan fell, Sakakida was sent to Corregidor to work in signal intelligence, deciphering Japanese codes and monitoring Japanese radio frequencies. Concerned that the Japanese might deal harshly with Japanese Americans, G-2 decided to send Sakakida and Arthur Komori to a safer spot—Australia, where MacArthur had established his new headquarters. Sakakida did not leave Corregidor, however. He requested (and received) Lt. Gen. Jonathan Wainwright's permission for Clarence Yamagata to use the plane seat that had been reserved for Sakakida. Since he had involved Yamagata in translation assignments, Sakakida felt responsible for him, and he feared that the civilian Nisei was at additional risk due to his former attachment to the Japanese consulate.

When American surrender in the Philippines seemed inevitable, Sakakida was slated to be General Wainwright's interpreter at the talks. He remembers this:

> On 6 May 1942 I was called to make a brief broadcast to Lieutenant General Masaharu Homma and the Japanese Forces over the Voice of Freedom network operating from Corregidor, stating that Brigadier General Lewis C. Beebe [Lieutenant General

Wainwright's chief of staff] would depart for Cabcaben, Bataan, to make necessary surrender arrangements. I was included in the party and we headed for Bataan. At our destination we were met by Japanese soldiers. Each individual's identity was demanded. A sergeant came up to me. . . . He knew that I was a Nisei who had been making the various Japanese language propaganda broadcasts as well as interrogating the Japanese POWs. . . . He slapped me to the ground, breaking my glasses and causing cuts on my face. I was not allowed to accompany General Beebe and his staff.[1]

The Americans were returned to Corregidor to make necessary preparations for the surrender, and Sakakida destroyed his code-deciphering material. Since he was listed as a civilian on the surrender list, he checked his personal belongings to be sure nothing could be found to link him with the military. He describes his experiences during ensuing weeks:

On May 7, following the call-out of General Wainwright and his staff officers, I was called and escorted to the field office of the Commander of the Kempei Tai [military police]. My interrogation continued for two days. I repeated the story I had given the Japanese at the hotel when I first arrived in Manila: that I was a crew member but had jumped ship to avoid the military draft.[2]

Sakakida was then transferred to Bilibid Prison in Manila, where he was interrogated by the Kempei Tai for three hours each day for approximately ten days. Several former Japanese POWs testified that they had seen Sakakida wearing an American uniform. Sakakida countered this by saying he had been taken to Bataan with only the civilian clothes he was wearing and had to borrow uniforms from Americans while his civilian clothes were being washed.

The Sergeant [in charge] was unconvinced and resorted to the infamous Kempei Tai technique, tying my hands in the back and the rope thrown over the rafters to keep me dangling, barely on my toes, while undergoing the same questioning. . . . A lower ranking member of the Kempei Tai did the beating. When he realized he was not making any progress in his interrogation I was stripped and, while he continued his interrogation, the guard inflicted cigarette burns starting around my lower thighs, lower abdominal area, and ending on my private parts. . . . No matter how they tortured me, to include their water treatment [pumping the stomach full of water, then forcing regurgitation] I stuck to my story. They finally gave up.[3]

The Kempei Tai then questioned him about his citizenship. Sakakida had renounced his Japanese citizenship after joining the military in Hawaii, but he explained this to his interrogators by saying that his aged mother had disowned him and had his name removed from the family records. Having apparently convinced them, Sakakida was taken to the chief judge advocate's office in handcuffs and told that he was to serve as an interpreter there.

My activities were confined, so whenever possible I volunteered to remain at the office with the Duty Officer to take care of his needs. This gave me an opportunity to browse around the office, as well as to determine the location of classified documents. The Duty Officer was normally gone for approximately thirty minutes every three hours and this afforded me sufficient time to read over whatever classified documents were on hand. . . . I sensed that I was being accepted as their own kind. I started to receive a little more freedom around the office. They finally allowed me to maintain the incoming and outgoing document log, which gave me some free hand with the documents. The Japanese military . . . kept their documents in footlockers to make evacuation or relocation easier.[4]

With easy access to Japanese documents, Sakakida began figuring a way to transfer information to U.S. forces. The first step was to give himself the chance to be in contact with other people. He had been warned not to bring females into the judge advocate general's compound, so he arranged for a Spanish lady living nearby to visit him so that he could show her around the building. Because of this violation of rules, he was immediately transferred from his quarters in the compound to the former British Club, where other civilian employees were billeted.

The second step was to find the right contact. By this time many Filipino guerrillas had been imprisoned, including Ernesto Tupas, a sergeant in the Philippine Scouts who was assigned to G-2, U.S. Army, and had participated in the Bataan campaign. When Mrs. Tupas asked the judge advocate's office for a pass to visit her husband, Sakakida got a brilliant, but risky, idea.

> I met with Tupas to determine his interest in conducting a prison break. . . . Arrangements were made for 4 sets of Japanese uniforms and one set of the Officer of the Day uniform. On the designated night, four guerrilla members were dressed in the Japanese soldiers' uniforms, and I took the part of the Officer of the Day. We were in complete control of the prison in minutes and liberated some 500 imprisoned guerrilla members. I did not participate in the fighting. Immediately following the entry of the guerrillas into the main entrance of Muntinglupa Prison, I made my way back to Manila, to give myself adequate time for the morning Roll Call at 0600 hours. I did not want to compromise myself.
>
> I was able to provide whatever intelligence I obtained to Tupas and his group for whatever dissemination they could make for the benefit of the U.S. Forces and the Filipinos.[5]

How did Sakakida manage to avoid the strict 10 P.M. roll call so that he could help free the Filipino guerrillas? Sakakida's answer:

> The senior Japanese civilian within the dormitory I was in and who exercised his authority in having the civilian guards permit my exit from the compound following the 10 P.M. roll call was convinced that I needed to see a "comfort woman" [the Japanese term for prostitute].[6]

How did he manage to continue giving information to Filipino guerrilla forces?

> I had one native contact and we met an average of three nights a week. I never provided my information in writing. I verbally provided the contact, in detail, whatever information I had, and made sure he took notes. I had him repeat the information back to me. To assure ourselves that we were not under surveillance,

we utilized either a boat or a delivery truck. It was a small boat with only the two of us. We normally sailed on the Pasig River, pretending we were fishing. When we utilized a truck we cruised on major roadways.[7]

Sakakida started this arrangement in early 1943. Not having access to U.S. intelligence, he had no knowledge about the outcome of the information he passed on to the guerrillas. He remembers giving information that the Japanese were planning to invade Australia. A Japanese lieutenant in the judge advocate general's office was assigned to the forces preparing for the invasion. In the spring of 1943 that lieutenant returned to Manila and told how his convoy had been intercepted by U.S. forces; he was among the few survivors.

In addition to military intelligence information, including shipping schedules, Sakakida provided the guerrillas with various Civil Military Government plans, which were of importance to Filipino natives.

Sakakida also learned that there were plans to send him to Hawaii via submarine to perform intelligence work; throughout Japan's occupation of the Philippines he feared this would happen.

There was at least one attempt to trap Sakakida into revealing his military training. A Japanese warrant officer assigned to the judge advocate general's office ordered him to clean an American .45-caliber automatic. Instead of "field stripping" it in true military fashion, however, he polished the handle and barrel to a high gleam, then handed it back.[8]

Unknown to Sakakida, record of his commission as an officer in the U.S. Army waited in official files—if he survived.

Another Nisei, Yoshikazu Yamada, tended some of the first Americans wounded in the Japanese attack on the Philippines. When drafted, Yamada was a graduate student in chemistry at the University of Michigan and was attached to the army Medical Corps unit at Del Monte Air Base on northern Mindanao. The first casualty he treated was a B-17 tail-gunner who had been shot in the chest. With only two surgeons available, Yamada had a chance to use the surgical procedures he had been taught so he could replace physicians if they were wounded. As the Japanese began closing on the airfield, Yamada was shot at by both sides when Americans mistook him for the enemy.

When it became obvious that no help would be forthcoming for the small Del Monte airfield, its personnel began evacuating. Yamada suffered a severe back injury during a night evacuation and spent two months recuperating in Australia. On recovery he was assigned to the language section of the office of the director of intelligence there. He would eventually work in ATIS with graduates of the Military Intelligence Service Language School.

MacArthur had ordered the establishment of ATIS on September 19, 1942, remembering the linguistic abilities and the valuable assistance of Nisei in the Philippines. Isolated in his new command post in Australia, MacArthur badly needed information about the enemy facing the Allies in the Pacific. As Maj. Gen. Charles Willoughby, intelligence chief (G-2) for MacArthur's forces, explained:

> According to the MacArthur records . . . the Japanese had found . . . they could label their minefields, carry personal diaries, use their spoken language freely, and even handle military documents with little regard for security.[9]

MacArthur realized he would not get much intelligence help from Washington, which was concentrating on the war in Europe. Moreover, he concluded that the best way to gain knowledge of the Japanese was to employ Japanese Americans. According to Willoughby:

> MacArthur, unlike the panicky Californian authorities who insisted on herding second-generation Japanese Americans into concentration camps, had complete confidence in the Nisei. His G-2 employed hundreds of second-generation Japanese from Hawaii and California in linguist detachments, to be sent into the field with the combat forces.
>
> ATIS intelligence teams accompanied the troops in all initial landing operations. Captured maps and orders processed by ATIS revealed enemy strength and dispositions and plans of attack. Diaries contained excellent clues to the psychology and the state of morale of the Japanese troops.
>
> Other documents indicated the enemy's problems of food and supply, his order of battle, the effect of our air attacks, his relations with the natives, the relative effectiveness of Allied and Japanese weapons. . . . Spot interrogations of prisoners taken in battle were at times of such importance that they caused a shift in Allied plans of attack.

Col. Sid Mashbir, a former language student in Tokyo, must be credited with developing ATIS to a high degree of efficiency. The Japanese were not able to match MacArthur's translating services.[10]

ATIS was a comparatively insignificant organization until Col. Sidney F. Mashbir arrived on the scene on October 6, 1942. He found ATIS divided into four separate units with eight Nisei linguists, three enlisted clerks, Australian linguistic officers, guards, and maintenance detachments. There was little coordination between ATIS and the Military Intelligence Service Language School, whose graduates, as a result, were scattered throughout the Pacific. Within a few weeks after his arrival, Mashbir integrated the four units to create an inter-Allied, interservice organization. He then established a system to test each Nisei linguist, classify them according to their competency in Japanese and English, and pair Nisei who were good in Japanese but poor in English with men who were poor in Japanese but good in English. All linguists were reexamined every six months.

To rescue every scrap of captured Japanese writing for possible intelligence, Mashbir brought a paper expert from the National Bureau of Standards in Washington, D.C., to create a Document Restoration Section. There, soiled paper, some stained with blood and body excreta, was cleaned and scientifically treated to make it readable. In addition to diaries and personal effects found on dead or captured Japanese soldiers, each enemy unit kept a war diary, rolls of names with rank and serial numbers, intelligence papers, pay books, and postal savings books.

By the end of the war, according to a report of General Willoughby's dated October 29, 1945, Nisei linguists had translated 20,598,051 pages, and ATIS had become "a field agency reaching into every Regiment, Division, Corps and Army in all our campaigns."

Mashbir had more than three thousand Nisei linguists working in and out of ATIS headquarters. They interrogated fourteen thousand prisoners, translated two million documents, and worked with front-line troops in every unit in every Pacific campaign. The remaining graduates of the MIS Language School (another three thousand) were serving in other parts of the world or were retained at the school as instructors to cope with the growing number of Japanese Americans volunteering to serve as linguists, including hundreds from the internment camps.

For linguists serving with frontline troops, ATIS devised a rotation plan: men served approximately three months with combat units, then were brought back to the rear.

Already in Australia when Mashbir arrived to take over ATIS was Arthur Komori, the CIC (formerly CIP) undercover agent who had worked in the Philippines before the war and had been evacuated on MacArthur's orders. Following Komori's advice, based on experience in handling prisoners in the Philippines and on a knowledge of Japanese psychology, ATIS established a procedure for interrogating prisoners that differed from the strict treatment given German prisoners. First, a Japanese prisoner's wounds were treated. Then he was offered a cigarette. During conversations no threats were made. The procedure succeeded. A prisoner who had worked in a Japanese naval shipyard made detailed drawings of every type of ship Japan was using. Other prisoners explained various Japanese armaments. But the work of ATIS went beyond the war itself. Its translations would be used to help convict Japanese officers who had tolerated or ordered atrocities.

Throughout the war the Nisei worried about two inescapable facts. First, the teams sent out from the Military Intelligence School were headed by Caucasian officers who usually didn't know as much Japanese as the men under their command. The conclusion was obvious: the "brass" didn't trust the Nisei but, at the same time, was willing to send them to the front to risk death from the enemy and, also, because of their Japanese faces, at the hands of American soldiers. Second, there were no significant promotions in rank for the MISers, though more than three-quarters of them had attended college. It was not until July 29, 1945, less than a month before war's end, that the War Department finally issued a "Table of Distribution," allowing some of the ATIS Nisei to be commissioned as officers.

Despite such obstacles, Mashbir built ATIS into one of the great intelligence centers of the Pacific. Teams of Nisei streamed from there to join American and Allied forces throughout the Pacific. Many wound up on New Guinea, where they participated in one of the longest and most torturous campaigns of the war.

CHAPTER 4

THE KILLING FIELDS OF NEW GUINEA

I t was inevitable that New Guinea would become one of the worst killing fields of the Pacific. Whoever occupied it could command Australia, which both Japan and the Allies needed. New Guinea was vital to Japan because it would provide a base from which the Japanese could dominate neighboring islands and disrupt Allied lines of communication. It was just as vital to the Allies for the same reasons.

By March 17, 1942, when General MacArthur arrived in Australia from the Philippines, Japan had established a fleet base at Rabaul on New Britain in the Bismarck Archipelago, bombed the northern Australian city of Darwin, and landed forces on New Guinea in hopes of securing a base for an eventual invasion of Australia.

At more than 319,713 square miles (344,927 square miles including politically attached islands), New Guinea is the world's second largest island, with jungles and rugged mountains, numerous harbors and offshore islands, and one end pointing at Australia and the other end toward the Philippines. It would take most of World War II to free it of Japanese troops, although the costly battles waged over its tortuous terrain were overshadowed by the more spectacular campaigns on Guadalcanal in the Solomon Islands and in other Pacific areas.

Throughout the long campaign to save New Guinea, the Nisei used their language skills to unmask the enemy both by interrogation of prisoners captured at the front and by translation of thousands of diaries and other documents found on dead or captured Japanese soldiers. Few prisoners were taken, because Japanese soldiers, following the Bushido custom of ancient warriors, considered it a disgrace to surrender; they would rather commit suicide. When they were hungry—indeed starving—they still refused to surrender; instead, they ate whatever they could forage and, in some instances, the flesh of dead comrades and captured enemies.

The Allied soldiers did not know their enemy because he lived and thought so differently. Although downed Japanese aircraft and captured weapons could be studied by aeronautical and weapons experts (aided by Nisei who translated instruction pamphlets), the Japanese soldier was an enigma. Since relatively few Japanese were captured, soldiers' diaries were studied assiduously after the MISers had translated them. The diaries were scrutinized not only to learn troop movements but also to understand the moral, religious, and patriotic beliefs of the enemy and his physical conditions. What might have been interesting or bizarre passages to a casual reader were, to the military, essential guides to strategy.

The Japanese hoped to launch an attack on Australia by sea from Port Moresby, New Guinea. After successive defeats at sea thwarted efforts to capture Port Moresby, the Japanese abandoned this plan and prepared to take the city by moving troops overland through the Owen Stanley Mountains. It would be one of history's most gruesome military campaigns.

Australians began their drive north from Port Moresby to meet the Japanese troops somewhere on the Kokoda Trail, which ran over a spine of jagged mountain peaks rising to more than thirteen thousand feet, shrouded in dense jungle, permeated with steep, rocky gorges through which frothing rivers cascaded to the sea. It is one of the most brutal areas in the world. In the rainy season, an inch of rain could fall in a few minutes, turning the earth into knee-deep black mud. Boots rotted off men's feet. Dampness exacerbated the misery of malaria. Jungle sores broke out on exposed limbs. Mosquitoes and other insects bit into exposed flesh.

On July 21, 1942, fourteen thousand Japanese troops began landing on the north coast of New Guinea and moving through the Owen Stanley Mountains toward Port Moresby. Eight days later they wrested from the Australians the settlement of Kokoda and its vital airstrip and prepared for their final drive on Port Moresby.

Major General Tomitaro Horii, commander of the South Seas Detachment, left for the front to take personal command of the operation. By September 14 his force had reached Imita Ridge, thirty-two miles from Port Moresby. But two days later Australian troops stopped the Japanese advance in hand-to-hand battles at Ioribaiwa. It was at this point, ten days later and almost within sight of their objective, that General Horii finally ordered a retreat over the nightmarish Kokoda Trail to the coast. During the retreat, General Horii died when the swirling current of the Kumusi River overturned the log raft he used for the crossing. What was left of Japan's South Seas Detachment was a bunch of starving men wearing blankets and rags to replace uniforms and boots that had rotted in the incessant rains and mud. Australian troops destroyed the Japanese rear guard at the Kumusi River crossing, marking a tragic end to one of the most determined and bitterly fought campaigns that Japanese soldiers would experience.

Diaries found along the Kokoda Trail began to reveal to Americans and Australians information about Japanese troops that questioning of prisoners could seldom equal. The diaries described psychological difficulties, troop strengths, strategies, morale, and the inadequate Japanese supply situation, which had left troops scrounging for anything they could find to eat. The diaries found on their bodies also expressed last thoughts, hopes, anxieties, and pathetic struggles to remain alive. They spoke of love of families back home, hate for the enemy, incessant hunger, loyalty, patriotism, loneliness, weariness, the failure of weapons and plans, their health, recurring bouts of beriberi and malaria, and, in some cases, the arrogant disregard of officers for their troops. Some diaries, found in muddy foxholes, contained poetry of exquisite and unique beauty. One Japanese trooper expressed an amusing change of esteem for the Australian soldiers:[1]

29 Aug 1942. The enemy (confronting us) is none other than AUSTRALIAN soldiers. They are a bunch of exiles. We don't think much of their strength. They are not worthy to be our enemy!

Four days later the same diarist had changed his mind:

3 Sept. These AUSTRALIANS are mighty warriors, who refuse to recognize the strength of JAPANESE might!!

Diaries showed that Japan, caught between the battles for Guadalcanal and for New Guinea, was reinforcing the latter. And orders issued to a Japanese unit for a landing on New Guinea showed the scarcity of supplies. The orders concluded with the instruction:

> Every man will carry two meals (1 mess tin of boiled rice and 1 pkg. of rice wrapped separately in cellophane) and B emergency rations and sweets for one meal. Be sure to take drinking water.

An officer's diary entry commented on the effectiveness of Allied troops:

> Reasons why the enemy's whereabouts have been discovered:
> 1. Enemy positions have been revealed by the sounds of voices and the glow of cigarettes.
> 2. The ease with which patrols can penetrate into enemy positions.
> 3. Enemy positions are deployed in all directions.
> 4. Contrary to expectations their patrols at night are most vigilant.
> The training we received in patrol work in the homeland is absolutely valueless in the jungle.

A first lieutenant captured at Sattelberg, New Guinea, in November 1943 lamented Allied air superiority and Japanese lack of rations. His diary, written at various New Guinea locations, included diagnostic comments that must have been of significance to American and Australian commanders. The Nisei translator listed them under the heading "Interesting Items":

> 1. To put it briefly, we are about a century behind Germany and America in air superiority. It is childish chatter to talk of our air superiority in China, where we opposed poorly equipped armies. You have to experience a bombing by formations of Lockheeds and North Americans, or 50 or 60 bombers to truly appreciate what air superiority means.
> 2. The present war is a war of supply. Shipping is the secret of victory or defeat.

3. Suggestion that Allied air superiority cannot be permanently maintained, usual references to the unbeatable fighting spirit of the Imperial Army. "The spirit of Satsuma is in our blood." Reference made to the bombardment of Kagoshima by the "arrogant English" in 1863. "Most hateful and cursed Americans and British."

4. Comment following Allied landing at Hopoi (3 Sep '43). "This made me actually aware of their power, both in the air and in control of the sea. Since the beginning of the campaign we have had no ships to transport men or rations. There must be a drastic change in our strategy."

5. Allied forces have severed main Japanese supply lines by landing at Nadzab (in New Guinea), the key point of our escape route. What must be the feelings of the 18 Army Commander? Our glorious colours had to be withdrawn.

6. Comment on Allied propaganda leaflet: "It was laughable. We can but visualize the enemy department, drugged by the present victories, and smile sardonically. Such an illiterate style of writing could not impress."

7. Allied roads built through the jungle are something of which their materialistic civilization might be proud.

8. We left Sio with ten days rations; this can be made to last 25 days . . . As we have no food, we fight whilst only eating grass. However we must not complain about it to our superior officers. If we only had salt and matches we could cope with anything.

Another Japanese soldier poured out his gripes about the lack of food.

17 Nov . . . You won't find many smiling faces among the men in the ranks in New Guinea. They are always hungry; every other word has something to do with eating. At the sight of potatoes their eyes gleam and their mouths water. The div comdr and the staff officers don't seem to realize that the only way the men can drag out their lives from day to day is by this endless hunt for potatoes. How can they complain about slackness and expect miracles when most of our effort goes into looking for something to eat!

You would hardly think div HQ could be misinformed. They are comparatively close to us. But there's no getting away from it. Army must think we have plenty of everything and are getting along all right. What a laugh! We have a perfect illustration in this theatre of the good old Chinese saying:

> "To hell with the boys on the firing line
> As long as the bigwigs are doing fine."

Some poems translated by Nisei were published in ATIS reports "as a matter of psychological interest." The following lines revealed the feelings of a wounded Japanese prisoner of war:

You may fall or not, flower of the cherry
The warrior falls in righteousness.

• • •

If one falls when one should,
His name is lamented to the end of time.

• • •

He doesn't want to be prisoner, and joins his hands,
And prays to be killed
The Japanese soldier.

My comrades are crossing the Seas
To the Shrine at KUDAN,*
But I, like a caged bird,
Cannot join them.

My comrades have been scattered by the wind,
But they will bloom again as flowers of KUDAN.
My name was scattered too,
But alas! I shall not come to fruition.

• • •

For my Sovereign and my Country,

---

*"Kudan" refers to the Yasukuni Shrine to the War Dead on Kudan Hill, Tokyo. "Falling" usually refers to the scattering of the petals of the cherry, which fall at the height of their beauty and do not wither on the tree, hence a simile for a soldier's death in battle.

My name was lost on the battlefield,
But I cannot lose this five-foot body of mine.
The comrades I talked with yesterday
Have become protective Gods of the Nation.
I, alas! am not yet dead,
And my carcass in enemy land, still unburied.
Without hope, without ambition, without money
I do not wish to return to my homeland,
Neither do I wish to die.

Nisei linguists were also on the front lines to question prisoners and to do spot translations of captured material in hopes of obtaining information that could be put to immediate use.

Minoru "Min" Hara tells a story of MISers on New Guinea's front lines. His team of MIS men, led by George Hayashida, a veteran of the Attu-Kiska campaigns in the Aleutian Islands, landed at Maffin Bay in the Wakde-Sarmi sector of Dutch New Guinea (now called Irian), in May 1944. There he interrogated prisoners of war, remnants of the Japanese Tenth Air Force. They couldn't retreat along the beaches because American fighter planes would strafe them, so they had walked through the jungle, each man carrying as much food as he could, plus a bag of salt and matches, which they protected from the rain and damp of the jungle by placing them in condoms. When they began dying of starvation, some men began practicing cannibalism. One man, whose right buttock was missing when he was captured, told Hara: "When I fainted, my buddy thought I was dead and chopped it off."

That was the way it was, the soldier told Hara: When a man fell on the trail, his buddies had to leave him there and keep on walking. Otherwise, they would ultimately die themselves.

Hara's notes reveal even more misfortunes of the Japanese prisoners, as well as the conditions under which the MIS men worked.[2]

Most of them were on the verge of starvation since they were all skin and bones. We made them nigri (rice balls) and told them to go easy since they haven't eaten for over a month, but some just didn't listen. I saw one of them gulp down three rice balls (bigger than our baseball) in a few minutes and I heard he died the following morning. I remember making a bathtub out of a

50-gallon drum so we could clean up one of the POWs. His physical condition was in such a poor state, from malnutrition and skin infections, washcloth could not be used since his skin peeled off and blood poured out. Fortunately for the prisoner our Field Hospital received their first supply of penicillin so I believe he survived. . . .

Our Division Command Post moved up to a forward Sector a few days later when the Japanese Forces started to lob artillery shells so we had to immediately evacuate to a safer ground. Battle of Lone Tree Hill commenced (May 1944 at Maffin Bay, Wakde-Sarmi Sector, Dutch New Guinea). . . . Enemy opposition was so intense, taking prisoners was out of the question. Besides they fought till the last man. . . . Our foxholes were about five yards from the shoreline, water started to seep in from the sea when the tide came up, tropical rain came down in torrents, had to keep our rifle and ammo above water so I held it on top of my helmet all night. We couldn't afford to stick our heads up for fear of a sniper putting a bullet between our eyes. We had to jiggle our helmets on top of our rifle barrels before standing up in the morning. Took us over a month to overrun Hill 225 for this Battle of Lone Tree Hill. Due to this stiff opposition we hardly took any prisoners. In most cases, the enemy was annihilated or pushed inland while we occupied the shoreline area anywhere from a 1/4 to 1/2 mile deep. Our backs were to the sea so all units had a front line, even our Division Headquarters. . . . We experienced constant harassment from enemy infiltrators and snipers all along the front.

It was during the Battle of Lone Tree Hill at Maffin Bay in May 1944 that TSgt. Yukitaka "Terry" Mizutari was killed when the enemy came through the jungle to infiltrate American positions near the shoreline. As a longtime dedicated leader of a MIS language team, Terry had won the affection of both his Nisei comrades and his white officers. He had been in the Hawaii National Guard when Pearl Harbor was bombed, and was a member of Hawaii's 100th Infantry Battalion before he was transferred to the Military Intelligence Service because of his language skills.

Min Hara continues the story of his detachment of MISers:

Sep 44: We sailed for our next beachhead on LSTs. Aerial photography showed no enemy troop concentrations so the few escorting destroyers did not have to bombard the beaches. Our landing at Cape Sansapor, Dutch New Guinea, was unopposed . . . Prisoners from the remnants of the 10th Japanese Air Division, totally destroyed on the ground at Hollandia, Dutch New Guinea, started to come in by the hundreds. Taiwan and Korean Labor Force prisoners came in willingly, but the die-hard Japanese had to be captured with the force of arms. We were kept busy for several weeks, interrogating and processing. The Labor Forces were being used by the Japanese Army to construct their airfields throughout the Southwest Pacific. . . .

Due to the life or death situation, cannibalism was practiced by the Japanese troops during their 500-mile trek through the dense jungles. Whenever a large group of prisoners came in, I was able to pick each and every Japanese that practiced cannibalism by just looking at their eyes. Their fierce looking eyes reminded me of a hungry Bengal Tiger. Upon interrogation, their only comment was, "It's a matter of survival." I asked several of their combat veterans if it's true that all dying soldiers shouted, "Tenno heika banzai!" (Long live the Emperor!) and their snickering answer was, "Maybe one soldier in 10,000." Another interjected, "One in 20,000 is too high!" They said all they ever heard was the word "Oka San" (mother) on their dying lips.

The scars the Nisei acquired as they fought with their language skills beside Australian and American troops were not only from physical hardships. It was painful for them to think of the treatment of their families back home. Mamoru Noji was one. Despite the fact that his family was in an internment camp, he would fight his special kind of war as a linguist with American troops on Guadalcanal and New Georgia in the Solomon Islands, at Aitape in New Guinea, and, finally, on Luzon when General MacArthur returned to the Philippines. And while he was serving in the Pacific, the American Legion post in his hometown of Hood River, Oregon, deleted from its Roll of Honor the names of Japanese-American servicemen, including that of Mamoru Noji.

This was the news from home that reached so many Nisei as they climbed mountains and fought through jungles and sailed the rough seas of the Pacific.

By 1943, Nisei linguists had spread in other directions. In the newly finished Pentagon, just outside of Washington, D.C., Jim Matsumura led a team that was feverishly translating the constant stream of reports sent from the Pacific to keep up to date the Japanese Order of Battle, a vital reference for the United States. With Matsumura were Kazuo Yamane, Seishin Kondo, and John Kenjo. Later Matsumura, who had studied in Japan and been retained initially at Camp Savage as an instructor, worked with an enlarged team of approximately fifty at Camp Ritchie, Maryland, when the Pacific Military Intelligence Research Section (PACMIRS) was created. It was a centralized agency coordinating all theater document sections. There, in the last stages of the Pacific war, Yamane discovered a crate of documents captured in Saipan and marked "routine" by navy intelligence experts at Pearl Harbor. Examination of the crate's contents was going to be delayed because of the pressure of work, but Yamane insisted on looking through it. He found a thick book listing a highly classified Japanese Imperial Army document. It turned out to be the Japanese army's ordnance inventory, listing the condition, location, and quantity of weapons, and where spare parts and other materials could be found.

Yamane remembers that he discovered the contents of the crate on a Friday, whereupon weekend liberty for the entire PACMIRS crew was canceled. Based on what they learned, strategic planners added new targets to the B-29 bombing list; when Japan finally surrendered, American occupying forces were able to proceed directly to arms caches to seize and disarm them. This was an important factor in preventing the loss of lives that surely would have occurred if the ordnance materials had been found by Japanese refusing to surrender.

Yamane, who had studied in Japan, had been a member of the 298th Regiment of the Hawaii National Guard and was on leave from Schofield Barracks when Pearl Harbor was bombed. He was among the thousands of servicemen trying to get to their posts through miles of traffic jams, which Secretary of the Navy Frank Knox and propagandists later claimed were caused by saboteurs.

The Nisei linguists were, in short, working in every possible effort and in every possible place to win the war for the United States. They had swallowed their pride, accepted the harsh rebuffs and the incarceration of their families, and pitted their unique skills and knowledge against America's enemy. But the secrecy they had to maintain denied them public acknowledgment of their deeds.

Nowhere were their contributions greater than on Guadalcanal, where, simultaneously with its efforts to conquer New Guinea, Japan had begun to build an airfield from which it planned to cut the U.S. supply line to Australia. Americans would hear urgent, daily radio reports, read hundreds of newspaper and magazine articles, and even see a movie about Guadalcanal. But nowhere did they learn that the Nisei were there, too.

CHAPTER 5

THE PROVING GROUND

Guadalcanal was a turning point in the Pacific war and a proving ground for Japanese-American Military Intelligence Service linguists. But it took the courage, training, and understanding of one man to show what the Nisei could do to help win American victories.

John Alfred Burden was one of those unique personalities who appears throughout history when they are most needed. Born in Tokyo in 1900 of missionary parents, he attended the same schools as Japanese youngsters. When he was fourteen years old, his parents gave him fifty dollars and a steamship ticket to the United States and told him to get an education. He did, supporting himself with a variety of jobs—from dishwasher to X-ray technician. Finally, at age thirty-six, he received his medical degree and, although overage, was accepted in the army reserve as a lieutenant because of his Japanese-language skills. He settled in Hawaii on the island of Maui, first as a plantation doctor and later as a doctor with an agricultural firm.

As noted earlier, when war broke out he was sent to the Fourth Army Intelligence School at San Francisco's Presidio, given a crash course in military Japanese, and graduated with the school's first class. Burden was promoted to captain and attached to the Ohio National Guard's 37th Division, which was commanded by Maj. Gen. Robert S. Beightler. He and two Japanese Americans were assigned to the general's ship, directly under the charge of Major Eagen, the assistant division G-2.

They sailed on June 6, not knowing their destination, and ended up weeks later at Suva, Fiji. To keep busy, Burden volunteered to conduct an air inspection of camouflaged gun positions. After reading Burden's report, General Beightler made him a camouflage officer, which entailed use of a Piper Cub observation aircraft and the general's aviation aide, a pilot named Thomas Lanphier (who was later one of two men credited with shooting down a plane carrying Adm. Isoroku Yamamoto, the architect of the Pearl Harbor attack). In his spare time, Lanphier also taught Burden to fly. The crusty doctor-turned-soldier was still marooned on Fiji when the United States began its battle for Guadalcanal (Operation Watchtower) on August 7, 1942.

The American invasion of Guadalcanal was one of the few times throughout the Pacific war that Nisei of the MIS did not go in with the assault troops. Although Nisei graduates of the army's language school had been rushed to the Aleutian Islands when the Japanese invaded there prior to the Battle of Midway, and pleas for linguists were streaming in from Guadalcanal, few military leaders knew that Japanese Americans were available for this job. It would be nearly two months before Major Swift, recuperating from a bout with yellow fever, would help establish ATIS in Australia as a control center for Japanese-American linguists in the Pacific. At the time of the Guadalcanal landings, most were still scattered from the Aleutians to Fiji, although some had been added to the teaching staff at the school, which had by then been relocated to Camp Savage, Minnesota.

When Australian coastwatchers and American radio intelligence reported that the Japanese were landing airfield construction crews on Guadalcanal, it became inevitable that the southern Solomon Islands would become a crucial Pacific battleground. There was little choice for either side. A Japanese airfield on Guadalcanal would threaten the Allied position in the South Pacific. On May 3, Japan had seized the island of Tulagi (opposite Guadalcanal), which was suitable for a seaplane base. However, the Japanese still needed airfields from which to launch bombers to strengthen their hold on New Guinea—thus the move to occupy Guadalcanal.

For the Americans, Guadalcanal could serve as the first step in taking the rest of the Solomon Islands and, eventually, the Japanese fleet base at Rabaul, which was a main obstacle in recovering the Philippines. The day the U.S. Marines landed, they quickly overran the airstrip on Guadalcanal. For the next four months the Americans would fight to hold it in desperate land, sea, and air battles. Japan's Korean labor force, which had completed about three-fourths of the airstrip, was taken by surprise and fled, leaving behind trucks, machinery, and supplies, which marines used to complete the job. This airstrip, renamed Henderson Field, was used by the fledgling "Cactus Air Force" of marine and army flyers in support of marines battling waves of enemy troops sent to Guadalcanal to try to recover the airfield.

The marines managed to hold it against the enemy's brutal assaults. While battles were still raging around the airstrip, indefatigable Seabees defied death to fill craters as fast as Japanese bombs and shells dug them into the earth, so that the Cactus Air Force could get off the ground. Realizing the importance of the island, the Japanese unloaded a constant stream of reinforcements to bolster the battered units fighting along the craggy, volcanic heights of "Bloody Ridge."

During the first weeks of combat on Guadalcanal, the few linguists available to the marines were Caucasians, highly competent but usually unable to understand the Japanese psyche and therefore unable to entice Japanese soldiers to surrender.

By mid-October marines were still fighting to retain command of Henderson Field. General MacArthur's warnings were incessant and urgent: if Japan captured New Guinea and Guadalcanal, Australia would be lost.

The global Anglo-American strategy had been to defeat Hitler while holding off the Japanese in the Pacific. But it had become obvious that Guadalcanal could spell the beginning of American victory or defeat in the Pacific. On October 24, 1942, President Roosevelt ordered the Joint Chiefs of Staff to get every possible weapon to the island—even if it meant a delay in commitments to Allied countries fighting in Europe and the Mediterranean.

As the battle raged on Guadalcanal, Captain Burden was still in Fiji, and Nisei graduates of the Fourth Army Intelligence School were scattered in a haphazard way throughout the Pacific, many of them wondering if they would ever get a chance to do something in this war. What happened next is described by Captain Burden:

Each member of G-2 (in Fiji) had to take their turn at night duty on the switchboard which monitored all calls coming from the West. I was on that shift one night after the Battle of Guadalcanal started when a call came through from Guadalcanal asking for a Japanese Language Officer. I knew I was the only one in the area, so I went home, packed my bag, and told my roommates I was going to Guadalcanal, but nothing happened so I unpacked.

The next night I had the Duty, the request came through marked "Urgent." I went home and packed again, but again nothing happened.

One day I saw Colonel Sears [the division G-2] talking to Admiral Nimitz. He motioned me over and introduced me to Admiral Nimitz, then said: "I understand you're looking for a Japanese Language Officer."

Nimitz said: "They are hounding me to death but I don't know where I can find one."

Sears then said: "I do."

Nimitz said: "Where?"

Sears said: "Captain Burden here is one."

Nimitz told me to pack my things and catch the first plane to Guadalcanal. I arrived the next day and reported to General Patch. I asked him to send for the Kubo brothers (Tadao and Takashi) and they arrived a few days later. Then I located Kei Kiyoshi Sakamoto (in Boro Boro) and had him transferred. An officer from the 37th who had been in Tonga told me about a Nisei on Tonga who was driving the general's jeep because they didn't know what to do with him. I sent for him and it was Tateshi Miyasaki, the first [linguist] sent out from the Presidio on a secret mission and no one had heard of him since. He was my right hand all through the Solomon Islands campaign.[1]

It was the Kubo brothers who interrogated the first Japanese pilot captured by the Americans. Burden's Nisei linguist teams translated war maps, captured documents that yielded information of immediate use in the fighting, and diaries that showed that the Japanese command was repeating on Guadalcanal what it had done on New Guinea— failing to provide its troops with sufficient supplies, including food.

Japan's navy commanders hesitated to expose their ships to American land-based planes, thus cutting off supplies for troops. One Japanese officer on Guadalcanal, however, flew to Admiral Yamamoto's flagship, which had been nicknamed "The Yamato Hotel" because of its luxurious accommodations. There he told the admiral that Japanese troops on the island were starving, eating grass to survive. Yamamoto assured the colonel that supplies would be forthcoming. But it didn't happen.[2]

Japan now planned another major attempt to recapture Guadalcanal. Z day was set for November 11, but it would be delayed a few days. Again, the Japanese navy failed to deliver necessary supplies.

Diaries taken from dead Japanese were yielding interesting facts, but Burden and his teams of MISers needed more. They needed live prisoners to interrogate about immediate Japanese plans. Burden's first break was when he was allowed to make a loudspeaker broadcast urging Japanese soldiers who had been surrounded in a gully to surrender. About a dozen did so, and the MISers were able to get information from them about their units, living conditions, and the orders they had received. It was an example of what interrogation of prisoners by Nisei linguists could do to help win the war.

As Burden remembers the situation:

> The reason the Japanese would not surrender was because they had been indoctrinated that they would be tortured by the Americans if they were captured. No one would surrender under these circumstances.
>
> I think I was successful in my broadcast because I assured them they would not be tortured but would be given food and medical care. After the first sergeant came out I asked him to do most of the broadcasting as he knew them all by name and could assure them how well he had been treated. He himself was very helpful and I took him with me on trips to examine Japanese positions. One time I had a few anxious moments. I saw him pick up a couple of hand grenades and then head for me. I held my breath but he only wanted to show me the two types of grenades the Japanese used. From then on I trusted him.[3]

While MISers on Guadalcanal were still struggling for recognition, ATIS had a major breakthrough. On Goodenough Island, off the New Guinea coast, a document of incalculable value was found.

Dr. Edward J. Drea, chief of the Research and Analysis Division of the U.S. Army Center of Military History in Washington, D.C., describes the significance of this discovery and its translation by ATIS in his book *MacArthur's Ultra.*

> [It was] the current Japanese Army List, a register of forty thousand active duty Japanese officers, by rank and assignment, as of October 15, 1942. This invaluable reference document was turned over to MacArthur's Allied Translator and Interpreter Section where Japanese linguists worked day and night to translate every name and its accompanying data. Within two months, the translation, entitled *Alphabetical List of Japanese Army Officers,* had been . . . distributed to Allied units from Alaska to India.
>
> Henceforth MacArthur's order of battle specialists could correlate the personal names of Japanese officers with specific Japanese units. . . . Comparing Japanese officers' names in deciphered communications against those in the register became a convenient and reliable means to verify an order of battle. The list filled a void because the information on Japanese formations provided to MacArthur's theater by the War Department was so elementary it was useless.[4]

The ATIS translation, which filled five volumes, covered the entire composition of the Japanese army. It was copied onto three-by-five-inch cards, which filled thirteen file drawers. Taro Yoshihashi, who was put in charge of the files, was responsible for correlating its information with advance information concerning Japanese troop movements.

Describing the value of Japanese-American linguists, Burden advised U.S. Army officials:

> The use of Nisei in the combat area is essential to efficient work. There has been a great deal of prejudice and opposition to the use of Nisei in combat areas. The two arguments advanced are: (1) Americans of Japanese ancestry are not to be trusted and (2) the lives of the Nisei would be endangered due to the strong sentiment against Japanese prevailing in the area. Both of these arguments have been thoroughly disproved by experiences on Guadalcanal and I am glad to say that those who opposed the

use of Nisei the most are now their most enthusiastic advocates. It has been proven that only the Nisei are capable of rapid translation of written orders and diaries, and their use is essential in obtaining the information contained in them.[5]

Captain Burden also experimented with psychological warfare by dropping leaflets from a plane, urging the Japanese to surrender. On one flight the plane was shot down, but Burden and the others on board managed to swim to shore.

On December 9, 1942, Lt. Gen. Alexander M. Patch, commanding general of the XIV Corps, replaced Maj. Gen. Alexander A. Vandegrift as commander on Guadalcanal. This would be Patch's first contact with Nisei linguists of the MIS; he would later carry with him to Europe his admiration for Japanese Americans. In France, the Nisei 100th/442nd Regimental Combat Team served in his Seventh Army, and later, in Germany, the Nisei 522nd Field Artillery Battalion fought with Seventh Army in the closing days of the war. Whenever the general discussed the Nisei combat units with reporters, his pride in their courage and fighting record was obvious.

On December 28, Japanese army and navy commanders informed Emperor Hirohito of their intended withdrawal from Guadalcanal. Their plan was to divide responsibility. The army would conduct the defense of the northern Solomon Islands, including Bougainville, the largest island in the chain; the navy would defend the middle Solomons and reinforce the army's defense of crucial points on New Guinea. The withdrawal took almost two months, and the Americans were unable to prevent it.

Organized resistance on Guadalcanal ceased on February 9, 1943. Thirteen thousand Japanese had escaped to fight somewhere else.

By the end of 1942, additional teams of MISers had begun landing on Guadalcanal to be shipped out with army, navy, and marines when American forces began invading the other Solomon Islands. On New Georgia, Richard Matsumoto and Shigeo Yasutake received Bronze Stars for their rapid translations of vital enemy documents that provided information essential for the success of immediate maneuvers on that island.

Kazuo Komoto led another team to New Georgia. He was wounded there and evacuated to the United States, where he had a chance to visit his young brother in an internment camp and show him his Purple Heart.[6]

Mamoru Noji had been in the final struggle for Guadalcanal, but it was during the invasion of New Georgia that he got his "real baptism of fire," and had his first "interrogation duty"—a pilot who had been shot down, an enemy he still remembers and wonders about.

"We were told that prisoners might attempt suicide," he recalls. "I tried to talk him out of any notion like that. I do not know how successful I was."[7]

Captain Burden was sent with MIS teams to Vella Lavella in the Solomons, where his right-hand man, Tateshi Miyasaki, was almost killed. Miyasaki was stripped to the waist, with no U.S. Army identification on him, when three New Zealanders mistook him for an enemy soldier. They were pointing their rifles at him when Burden yelled: "He's O.K. He's one of my boys!"

For his work in the Solomons, Burden was awarded the Silver Star, the Bronze Star, the Purple Heart with Oak Leaf Cluster (second award), and the Legion of Merit. From there he was sent back to the language school to lecture MIS students on the techniques of interrogating Japanese prisoners. He was then sent to China, where he oversaw the review of all communications from the Office of Strategic Services (OSS), the Counterintelligence Corps (CIC), and Chinese army sources. For his work there, Chiang Kai-shek personally awarded him The Order of Three White Doves.

Because of the secrecy surrounding the MISers, nothing about their activities, even those of extreme importance, could be made public. Consequently, it has remained unknown that they contributed to one of the most stunning and devastating blows to Japan's morale— the death of Admiral Yamamoto, commander in chief of Japan's Combined Fleet.

Yamamoto had gone to Japan's fleet headquarters at Rabaul on New Britain and wanted to tour Japanese bases in the Solomon Islands before leaving the area. In the late afternoon of April 13, 1943, this encoded message was sent from Rabaul to base units, air flotillas, and garrisons:

Commander in Chief Combined Fleet will personally inspect
Ballale, Shortland, and Buin on April 18. Schedule as follows:

0600 leave Rabaul in medium attack plane (escorted by six fighters); 0800 arrive Ballale and proceed immediately by subchaser to Shortland, arriving 0840. . . . 1400 leave Buin by medium attack plane; 1540 arrive Rabaul. . . . To be postponed one day in case of bad weather.

The message was intercepted and decoded by American monitors at FRUPAC (Fleet Radio Unit, Pacific), FRUMEL (Fleet Radio Unit, Melbourne), and NEGAT (a U.S. Navy radio intercept station in Washington, D.C.).[8] The message was given to Admiral Nimitz the next day, then sent to Adm. William F. Halsey's headquarters in New Caledonia, with later instructions to intercept the Yamamoto flight. Vice Admiral Marc A. Mitscher on Guadalcanal received a message from Halsey's headquarters detailing Yamamoto's travel plans and asking if fighters based there could shoot down the admiral's plane. Mitscher replied that his P-38s could, and he began making plans.

Meanwhile, Brig. Gen. Ennis Whitehead, deputy commander of the Fifth Air Force, stationed at Port Moresby, New Guinea, was confronted with a Japanese message of unknown origin that had been sent to several locations that Yamamoto was scheduled to visit. Whitehead was concerned that the original message describing Yamamoto's flight plans might be a ploy to entice American airmen into battle. The messages intercepted near Port Moresby were sent in kana, a special form of the Japanese language. They had been intercepted by Signal Corps radio operators stationed around Port Moresby. Needing an expert linguist, Whitehead contacted ATIS headquarters in Australia, and Sgt. Harold Fudenna was flown to Port Moresby.

Fudenna had recently graduated near the top of his class from the MIS Language School and was assigned to the Fifth Air Force's 1st Radio Squadron. When he arrived at Port Moresby, he was given the intercepted messages. The text was in English letters of the alphabet representing Japanese characters, but they were run together with no break between words. It was Fudenna's task to separate the Japanese kana words and translate them into English.

Early on April 18, 1943, just before American P-38s were due to take off from Guadalcanal on their hunt for Admiral Yamamoto, General Whitehead summoned Fudenna to his quarters to review the translation. The general warned Fudenna that he would hold him responsible

for its accuracy. Fudenna assured him that these new messages verified the original coded message: Yamamoto would be on the flight.
Fudenna then returned to his tent to rest. A few hours later General
Whitehead visited him to thank him for his part in the successful mission.[9]
Fudenna never received any other recognition, and the matter was
forgotten. To prevent Japan from learning that the United States had
cracked its codes, the U.S. announcement of the battle contained no
reference to Admiral Yamamoto's presence on the planes shot down.

Fudenna later was sent to the War Department in Washington, D.C.,
where he was attached to a classified air force section studying information about aircraft factories in Japan. At war's end, he was a master sergeant attached to a team that inspected aircraft factories in Japan to determine the effectiveness of American B-29 raids on critical
aircraft parts factories.

Still climbing the Solomon Islands chain, American forces, including teams of MISers and Seabees, began landing on Bougainville on
November 1, 1943. From there Americans would intensify their air
strikes against Rabaul, the Japanese South Pacific command center,
which lay 225 miles north of Bougainville. Japan was just as adamant
about its future in the Solomons. Humiliated by the defeat on Guadalcanal,
it was determined not to relinquish Bougainville.

Seabees began clearing the almost impenetrable jungle swampland
to build an airstrip. Before the enemy could hack their way through
the jungles to confront them, a marine patrol fought for nineteen days
through swampland, enemy shelling, and drenching rains to capture
the mountainous ridge overlooking strategic Empress Augusta Bay. From
there the Americans had a complete view of enemy movements in all
directions. Loss of this ridge could spell success or failure in this initial
phase of the Bougainville campaign. Living off emergency K rations,
and with low supplies of machine-gun ammunition and hand grenades,
the marines fought off enemy attempts to recapture the ridge until
November 23, when American troops were able to cross the Torokina
River, running below the ridge. Victory in this attack gave the United
States its first firm base from which to conquer the island, but it would
take many more months of bitter jungle fighting to achieve that goal.

Meanwhile, more MISers were landing on the island. Yukio Kawamoto
was one of them. Kawamoto had attended Japanese language school

as a youngster, had been tutored in the language by his mother, and had studied Japanese at the University of California before volunteering for the Military Intelligence Service. Living conditions in the jungle were hellish, recalls the retired State Department official. It rained every day except three while he was on Bougainville. Incessant dampness and the heat created skin infections—jungle rot. The men slept in hammocks covered with plastic and mosquito netting. "You find two coconut trees, string it up and you've got a bed," is how he describes it. And the mess hall: "A couple of posts with a canvas roof." From Bougainville, Kawamoto would be sent to the Philippines; finally, after twenty months of army service, he went home to get his elderly parents out of the internment camp at Topaz, Utah.[10]

The final Japanese offensive on Bougainville was launched in March 1944. The MISers' interrogation of prisoners had given American troops advance warning that the main thrust of the enemy attack would begin before dawn on March 23. In the resulting battle, five thousand Japanese were killed and three thousand wounded, while American casualties numbered one-twentieth that number. This action effectively ended combat on that island. Two MISers, T3g. Roy Uyehata and T3g. Hiroshi T. Matsuda, whose interrogation of prisoners provided the vital warning, received Bronze Stars for their performance as interrogators and translators.

A poem written by a Japanese soldier and translated by these two men was printed in *Newsweek*. One verse explains what drove the Japanese on Bougainville through the devastating enemy fire:

> To avenge our mortification on Guadalcanal
> Will be our duty true and supreme.
> Strike, strike and strike again
> Until our enemy is humbled forevermore.

While Nisei of the Military Intelligence Service were grappling with the enemy on Guadalcanal, the men of Hawaii's 100th Infantry Battalion had been struggling for a chance to fight America's enemies—*anywhere!* By the time Bougainville was conquered, the 100th had shown, on the battlefields of Italy, what Japanese Americans would do for the United States.

Getting there hadn't been easy.

CHAPTER 6

THE STRUGGLE AGAINST ODDS

From the day Hawaii's 100th Battalion arrived at Wisconsin's Camp McCoy, the men were scrutinized for signs of questionable loyalty. The FBI watched them. The U.S. Army watched them. White officers from the Islands didn't have to; they knew better.

Through all the months of uncertainty, the One Puka Puka made the best of this new land. When the men saw snow for the first time, they loved it. They rolled in it. They tried to ski and broke arms and legs. They built a snowman and decorated him with a lei of charcoal. They ice-skated, even though they fell down more than they skated.

The increasing demand for Japanese linguists caused the army's intelligence branch to raid the 100th; sixty-seven men were transferred to Camp Savage, Minnesota, for language training. Among them was Don Kuwaye, who wound up in the China-Burma-India Theater as a team leader of MISers interpreting Japanese conversations on tapped wires. (At war's end he would return to Hawaii to become executive secretary of the 100th's veterans club, editor of its magazine *Puka Puka Parade,* and one of my best friends, whose memory I cherish.)

In autumn of 1942, two officers and a group of enlisted men disappeared mysteriously from the 100th. When they reappeared about five months later, they had a strange tale to tell. It seems that bright War Department officials in Washington got the idea that Asians might have a special scent that dogs could be taught to track. This, it was believed, would help infantry men searching for Japanese in jungle areas. The Nisei GIs were sent to Cat

59

Island, near Gulfport, Mississippi, a semitropical area, complete with snakes and thick vegetation. They were to act as "bait" for the dogs in training. The dogs, however, flunked; they couldn't distinguish between the scents of Asians and Caucasians. But while the men were on this trip they made the best of it. The swimming was good. The fishing was excellent. By the time the Nisei reappeared, the 100th Battalion had been shifted to Camp Shelby in Hattiesburg, Mississippi. It was there that the battalion met up with the newly formed 442nd Regimental Combat Team.

As government officials watched the 100th during 1942, they began considering the formation of a Japanese-American combat team. One of its staunchest advocates was Elmer Davis, director of the Office of War Information (OWI), who wanted to counter the racist propaganda that Japan was spreading throughout the Orient. In a letter to President Roosevelt, dated October 2, 1942, he wrote:

> Loyal American citizens of Japanese descent should be per mitted, after individual test, to enlist in the Army and Navy. It would hardly be fair to evacuate people and then impose normal draft procedures, but voluntary enlistment would help a lot.
> This matter is of great interest to OWI. Japanese propaganda to the Philippines, Burma and elsewhere insists that this is a racial war.[1]

The White House forwarded Davis's letter to Secretary of War Henry L. Stimson, who passed it on to Assistant Secretary of War John McCloy. From there the idea went the rounds of Washington and Hawaii military offices for reaction. The final recommendation was to train a special Nisei unit somewhere other than the West Coast, and then use it in the European Theater, because its presence in the Pacific would enable the enemy to infiltrate Allied lines in disguise.

The question of a new military unit of Japanese Americans was still unresolved when McCloy visited Hawaii in late December 1942 to confer with Lt. Gen. Delos C. Emmons, chief of the army's Hawaiian Department. There, McCloy saw a unique cadre of Japanese-American college men performing the only work they had been permitted to do to help in this war. Supervised by the U.S. Army Corps of Engineers, they were digging ditches, quarrying rock, and building warehouses, roads, and barracks. The Varsity Victory Volunteers (VVV), as they called themselves, were the Japanese-American members of the University of Hawaii ROTC program—young men who had stood ready after the Pearl Harbor attack but were dismissed because they were of Japanese descent. For twenty-six days and nights following the attack, they had guarded public utilities and other strategic areas on Oahu. After their dismissal they had returned to classes, smarting from the rebuff but still wanting somehow, somewhere, to serve their country in its crisis.

Ted Tsukiyama tells the rest of their story.

A group of us were sitting under a tree at the Manoa campus one day . . . when we were approached by Hung Wai Ching, secretary of the University YMCA and, also, a member of the Morale Committee of the military governor, General Emmons. . . . I recall him asking: "You think the only thing you can do is to hold a gun?" He also said: "Don't you think there are other ways in which you can serve your country, especially when they are crying for manpower for defense?"

Hung Wai opened our minds to other options to be of service to our country and to demonstrate our loyalty. The boys decided to offer themselves as a non-combat labor battalion.

A petition to the commanding general was drawn up and signed by 169 of the university boys. It read:

"We, the undersigned, were members of the Hawaii Territorial Guard until its recent inactivation. We joined the guard voluntarily with the hope that this was one way to serve our country in her time of need.

"Needless to say, we were deeply disappointed when we were told that our services in the guard were no longer needed. Hawaii is our home, the United States is our country. We know but one loyalty and that is to the Stars and Stripes. We wish to do our part as loyal Americans in every way possible and we hereby offer ourselves for whatever service you may see fit to use us."

On February 25, 1942, General Emmons accepted our petition.

. . . [We] were now accepted as non-combat civilian laborers assigned to the 34th Engineers at Schofield Barracks.

We were armed with hammers, saws, picks, shovels and sledge hammers. We dug ammunition pits, built secondary roads, culverts, warehouses, portable field huts, iceboxes and even flytraps. One gang operated a stone quarry.

There was no rank. We wore blue dungaree uniforms, lived in Army barracks and ate three square Army chow meals per day. We got paid less than $90 per month. For 11 months we performed labor battalion work. . . . We felt trusted, accepted, useful and productive. . . . One day the quarry gang looked up from their work and there was the Assistant Secretary of the Army, John J. McCloy, with Hung Wai Ching, inspecting the quality of their quarrying work. The War Department was soon convinced. . . . A call went out for volunteers. . . . The men of VVV volunteered again.[2]

The sight of Japanese-American college men quarrying rocks because it was the only contribution they were allowed to make toward the war effort was, undoubtedly, still fresh in McCloy's memory when he returned to Washington in the last days of December. A plan for the proposed unit was approved by the army chief of staff, Gen. George C. Marshall, on January 1, 1943, and four weeks later the War Department announced its final plan for the Japanese-American unit. A call would be made for volunteers—fifteen hundred from Hawaii and three thousand from the U.S. mainland.

Three days later, in a letter to Secretary of War Stimson, President Roosevelt issued his endorsement of an all-Nisei combat team. The letter was drafted by the War Relocation Authority and includes a phrase that has been widely quoted as reflecting the president's views on America's racial minorities (contrary to his endorsement of Executive Order 9066, which paved the way for incarceration of Japanese Americans). The wording was actually inserted by Elmer Davis, chief of the Office of War Information:[3]

The principle on which this country was founded and by which it has always been governed is that Americanism is a matter of the mind and heart; Americanism is not, and never was, a matter of race or ancestry.

In answer to the army's call for fifteen hundred volunteers from Hawaii, nearly ten thousand Island Nisei rushed to recruitment depots. Overwhelmed by the response, the War Department increased the Islands' quota. Some Island Nisei who didn't make it, because of physical disabilities or because others had beaten them into the long lines of applicants, went home and cried.

Among the Islanders was young Daniel Inouye, who wanted to be a doctor. As a start, he had enrolled in a Red Cross first-aid course and obtained his certificate to teach it. On December 7, 1941, he was listening to the radio while getting dressed and heard Webley Edwards of KGMB shout into the microphone: "This is no test! This is the real McCoy. Pearl Harbor is being bombed by the Japanese."[4]

Without stopping to eat breakfast, Inouye pedaled his bike to his first-aid station, where Honolulu's dead and wounded were being taken, and worked three days and nights, catching bits of sleep when he could. Thirteen months later, when the army announced that it would form a new Nisei combat regiment, Daniel Inouye was one of the thousands who rushed to volunteer. Though he passed the physical exam, he was not included in the first list of men accepted, so he stormed the draft board wanting to know why. He was told:

> You're putting in 72 hours a week at the aid station, which we consider an essential defense contribution, and you're enrolled in a pre-med course at the University and Lord knows we'll be needing doctors. Does that clear it up for you, Inouye?

Not one to give up easily, he resigned within the hour from both the aid station and the university. Two days later the draft board ordered him to report to Schofield Barracks for induction.

When the final count was taken, 2,686 Hawaii men had been accepted for the new Nisei combat team. Inouye was number 2,685.[5]

Unlike the hurried, secret shipment of the 100th Battalion during the Battle of Midway, the whole Territory of Hawaii knew about the new cadre of Japanese-American soldiers. On March 28, 1943, the largest crowd Hawaii had ever seen gathered at Iolani Palace for a farewell ceremony.

Alien Japanese parents, however, did more than encourage their sons to fight for the United States. It went deeper than that. They had carried with them to their new land basic philosophies and values gleaned from a traditional Japanese upbringing, which they had passed on to their families.

When Dan Inouye was leaving home to report to Schofield Barracks, his father asked him: "You know what *on* means in Japanese?"

Inouye answered: "Yes. *On* is at the very heart of Japanese culture. *On* requires that when one man is aided by another he incurs a debt that is never canceled, one that must be repaid at every opportunity without stint or reservation."

"The Inouyes have great *on* for America," his father said. "It has been good to us. And now . . . it is you who must try to return the goodness of this country. You are my first son and you are very precious to your mother and to me, but you must do what must be done."[6]

Conversations like this went on in many Japanese households as parents who had been reared in the ancient customs of Japan warned their sons: Fight with honor. Die if you must. But do not bring shame on your family. *Hagi* (shame) was probably the most menacing word in the Japanese language to the young Nisei. Years later, Lt. Col. James Hanley, commander of the 442nd's 2nd Battalion, confessed that the quickest way to discipline his men was by threatening to write a letter home to the father. "*Hagi*—don't bring shame to the family. It worked every time," he said.[7]

On April 4, the Nisei boarded a train near Schofield Barracks for the ride into Honolulu and the one-mile walk from the railroad depot to Pier 11, where the *Lurline,* the prime luxury liner of the Matson Navigation Company fleet, waited. Their departure from the Islands was supposed to be secret, but thousands of relatives and friends jammed the streets to wish aloha to the rather motley crew of short, black-haired men burdened with duffel bags bulging with ukuleles, banjos, and guitars. They would carry their Hawaiian music with them wherever they went.

From the mainland internment camps, twelve hundred volunteers were also accepted. This was the beginning of the 442nd Regimental Combat Team, which began assembling at Camp Shelby. First to arrive were the mainland men. To those coming from the tarpaper barracks at the camps, the facilities at Camp Shelby looked even worse. Roofs leaked, doors hung from one hinge, floors sagged, and rain made the outdoors one great, muddy swamp. When they weren't training, the men tried to make their new home habitable.

During a mid-April cold snap the volunteers from Hawaii finally arrived, shivering in weather unlike anything they had ever experienced in the Islands. They wrapped themselves in coats, blankets—anything that was warm.

That same day, April thirteenth, General DeWitt, who had ordered removal of Japanese from the West Coast to internment camps, testified before the House Naval Affairs Subcommittee in San Francisco, saying: "A Jap's a Jap. You can't change him by giving him a piece of paper."[8]

Two days after the Island Nisei reached Camp Shelby, Mississippi's veteran congressman, John Rankin, warned the U.S. House of Representatives that Hawaii-born Japanese "are being sent into the South where we don't want them and where an invasion would surely occur if the Axis ever attempts it."

These same American-born Japanese, Rankin shouted, had formed the fifth column in Hawaii, which made Pearl Harbor possible. "Instead of sending these Jap troops into Mississippi as they are now doing, they should be put into labor battalions and be made to do manual labor."[9]

The Nisei faced another challenge in the small town of Hattiesburg: the South's "Jim Crow" laws, separating everything from bus seats to toilets into black and white. Some men flaunted the color barrier by using whatever facilities were convenient, until their Caucasian officers ordered them to use the white facilities. Although the men were generally treated like whites, there were subtle differences; at the USO gatherings, for example, few white girls would dance with them. The Nisei let it be known that they resented any type of racial segregation.

There was one white man in Hattiesburg who was different. Earl Finch was a lanky, genial local rancher who happened to meet a couple of the Nisei in town one day. He casually invited them to dinner at his home, which he shared with his mother. From that beginning grew an unprecedented friendship. Finch entertained the Nisei at his ranch and took them on excursions to New Orleans, where they stayed at the best hotels, at Finch's expense. He arranged and paid for furloughs throughout the United States. When his Nisei friends began to return wounded from overseas, Finch met them on their arrival, traveled hundreds of miles to visit them in hospitals, and entertained them at parties when they were well enough to leave the hospitals. And when the internment camps closed after the war, he helped Nisei soldiers resettle their families, many of whom left the camps penniless, having lost homes, businesses, and belongings.

To command the 442nd Regimental Combat Team, the War Department selected Col. Charles W. Pence, a man who had risen through the ranks the hard way. As an undergraduate at Indiana's DePauw University, he was not only a dedicated student but a star athlete on the university's football, baseball, and basketball teams—all while working his way through college at a variety of jobs. When he volunteered for the army in 1917 during World War I, the university gave him his degree early because of his high scholastic standing. After completing officer training he was sent overseas and was seriously wounded in France.

A quiet, steady, top tactician, Pence was professor of military science at Castle Heights Military Academy in Tennessee when he was appointed commander of the 442nd. He was to play a leading role during the combat team's action in Europe until he was wounded in France in October 1944.

The 442nd, almost as self-sufficient as a full-fledged army division, included the following units: 442nd Infantry Regiment, 522nd Field Artillery Battalion, 232nd Combat Engineer Company, 206th Army Ground Forces Band (which would also be a supporting force for the infantry), Antitank Company, Cannon Company, Medical Detachment, and Service Company.

With so many crapshooting experts from Hawaii in the outfit, the choice of a nickname for the 442nd was obvious: "Go For Broke." Its battle colors showed a fierce-looking eagle, holding arrows in one claw, an olive branch in the other claw, and the regiment's name streaming from a sharp beak. The regiment's shoulder insignia featured a hand holding the torch of liberty upright against a red, white, and blue background.

Shortly before the 442nd men began arriving at Camp Shelby, the 100th Battalion was sent to the Louisiana Maneuver Area to participate in war games with the 85th Division. In Louisiana, members of the 100th discovered the one thing that could make them run in fear: snakes. Hawaii had none, whereas Louisiana had some of the most fearsome: big water moccasins and deadly coral snakes. Coming from Hawaii, the 100th men loved nothing more than jumping into the water whenever there was a break in training. But the fastest way to empty one of Louisiana's swimming holes was for somebody to holler: "Snakes!"

By the time the 100th Battalion returned to Camp Shelby, fights between Islanders and mainlanders of the 442nd were in full swing. The two factions disliked each other intensely. Mainlanders considered the men from Hawaii inferior because of their pidgin English and happy-go-lucky ways. Islanders thought the mainlanders were "stuck-up" because of their correct English and polite manners. Mainland Nisei were nicknamed "kotonks" by Islanders—"kotonk" being the sound a mainlander's head made when it was banged against a barracks floor. Mainlanders called Islanders "buddhaheads," a term of contempt derived from the Japanese word *buta,* meaning "pig." The nicknames lasted through the battles in Europe and into the peace that followed, although the two factions finally did become friends. Sharing foxholes under fire worked wonders.

It was easy to distinguish a kotonk from a buddhahead. A haole (Caucasian) described the difference to me: "When a mainland Nisei goes into a pub he sits down and orders his drink. When a Hawaii Nisei goes to a pub he doesn't give a damn. He slaps down a wad of money and orders drinks for everybody."

Differences were put aside, however, when it came to fighting Germans; they all helped each other. Once when I complimented a kotonk on his pidgin, he explained: "I spent five days in a foxhole with a couple of buddhaheads and *had* to learn it."

Back at Camp Shelby after the Louisiana maneuvers, the 100th Battalion came under close scrutiny by a succession of top army brass, who were considering how and where to use the unit. By the summer of 1943 the Allies had beaten the Germans in tough battles in Algeria and Tunisia and controlled the Mediterranean Sea. With North Africa in Allied hands, the combined British and American forces were getting ready to launch an attack on Italy. Churchill called it "the soft underbelly of Europe" and anticipated that American and British forces might advance from Italy into the Balkans to thwart a Russian attempt to claim sovereignty there. It didn't happen that way, of course, but the British were the senior partners in the alliance and thus couldn't be ignored.

Meanwhile, army generals who had observed the 100th Battalion in Louisiana and Mississippi had reported their favorable reactions to General Marshall. In turn, he queried generals in the field, asking whether they wanted the 100th in their commands. Marshall later wrote:

> I knew that it was quite unwise and quite unfair to send them to the Southwest Pacific where they would be in contact with their own people. . . . so we sent messages to commanders in Europe and, as I recall . . . Eisenhower's staff people declined them. Then I offered them to General Clark and his reply was, "We will take anybody that will fight." So I sent this battalion [the 100th, from Hawaii] over to him. . . . Then we organized another one . . . and we finally built this up into a regiment [442nd]. . . .
>
> I will say about the Japanese fighting in these units we had: They were superb! That word correctly describes it: superb! They took terrific casualties. They showed rare courage and tremendous fighting spirit. Not too much can be said of the performance of those battalions in Europe and everybody wanted them . . . in the operations, and we used them quite dramatically in the great advance in Italy which led up to the termination of the fighting there.
>
> I thought the organization of the additional [442nd] battalions was very essential because we felt that unless we did something about the Japanese in this country, we would have a very hard time afterwards. I don't mean [with] the Army. I mean the civil population. As a matter of fact, even with their brilliant performance, some communities rather blackballed the men when they came home as veterans.[10]

So the 100th Battalion received the orders it had waited for so long: shipment overseas. The men had no way of knowing they had been rejected by Gen. Dwight D. Eisenhower but welcomed by Lt. Gen. Mark W. Clark. And they still didn't know whether they would get into the fight or just be used as rear echelon maintenance crews. They simply hoped they were getting closer to their goal.

When they marched in final review at Shelby, men of the 100th flew their battalion colors, which depicted the feathered helmet of Hawaiian chieftains and an *ape* (pronounced ah'pay) leaf, which old Hawaiians honored as a good luck sign. Flaring across the flag was the battalion motto: Remember Pearl Harbor. No one had a more valid claim to it. To Nisei from the mainland who reminded the Islanders that President Roosevelt had called December 7 "a day of infamy," the Islanders could retort: "We'll *never* forget Pearl Harbor. We were there. We saw our country being bombed. Not the president. None of you."

The 100th Battalion was headed for Camp Kilmer, New Jersey. From there, two trains with all the shades pulled down carried the men to New York, where they boarded a ferry bound for Staten Island, the bustling embarkation point. During the ferry ride a picture they had seen in newspapers and books since childhood came to life: the Statue of Liberty. They would never forget it.

At dusk on August 21, 1943, the 100th Battalion sailed from New York aboard the SS *James Parker,* which had been a peacetime tourist and banana boat. As the ship left the harbor, the men lined the rails, taking a last look at the New York skyline, many of them fingering mementos from home: a picture, a loving letter. For twelve days they sailed in a convoy of troopships, zigzagging through the Atlantic to escape Hitler's U-boats, until they finally landed at Oran, Algeria, on September 2.

Sweating under the hot North African sun, they were convoyed to a rocky, arid staging area near Fleurus, Algeria, which GIs had named "Goat Hill." They hated it. Tropical winds blew dust into everything: tents, food, rifles. Sand fleas bit them, and the itching the bites caused was horrible. The water was alkaline, so they started drinking wine, which tasted better anyway.

The 100th's big question remained unanswered. What was their assignment? As soon as the battalion was settled at Goat Hill, Colonel Turner and Major Lovell went to Oran to get the question answered at Mediterranean Base Section Headquarters. No one seemed to have any idea what to do with this unique outfit except assign it to guard duty, protecting supply depots against civilian thefts, which had been rampant in the area. Turner and Lovell battled back. The 100th, they told the assembled officers, had been trained for combat, not to guard against thieves. The following day Turner was ordered to report to Fifth Army Headquarters, where he was told that the 100th would join the 34th Infantry Division.

After this initiation to North Africa, the battalion was shifted a dozen miles away to begin its training program. Most men from Hawaii had never seen cork trees until a unit found itself in a grove of them. One Nisei blurted out: "I never know dat cork grow on trees!"

"Where did you think it grew? In bottles?" an officer asked sarcastically.

The 34th Division—a Midwest National Guard unit—had been the first American division sent overseas, initially to northern Ireland where it trained, then into the North African battles. Throughout American military history its record was one of the proudest. Forebears of its 135th Infantry Regiment were the first to answer President Lincoln's call for volunteers at the beginning of the Civil War, and had fought in more than twenty major battles.[11] It was while training in New Mexico for World War I that National Guard units from Iowa, Nebraska, Minnesota, and South Dakota were combined to form the 34th Infantry Division. Its insignia was a red bull head on a black background, from which it derived its nickname: Red Bull Division. The battalion of men from Hawaii would love this insignia for the rest of their lives.

Under the command of Maj. Gen. Charles W. Ryder, a West Pointer and veteran of World War I, the 34th had fought at Kasserine Pass and stormed Hill 609 in the fight for Tunis. The division slogan was "Attack! Attack! Attack!" Now the 2nd Battalion of the 133rd Regiment had become the military guard of General Eisenhower's headquarters. The 100th Battalion would fill the vacant spot. It was not the first time General Ryder had seen Nisei soldiers. As one of the generals sent into the Pacific immediately after the Pearl

Harbor attack, he knew the work that Nisei linguists of the MIS were doing there.

To introduce these new, strange soldiers to the 34th's men, Col. Ray C. Fountain, commander of the 133rd Regiment, told his officers:

> They are not Japanese, but Americans born in Hawaii. They aren't asking for any special consideration and we won't give them anything that isn't given all the other units. They'll be in there taking their turn with all the rest. And tell your men not to call them "Japs" or there'll be trouble.[12]

The 34th's band turned out to greet the Island men, and the Red Bulls flocked into the 100th's area. They shared bottles of wine, listened to Hawaiian songs, and began to sing them, although they stumbled on Hawaiian words. The 34th Division history says that "This enthusiasm for the 100th Battalion was to grow for the Nisei were to prove themselves one of the outstanding combat units of this war."[13]

It was the beginning of friendships that would become strong in the mountains and mud of Italy, where men of Asian and Caucasian descent would fight and die together—all Americans, with no thoughts of ancient pedigrees.

Battle-hardened Red Bulls dug in to train the newcomers, teaching them how the Germans fought the war, including sly tricks such as booby-trapping a fallen American soldier so that when his friends tried to retrieve the body they would be blown up. Grisly details like that weren't included in training back in the States, but the 34th Division men had learned such German tricks all too well.

Between workouts and training, the 100th's Aloha Team, which had been formed at Camp McCoy, started its baseball season. It didn't take long for the 34th Division to discover that the men from Hawaii were ace players, so some of them were recruited for the division team. Among them was Pfc. Yoshinao "Turtle" Omiya. The explanation for his nickname is simple: when he strapped on a catcher's protective padding it looked like a turtle's shell covering his small body. Also, he was just about the slowest runner on the team. He moved fast enough in the final game for the North Africa army baseball championship. When he got up to bat, the 34th Division had one man on first and another on second. Turtle socked a triple, driving in the two runs that won the game and the North Africa championship for the 34th Division.

The baseball season in North Africa was interrupted when the division was ordered to Oran to prepare for shipment to Italy, where British and American forces had landed at Salerno.

The Red Bulls and the 100th Battalion arrived there on September 22. Associated Press correspondent Relman "Pat" Morin filed this story:

> The first unit of American-born Japanese troops to enter an overseas combat zone went into action above the Gulf of Salerno today—all of them smiling with satisfaction.
>
> The smiles brought expressions of blank amazement from veterans and officers accustomed to seeing men enter combat with tense, drawn faces.
>
> These troops acted like they were going to a baseball game, which, incidentally, is their favorite pastime. . . .
>
> They have taken for their motto "Remember Pearl Harbor," and their smiles of anticipation were not forced today.
>
> "They are really anxious to get into action," their commander said. "I have been with them since this outfit was organized, and I would not trade my command for any other in the army. . . .
>
> "The men would rather be in the Pacific fighting the Japanese than the Germans."

Pat Morin's dispatch was the first time Americans became aware that Japanese Americans were fighting overseas. The 100th was to become a favorite among war correspondents, who loved the easygoing, good humor of these Nisei from Hawaii, and they never ceased to be astonished at the tremendous casualties they suffered.

CHAPTER 7

THE MOUNTAINS OF ITALY

M ost invasions of Italy have been from the north. Even Hannibal used that approach, moving his army through the Swiss Alps, along with a herd of elephants. But Belisarius, greatest of the Byzantine Empire's generals, launched his campaign to capture Rome from Tunisia, crossing the narrow point of the Mediterranean Sea between Africa and Sicily, then the island of Sicily and the narrow Strait of Messina, to land on the toe of the Italian boot. Until the Allied invasion of Italy, he was the only general to reach Rome (A.D. 536) from the south.

The Allies copied Belisarius. However, their operation on Sicily got off to an inauspicious start on the night of July 9–10, 1943, as paratroopers missed designated drop zones and Allied antiaircraft gunners on ships in the invasion fleet shot down Allied planes. The British sent 147 gliders from bases in North Africa, of which nearly half crashed into the sea. Only a dozen reached their assigned landing zones.

The situation on the invasion beaches the next morning exceeded expectations, but the spirited German defense in the British sector and the halfhearted efforts of the Italians in the American zone—coupled with Gen. Sir R. L. G. Alexander's often ambiguous orders—allowed the personalities of the two headstrong army commanders, the U.S. Seventh Army's Lt. Gen. George S. Patton, Jr., and the British Eighth Army's Gen. Sir Bernard Law Montgomery, to dominate the remainder of the campaign as the two generals vied for the honor of being first to reach Messina.

General Omar N. Bradley, one of Patton's subordinate commanders on Sicily, later said of the campaign: "Seldom in war has a major operation been undertaken in such a fog of indecision, confusion and conflicting plans."[1]

Unfortunately for the Allies, while Patton and Montgomery focused their attention on the port city at Sicily's northeast tip, three crack German divisions—more than a hundred thousand Axis troops altogether—managed to escape with most of their equipment across the strait to Italy, where their presence would be sorely felt in the months to come.

The next step in the Allied plan called for Montgomery's Eighth Army to cross the strait and land on the tip of the toe of the Italian boot. That operation commenced on September 3, to be followed a week later by the main attack: landings by Lt. Gen. Mark Clark's Fifth Army along a ten-mile arc of beach extending from Salerno south to Agropoli. Clark's objective was Naples, an important port and rail center in southern Italy, which the Allies needed as a base for further operations on the Italian peninsula. The Allies also hoped to cut off German forces drawn into southern Italy to contest Montgomery's landing.

On September 8, news of the Italian surrender, which had been secretly agreed to the same day Montgomery's forces began crossing the Strait of Messina, was broadcast to the world. Clark's forces, which included the British X Corps and the U.S. VI Corps, landed at Salerno the next morning, while the British 1st Airborne Division went ashore at Taranto in a hastily planned attempt to seize the Italian naval base there. It proved to be a wasted effort as the Italian fleet made a break for Malta the day before after hearing the surrender announcement.

Italy's King Victor Emmanuel III discharged Benito Mussolini from power, and Italian troops (except for some diehard Fascists in the ranks) laid down their arms and went home. Allied attention, meanwhile, shifted to preparation for a cross-Channel invasion of France, although German troops remained in control of Italy. Furthermore, they gave no indication they intended to give up. As the British Eighth Army advanced northward against minimal resistance, five German divisions raced toward Salerno to reinforce the 16th Panzer Division.

Beginning on the twelfth, the Germans launched a series of vigorous counterattacks that nearly made the forty-seven-year-old Clark's first combat operation since World War I a losing one. For nearly four days the operation's success hung in the balance. But the GIs and Tommies clinging to the beachhead fought tenaciously, and by the fifteenth the invasion site's safety was assured.

Replacements began pouring in and, after linking up with elements of Montgomery's Eighth Army, Clark began advancing toward Naples. Believing that good progress was being made, Gen. Dwight Eisenhower, the commander of Allied forces in the Mediterranean Theater, issued an order on September 26 for the offensive to continue northward, with Rome as the next objective.

The two major routes to the old imperial city were the same as they had been fourteen centuries before during Belisarius's assault. One, following the route of the ancient Via Appia, went up the west coast. The other, Via Casilina, went around the base of Monte Cassino into the Liri Valley and directly into the capital. Via Appia was known as Route 7 in modern Italy; Via Casilina had been renamed Route 6. Moving up both involved some of the most difficult fighting of the war.

As the Germans countered the Fifth Army's advance toward Naples, the bulk of their forces withdrew to the Volturno River, where they occupied the first of a series of defensive lines that soon changed the image of Churchill's "soft underbelly" of Europe into its "tough old gut."

The battles that followed ground up units, requiring a steady flow of reinforcements. Among them was the 34th Division, with its newly attached 100th Infantry Battalion, which reached Salerno on September 22.

From the SS *Frederick Funston,* on which the 100th Battalion had sailed from Oran, the men climbed into assault boats to head for shore. Still wet after wading the final few yards to the beach, the troops marched five miles to the regimental bivouac area, where two companies (E and F) were placed under Fifth Army control for use in guarding airfields and supply dumps. (This was necessary in order to reduce the size of the 100th, which was larger than a standard battalion. Heavy casualties later resulted in the 100th's Table of Organization being changed to incorporate its extra companies.)

Three days after they landed, the buddhaheads moved twenty-five miles south to Montecorvino Rovella, from which they would begin their journey through Italy. Colonel Ray C. Fountain commanded the 133rd Regimental Combat Team; General Ryder's Red Bull Division was attached to the American VI Corps, commanded by Maj. Gen. John P. Lucas.

As the 100th entered combat, Lucas, who would become one of the Nisei's most dedicated supporters and admirers, ordered this notice sent to all units under his command:

> 1. There has recently arrived in this theater a battalion of American soldiers of Japanese ancestry. The troops take particular pride in their American origin.
>
> 2. Your command should be so informed in order that during the stress and confusion of combat, cases of mistaken identity may be avoided.

The 100th Battalion finally headed into combat on September 26, first circling southeast—away from the battle raging around Naples—then north to begin the fight through terrain as treacherous as any Allied army would ever face: mountains so steep and rock encrusted that it was impossible in many places for mules to climb them or for men to dig foxholes. Mines were hidden in every conceivable place. Hundreds of hilltops provided choice locations for Germans to mount their guns for use against troops trudging through the valleys, draws, and gullies below.

The Nisei, still in summer-weight clothes and freezing, huddled deep in their coats as the trucks carrying them churned along rutted and bombed-out roads. The next day they marched through drenching rain, the heaviest of the month, and slept that night in mud. Early the following morning they were moving again, but slowly, because of heavily mined roads and bridges blown by retreating German troops. The Nisei waded across the Calore River, where the bridge was out, to reach the small town of Montemarano. There they came under the personal supervision of General Ryder, who gave them this initial indoctrination to war:

> You'll see your buddies hurt and killed, and maybe you'll get it next, but you'll keep on fighting. No matter what happens—your battalion may be blasted to company size, and your company to a platoon—you'll fill the place of the man that's hit, and you'll keep on fighting.[2]

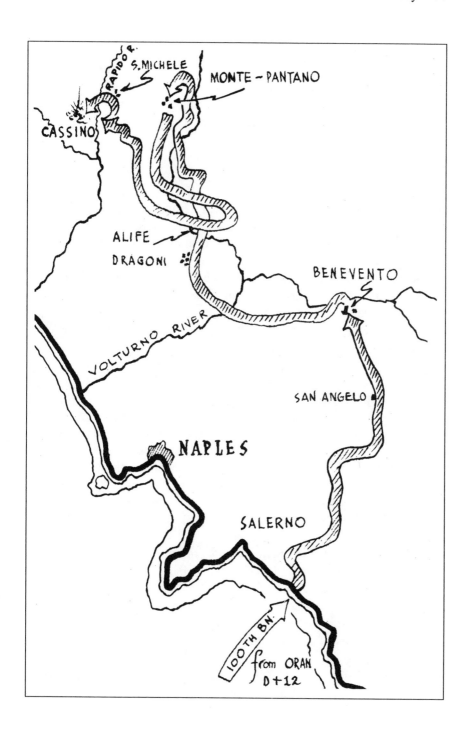

The men of the 100th Battalion slept wherever they could: in pup tents, in the remains of bomb-shattered houses, in stables. They were beginning to see the poverty and ruin that war had brought to Italy: hungry men, women, and children hovering around the edges of army encampments, waiting at garbage dumps for any food the GIs threw away, for discarded cigarette butts, for a chocolate bar that would tide a child through another day. It was all new to the Americans, and the Nisei were greatly affected by the painful sights: the wounded and dead civilians and soldiers in villages they walked through, the human and dog excrement scattered everywhere, the bombed houses, stray dogs wandering in packs looking for food, people searching for a place to sleep, their scanty belongings bundled under their arms, pushed in wheelbarrows, carried on their heads.

On September 28, in Montemarano, the Nisei met their first Wehrmacht soldier, waiting in a farmhouse and anxious to surrender his Luger pistol and a machine gun. It was the first enemy equipment the 100th captured; the men gave the Luger, a prize war relic, to Major Lovell. The prisoner was puzzled by their Asian features. Were they Chinese? he asked. When they replied that they were Japanese, he was sure that Japan had joined Germany's enemies. The Nisei also mystified German authorities, who thought the 100th Battalion was part of the Japanese army. Their language was even more of a puzzle: when Germans monitored Nisei radio transmissions, they couldn't understand their unique and inimitable pidgin. In fact, the Nisei took devilish delight in using their pidgin. Even the best professional linguist couldn't understand it if he hadn't lived in Hawaii. (Example: "*Hama hama* tommy gun *boltsu, hayaku,* eh? And *ammo mote kite kudasai.*" Translated, it means: Rush order on a tommy gun bolt and please bring up some more ammo.[3])

Later that day, still in Montemarano, the battalion suffered its first casualty. Sergeant (later 1st Lt.) Conrad C. Tsukayama, leading a mortar platoon, was hit by a fragment from an antitank mine set off by a passing jeep. Tsukayama was also the first to become a "reverse AWOL" when he left the hospital, without permission, to return to the battalion. In the many months of fighting that followed, this "reverse AWOL" by the Nisei was to become familiar to army hospital personnel throughout Europe. When they left without permission, it was always to get back to their outfits. ("Da boys need me," they'd argue.) The Nisei troops never went AWOL to avoid duty. This stemmed from their discipline, their sense of personal obligation. None of them would think of disgracing the battalion, anymore than they would their own family. They were all in this together. The shame (*haji*) of one would hurt the reputation of the battalion. No one wanted to be guilty of that.

"Sure, we all were scared," Ralph Ikeda later recalled. "But the saving grace was our 'mother hen' complex. Whenever we were caught in a machine gun cross fire or an artillery barrage we always thought 'who's going to get his now' because we somehow must keep the company together."[4]

The next day the battalion had its first battle—and its first combat death. They were heading north through Castelvetere on the Chiusano road when an enemy machine gun scattered the lead company at a bend in the road. They had to silence the gun in order to seize their objective. Sergeant Shigeo "Joe" Takata volunteered to do the job, and led a squad in a flanking movement around the gun. He was advancing toward the position alone, firing his automatic rifle, when a shell burst nearby and a piece of shrapnel hit his head. Although fatally wounded, he fought off death long enough to tell his men the location of the German gun, and they silenced it. Takata posthumously received the battalion's first battlefield award, the Distinguished Service Cross.[5]

After the war, 100th veterans would hold their annual memorial service on the Sunday nearest the date of Joe Takata's death, September 29. They never forgot this first man of the 100th Battalion to die on the battlefield.

That afternoon, near Chiusano, a company aide man, SSgt. Masaichi Goto, earned a Silver Star for gallantry when he went out under fire to treat wounded men. This would happen many more times throughout the war. If any man was in a tight spot, someone would help him. The Nisei's common background of Japanese heritage, Island birth, strong family ties, and the long months of struggling to prove themselves had molded these men into a group that was probably more homogeneous than any other Allied military outfit in World War II. The unusually close relationships worked to their advantage: no one could feel alone in this outfit.

Through torrential downpours and freezing weather the 100th moved north again to cover the advance of the rest of the 133rd Regiment. At Montefalcione, Yoshiharu Yoshida won a Silver Star for stopping a line of enemy armored cars. When he spotted the lead vehicle he let it approach to within thirty-five yards, then fired until it blew apart. The other cars turned and fled. Despite enemy shells falling around his post, he remained there to fire on any armored cars that might return. After seeing the lead vehicle demolished, none did.

With the fall of Benevento, an important rail center and road intersection, the 100th had accomplished its first major mission. Faced with the advance of Allied armies, the Germans had retreated to establish a new defense line across the peninsula, beginning below the Volturno River on the west coast and ending on the east coast at Petacciato. Opposing the Fifth Army from Benevento to the west coast was the German Tenth Army.

At the small town of Bagnoli, E and F Companies rejoined the 100th to begin replacing men who had been killed or wounded. And it was about this time that the battalion received its first praise from army authorities. The 34th Division news bulletin carried a message from General Clark to General Eisenhower praising the 100th Battalion's fighting abilities. At this time, also, General Ryder gave the 100th permission to wear the Red Bull insignia. After two years without any army "home," it was what the Nisei had been waiting for. The men of the 100th Battalion began to wear the Red Bull on helmets and uniforms, and they never stopped, not even when they later became part of the Nisei 442nd Regimental Combat Team.

The next destination was the Volturno River. Always seeming to be just up ahead, the Volturno rambles all over southern Italy. By October 10, the battalion reached a sector near Limatola, where it was held in reserve during this first crossing of the Volturno River. On the night of October 12–13, Fifth Army began its all-out assault of the Volturno on a forty-mile front, by rafts, on foot, swimming, and in small boats.[6]

Mike Tokunaga described his first Volturno crossing. "Our platoon leader told us to take off our pants and hold them on our heads to keep them dry," he told me. "So when we got to the other side there were Jerries shooting at us and I thought: My God! They'll get me with my pants down!"

Then it was on to the next crossing of the Volturno. About midnight on October 18–19, the battalion plowed through a current so swift that it swept men off their feet. The water was over the heads of shorter men and some went under, but strong Island swimmers saved them.

At these river crossings the Germans were always holding high ground, positioned to shoot down on the wet GIs struggling through the river, up the steep, slippery banks, and onto dry land from which they could shoot back. They then headed across open fields to attack the Germans entrenched in the surrounding hills and mountains.

After this second river crossing, the battalion faced the ancient villages of Alife and San Angelo d'Alife, where a tough regiment from the 3rd Panzer Grenadier Division had dug in behind mined areas and with machine-gun pits positioned to provide interlocking fire. On the path to San Angelo d'Alife, below the foothills of the Matese Mountains, the Nisei were stopped by heavy enemy fire. Caught in a murderous cross fire, many of the men were unable to defend themselves, and their friends were unable to help them. This was where the Nisei heard, for the first time, the dreaded "screaming meemies," the deadly, multibarreled Nebelwerfer rocket launchers, which they would encounter again at Cassino, and again and again at other German strongholds. No matter how often they heard the shrieking, it was terrifying.

In the battle that followed, Pfc. Thomas I. Yamanage, Browning automatic rifleman in a lead rifle squad, silenced an enemy machine gun and freed his pinned-down platoon. He killed the entire German crew but was mortally wounded. Another Distinguished Service Cross, the 100th's second such award, was posthumously awarded.

A haole (white) lieutenant, James C. Vaughn, crawled fifty yards to encourage a platoon that had become separated, then crawled another three hundred yards under intense fire to his company command post (CP), where he received orders to withdraw his platoon. Crawling back on the same route, he withdrew them and was wounded, though not before he silenced an enemy gun with his pistol. Another Silver Star.

Technician 5th Grade Satoshi Kadota, a medical aid man with a trapped unit, moved out to administer first aid to twelve wounded men and, under heavy fire, evacuated a large number of casualties. Another Silver Star.

Private Ted Shikiya, despite severe wounds, dragged a wounded man from a shelled area and was wounded again, this time fatally. Another Silver Star.

Corporal Donald Hayashi took over the command of a squad when its leader was hit, administered aid to wounded comrades, and held the position single-handedly for nearly two hours so that litter bearers could evacuate the wounded. Another Silver Star.

Trying to outflank the enemy at Alife, A and C Companies were stopped by enemy tanks. The rifles and machine guns they carried were ineffective against tanks, and they had no antitank gun. Their only possible defense was a bazooka that Pfc. Masao Awakuni carried. As the lead tank moved closer, Awakuni waited with his assistant, Pfc. Ichiro Obara, behind a stone wall. He didn't move, and the rest of the Nisei wondered if he was dead. If so, they knew they would be killed when the tank flattened their stone wall shelter. They watched the tank, fingering their useless rifles. "We were so tense and scared," Awakuni explained later. "You blink your eyes and all of a sudden it's there in front of you." But he held his fire.

When the lead tank was close enough, Awakuni finally began firing his bazooka. Before he knew it, he had fired all of his rounds. Fortunately, the other tanks turned back and were then hit by artillery fire. Three months later, on a Cassino mountainside, Awakuni hit another German tank with his bazooka and saved the lives of countless 100th men caught in the tank's sights on a lower slope. His nickname became "Tankbuster."[7]

Also significant in routing enemy forces in the fight for Alife was SSgt. Louis Sakamoto's pinpoint pitching. He responded to heavy fire from enemy positions by throwing hand grenades, one after another, until he had killed a number of Germans and forced the others to retreat. His platoon was then able to move up its mortars and devastate the rest of the troops. The skill of the Nisei baseball players had paid off on the battlefield!

It took the 100th forty-eight hours to seize Alife, but the Germans moved back to Hill 529, north of San Angelo d'Alife and dominating everything around it. The 100th and the 133rd's 1st Battalion converged on it and drove the Germans north again. The 34th Division history comments that "The redoubtable 100th Battalion picked its way through heavily mined fields and scaled the summits of Hill 529."

The fight to capture the small towns of Alife and neighboring San Angelo d'Alife cost the 100th twenty-one killed and sixty-six wounded, including Major Lovell, a man these soldiers would have followed anywhere. A half century later his leadership and "sheer guts" remain a legend among the battalion's survivors. Says veteran Leighton "Goro" Sumida:

On one occasion, I remember when our company (E Company) was moved up to take over A Company's place because they got shot up. We had one of the boys in the cornfield, wounded on the leg. . . . Lovell got good scolding from Colonel Turner because he went off the road and into the bushes to go get the person in the cornfield. He picked him up and carried him back. The Colonel said: "You've got no business going out there! Next time let the medics get him!" But that was the Major—all the men respected him.

In another encounter near Alife, Sumida described how Lovell could inspire his men simply by example. Sumida, serving as a scout, and a Browning automatic rifleman came to a bridge. "That's when we first heard that Screaming Meemie rocket," Sumida recalls. A soldier under the bridge was hit and killed, but the men on the bridge miraculously escaped unscathed. "We was all hugging the ground under the rocket barrage, but the Major—he behind the corner eating fruits and smoking his pipe. He look at us guys and said, 'What's the matter, boy?' We were kinda embarrassed."

Soon after traversing the bridge, the men reached a graveyard. Again, the shelling caused the men to dive helter-skelter. Sumida recounts with admiration how Major Lovell simply stepped forward, drew his pistol, started firing toward the point where mortar fire was originating, and "led the charge up the hill."[8]

Lovell's wounding at Alife was not the only bad news for the battalion at this time. Colonel Turner was criticized for poor scouting and tactics and was replaced as their commander by Maj. (later Lt. Col.) James J. Gillespie, who had fought with the 34th Division in the worst of the North African campaigns and had been wounded there. The 100th men didn't like to see the Old Man go, but the army had decided that an officer less involved personally with the welfare of his men would be more effective in combat. The Old Man had fought for them when others doubted. He had worried about their training, and planned for them to get the chance they wanted. He had brought them out of the shadow of suspicion. Now that they were beginning to die, he was sickened by their losses, even as he gloried in their bravery. He had always known they were brave men. Now others were learning it, too.

Everything in Turner's being had gone into the Nisei's fight for recognition as true Americans. The names of the dead and wounded were more than words on paper to him; the men had become part of his own family. The horrors and machinery of this war were already greater—and more complicated—than the war he had fought nearly three decades before. He had wanted to shelter his men, but that was not possible.

Commenting on this change, the 100th Battalion journal states:

> Colonel Turner's relief was a cruel blow to the officers and men. In sixteen months he had organized, trained, and led the 100th in combat, exemplifying the highest qualities of a leader. Ever-mindful of the welfare of his troops when they were committed, his thoughts were first and always for them.

To make matters worse, Major Lovell was evacuated to a hospital in North Africa, and they worried they might never get him back. Colonel Gillespie, however, who had risen from the ranks in the 168th Infantry to command its 1st Battalion, turned out to be one of the best commanders the 100th would ever have, a brilliant tactician able to acutely judge military situations.

In the final days of October the battalion moved toward its third crossing of the Volturno River, at its juncture with the Sava River. Here the Volturno flows in a series of shallow streams through a flat, broad valley above which a ridge of mountains rises about twelve hundred to eighteen hundred feet, with olive groves spreading along the slopes. The 34th Division was to cross the river in full view of the enemy along a five-mile front. The assault units included the 133rd Regiment with the 100th Battalion; the 1st Battalion, 135th Regiment; and the 2nd and 3rd Battalions of the 168th Regiment. The immediate objectives were Santa Maria Olivetto and Roccaravindola. The 34th Division's history describes that crossing:

> At midnight on the 3rd of November, the troops moved quietly down from the hills to their assembly areas, there to await preparation fire by the artillery which opened up at 2330 hours on the morning of the 4th of November. Guns laid down a terrific concentration upon enemy positions lifting their fire at zero hour. At 2400 hours, all Battalions moved into the broad valley,

entered the river bed and commenced the crossing of the several channels, which, though shallow, none-the-less flowed swiftly. The water had turned to icy cold with the advance of fall. The going was rough: the enemy pouring in heavy mortar and artillery fire; troops encountering numerous mine fields and booby traps which were planted thickly in the river bottom and up the approaching banks and the flat land that lay before the hills beyond. The enemy heavily strafed and bombed, adding still another serious impediment in the crossing. With uncanny skill, the Germans had hung wires between trees in the long grape vines and set vast networks of trip-wires. As the troops advanced in the darkness of the night, observers from our command-posts could determine the progress made by the repeated explosions of mines which told only too clearly the terrible cost being paid in this last crossing of the hated river.

On the south flank the 100th Battalion, suffering great casualties from booby traps, mines and machine gun fire, finally reached Highway No. 85 where the progress was temporarily retarded by an enemy detachment which fought stubbornly to hold the road. Continuing its drive it captured Hill 590 and by the 5th day of November, had reached and captured Hill 610.

That account of the third Volturno River crossing was written by Lt. Col. John H. Hougen, the judge advocate and historian of the 34th Division. CBS war correspondent Eric Sevareid heard this description of the third Volturno crossing from the men who made it:

They told me about the Volturno River action in November, when men of the Thirty-fourth had been stupidly driven to their death in a night advance through one of the thickest German mine fields ever ventured over. As the mines flashed off, the Germans poured artillery fire into the flat stretch of ground, and the men screamed and died. Some went out of their heads and ran blindly forward shrieking curses upon the enemy, to perish in shattering explosions. A few men of bravery beyond all words are said to have led their comrades, crawling on hands and knees so that they would catch the mine bursts in their bellies and save those behind them.[9]

In this disastrous crossing, Sgt. Matsutada Makishi and Cpl. Haru-yoshi Tateyama searched to locate their squad members, then led them in single file through the minefield. While trying to get others to safety, both men stepped on mines and were killed. Two more Silver Stars, posthumously awarded.

Four men from a wire-laying squad were awarded Silver Stars for their courageous actions putting in telephone lines for battalion intracommunications, but only one man lived to receive his: SSgt. Melvin Tsuda. Awards for the other three—Pvt. Harushi Kondo, Pvt. Edward Ide, and Pvt. Himeo Hiratani—were posthumous. The men were killed by machine-gun fire.

About 0230 on November 4, Baker Company was halted by machine pistols firing across the road. When Capt. Taro Suzuki and Capt. Young Kim went to investigate, a barrage of bullets began. Suzuki and the men behind him saw Kim jump off the road, hollering as he fell. Word went back to Baker Company that Kim had been captured or wounded. That was all the men had to hear. According to one of them: "What followed can only be understood if one is familiar with the close loyalty and esprit de corps of the 100th Infantry Battalion."[10] Staff Sergeant Robert Ozaki, a squad leader in the 2nd Platoon, screamed the order: "Fix bayonets!" The platoon charged, yelling "Banzai!" The enemy ran, leaving behind two of their American prisoners, delighted but puzzled. The Nisei had made the first recorded American bayonet charge in Italy. It wouldn't be their last.

By midnight of November 4, forty-two men had been wounded and eight killed, including Lt. Kurt E. Schemel, the first battalion officer to die. Schemel was one of the officers sent to the 100th after it arrived on the U.S. mainland for training. At first he had been stunned by his assignment to this unique battalion, but a warm friendship and understanding had grown between him and the buddhaheads. Like the Nisei, Schemel's parents had been born in an enemy country (Germany) but were living in the United States. And, like the Nisei in the Pacific, he would be fighting against his ancestral country.

The battalion was heading toward the hills outside of Pozzilli, and as they approached the town one of the most curious and poignant experiences in the unit's history occurred. At dawn, as they were crawling along a dry creek bed, several men rounded a corner and spotted an American soldier. He identified himself as "Thompson," a paratrooper

AWOL from his unit in the rear echelon at Naples. He said he had come up to the front lines looking for some excitement. He had been through Pozzilli and advised them that the town was heavily mined but didn't seem to be occupied. Then he offered to lead them around Pozzilli via a covered route to hills outside the town. They reached the hills safely, except for the heavy weapons company, which had failed to keep up with the rest of the battalion. Two men were sent back to lead them through the minefields, and Thompson went with them to help. On his way back, he stepped on a booby-trapped Teller mine and was blown apart. He carried no dog tags or letters, and there was nothing but a physical description of the man (blond, about twenty years old) to identify him. No one ever did. But the 100th Battalion men never forgot this strange man who had given his life to help them.[11]

The battalion pressed on into the hills, winning more decorations. In the attacks on Hills 590 and 610, F Company was pounded by artillery. E Company was stopped by a minefield. Lieutenant Lewis Key and his scout, TSgt. Kenso Suga, led a guard to cut trip wires and neutralize the minefield. They were awarded Silver Stars, but Lieutenant Key was killed a few days later and never saw his.

It was while fighting up Hill 600 that Lt. (later Capt.) Spark Matsunaga received a serious leg wound and was hospitalized. After being shipped back to the United States, he joined the Military Intelligence Service. Matsunaga eventually became a U.S. senator.

Ben Tamashiro was also wounded on Hill 600. He would become one of the battalion's most dedicated historians. And it was on Hill 600 that Turtle Omiya received the wound that plunged him into a world of darkness.

It was approaching 6 P.M. and the winter sky was darkening when a Dog Company contingent started climbing through the olive groves that blanketed Hill 600. Spark Matsunaga was up front, leading this tail-end group, which was already late because of a misunderstood radio call. Their heavy weapons would be needed in the coming battle, when Germans were expected to counterattack, shooting through lanes they had cut in the olive groves. Dog Company's men were climbing single file, hurrying so that their weapons would be in place to meet the Germans' next attack.

A man up front tripped a wire leading to a Bouncing Betty mine.

Unlike a regular mine, which blows up immediately when tripped, a Bouncing Betty is designed to spring into the air and explode, sending jagged scraps of metal in all directions. Turtle, a machine gunner in a Dog Company platoon, was carrying his weapon's tripod up the lower part of the hill, straining against the slope, head down and carefully watching the path as he climbed. When the man in front of him stopped suddenly, Turtle looked up quickly to see why. Years later, describing that moment to Ben Tamashiro, he said: "All I saw was a blue flash as shrapnel hit into my right eye."

If the small piece of metal had hit any other part of him, the wound would have been minor, perhaps leaving only a red spot on the skin. Maybe it would have merited a Purple Heart; maybe not. But for Turtle it meant the end of the world as he had known it. The tiny piece of metal shattered his right eye, and the concussion made his left eye useless.

Battalion medics tended Turtle, and all that night friends watched over him. Enemy counterattacks were so fierce and there were so many deaths and injuries on Hill 600 that he couldn't be moved out of the area until the next day. Then began his long journeys to hospitals: first in the war zone, then in North Africa, then in the United States. In February 1944 at Stark General Hospital in Charleston, South Carolina, a *Life* magazine photographer snapped the picture (printed in the issue of February 7, 1944) that would stun Hawaii. It was from this picture that Turtle's widowed mother learned what had happened to her son. The U.S. War Department had never informed her.

"Blind Nisei" the title read. It showed Turtle, clad in pajamas and a bathrobe, sitting cross-legged and barefooted on a hospital cot, leaning his head against a wooden wall, his arms resting against his knees, each blinded eye covered with a cotton swab held in place with two strips of adhesive tape that reached up to his uncombed thatch of black hair. Doctors had told the twenty-four-year-old Nisei that he would never see again.

Gifts and letters flowed into the hospital for Turtle. The nurses took over, lavishing care and affection on him. Letters to the editor also flowed into *Life*. Some criticized the magazine for publishing the picture of a Nisei. Others praised it as an answer to West Coast racists.

Earl Finch, the Mississippi rancher who was the benefactor of hundreds of Japanese-American servicemen, got the army to send Turtle to the seeing-eye-dog training center in Morristown, New Jersey. There Turtle met Audrey, the German shepherd who became his beloved companion. It was winter when they left the East Coast for Hawaii. They came home to the tiny frame Omiya house, which had been built next to the left-field fence of Moiliili Field, where Turtle had learned to play baseball, almost in his infancy.

Despite his blindness, Turtle could smile a wide handsome grin— even as his dark glasses hid the torment that denied him a full share of the life around him.[12] I last saw Turtle in July 1982 when he attended ceremonies marking the fortieth anniversary of the 100th Infantry Battalion. Two years later, on June 23, 1984, he began his long rest beside his many friends in the National Cemetery of the Pacific, Punchbowl, in Honolulu.

The fighting around Pozzilli continued, with more casualties and extraordinary acts of bravery. Captain Kim and two scouts, Sgt. Masaharu Takeba and Pfc. Yukio Takaki, routed four machine-gun nests and pulled in seven Germans. The next morning, after the battalion suffered heavy casualties, two counterattacking German companies were held up by three forward observers of Company D (Lt. Neill Ray, Cpl. Katsushi Tanouye, and Cpl. Bert Higashi), who poured out mortar fire until they were all killed by a tree burst—lethal shards of metal and sharp fragments of tree trunks and limbs cut loose when shells hit trees. Three more Silver Stars, posthumous.

Three platoons of the 9th Panzer Grenadier Regiment—about seventy men—tried to infiltrate behind the 100th's lines on a murky, overcast day, but Kim spotted them and ordered his patrol, hidden in a draw, to hold fire. He sat there calmly, letting the Germans come closer and closer. Watching through field glasses, several of the 100th's officers began to doubt that Kim saw the enemy approaching. The Germans began passing Kim and his patrol. Still they didn't fire. When the whole patrol had passed their hiding place and was cut off from any possible retreat, Kim gave the order to shoot. The Germans tried to run away, but several were killed and more than thirty were taken prisoner. Kim, the Korean who Colonel Turner thought might not want to serve in a Japanese-American outfit, was fast becoming a legend in this battalion of legendary men.

On Hill 600, two men from Company F won Silver Stars: Pfc. Kazunobu

Yamamoto, wounded and bleeding from the ears and nose, remained with his 60mm mortar, causing heavy German casualties because of his accurate firing. He left his gun only when someone found out about his wound and ordered him back. Another private first class, Michael Enga, kept dragging wounded men to safer positions, giving them first aid, then crawling under falling shells to get medics.

The 100th was, at last, pulled off the line for rest and reorganization. It was November 11, Armistice Day at home. For the first time since coming overseas, it was payday for the Nisei. But pay had to be made in slit trenches because occasional bombs fell on Pozzilli. A count of the ranks now showed 150 men per rifle company.

Since going into action in September, the battalion had rarely experienced a dry day. It was Italy's wettest season, with day after day of rain and fog. Cold weather had set in early, and, still in summer-weight clothing, the men suffered horribly. Supplies had not yet caught up with the battalion. Sometimes the men were lucky enough to find heavy garments that had belonged to Germans, and they wore them, happy for the warmth. The terrain through which they had been fighting was, like most of Italy, difficult.

Medics worked around the clock, evacuating patients, giving first aid under fire, carrying men back to aid stations. Litter bearers were killed. Wounded men died from exposure as well as from loss of blood because sometimes it was more than a day before they could be evacuated. Since the battalion had gone into action, the casualty list showed 3 officers and 75 enlisted men killed or dead of wounds, 18 officers and 239 enlisted men injured or wounded, and 1 man missing in action.

Mail caught up with the battalion at Pozzilli, and the men had time to write letters home. Many of them, unable to write Japanese, had to write in English to relatives who knew only Japanese. Or they had to find someone who could help them write in Japanese.

While the battalion was still at Pozzilli, Chaplain Israel Yost conducted a memorial service for the battalion's dead. During the ceremony he told the story of a Caucasian soldier who, seeing a burial detail carrying one of the 100th's men, had stopped and laid flowers beside the body. At that time the 100th men didn't know Israel Yost well. Yost, a lanky, bespectacled, Pennsylvania-Dutch Lutheran, was not very familiar with Japanese Americans or the Buddhist faith, or the mangled Island pidgin the men spoke. Before the war was over, however, the men would know him well. Yost was a man dedicated to helping others, and he was always there, even where he shouldn't have been—on the battlefields. Already he had been wounded, and it wouldn't be the last time.

By November 15, the Fifth Army had reached the German winter line, and General Clark halted the advance to rest his troops. Then, for the first time in Italy, the 100th received bedrolls. Hot food was brought up by pack mules or on the backs of men. The respite was short-lived.

By Thanksgiving Day, November 25, the battalion was back in the hills. The holiday meal was cold turkey sandwiches. Some of the meat arrived in good condition, but some of it was green. The men just scraped away the spoiled part and devoured the rest, then got back to the business of fighting, even though a few had diarrhea. Facing them was even worse terrain—a mass of mountains, valleys, and plains with peaks rising to more than six thousand feet. This was the Germans' winter line, the last line of defense before their heavily entrenched Gustav line at Monte Cassino, where the Germans hoped to stop the Allies cold. The Germans were using new devices: a booby trap with a delayed fuse, which could blow up even a week after the wire was tripped, and a flamethrower that could disorganize patrols.

One night, in the hills near Colli, Pfc. Leighton Sumida of Able Company heard a German patrol advancing. He froze against a stone wall and waited for his machine gunners to fire on the Germans. Nothing happened. He wondered why, because the Germans were noisy enough for his buddies to hear. The next morning he asked them: "How come you nevah fire?" The answer: they knew he was out front and were afraid they might shoot him.

The day after Thanksgiving, the 100th began reconnoitering a new range of hills. Lieutenant Masanao Otake led a ten-man patrol to observe conditions on Hill 905. After a few hours of slow, careful searching, Otake spotted three Germans. He killed them with submachine-gun fire, but a German machine-gun nest opened up on him. With his patrol covering his advance, he lobbed grenades and sprayed the nest with his machine gun. He then checked each slit trench for his own wounded and supervised their evacuation. A Silver Star.

The Fifth Army attack plan for December was to flank German positions in the Liri Valley, hoping this would avoid facing them at Cassino, where they were expected to make a strong stand behind their Gustav line. The 100th's job seemed almost insurmountable. It would mean fighting above the timberline, through ridges and mountains, in snow and freezing cold. The men would be short of supplies and rations; with few passable roads or trails, only mules could be used to replenish ammunition and food supplies. On some of the steep slopes, men would have to pack supplies and water on their backs to the hungry, thirsty troops above. If the 100th men needed encouragement at this time, they got it. Word came down that General Ryder and General Lucas "were well-pleased with the 100th's preceding actions."

At dawn on November 29, rifle units, supported by heavy machine guns and 81mm mortars, began crossing the barren, frozen heights. When the fighting started, Pfc. Chester Hada carried a sound-power telephone to within forty-five yards of the German line to report enemy activity and movements, then crawled closer to transmit information about the terrain. He won a Silver Star for his audacity.

Another private first class, Kazuo Ihara, helped neutralize mines and led a BAR (Browning automatic rifle) team to fire on the Germans. When enemy mortars wounded several men in his platoon, he administered aid and helped evacuate six men. As he attempted to bandage another, he was killed by a mortar shell. A Silver Star, posthumous.

In this fight, where men sacrificed themselves to save other men, there were heroic feats that would become folklore in the battalion:

During a flank attack on high ground, Pvt. Shizuya Hayashi rose, in the midst of enemy grenades and machine-gun fire, attacked a machine-gun nest with his automatic rifle, and destroyed it, killing eleven of the enemy, two of them as they tried to flee. When his own platoon had advanced two hundred yards, an enemy antiaircraft gun opened up and Hayashi fired at it, killing nine more and capturing four. The remaining Germans withdrew. His Distinguished Service Cross (DSC) was awarded "for his courage, superb marksmanship and indomitable determination."

Corporal Masaru Suehiro, already wounded, stayed at his exposed 60mm mortar observation post directing fire until an enemy machine-gun nest was destroyed and a threatened attack was dispersed. Another DSC.

Company B's "two-man army," which evolved during this action, was to become one of the great legends in the 100th's history. Lieutenant Allan Ohata and Pvt. Mikio Hasemoto were part of a squad attacked by forty Germans armed with machine guns, machine pistols, rifles, and grenades. When the fight was over, Ohata and Hasemoto, standing side by side at the head of their squad, had killed thirty-eight, wounded one, and taken one prisoner. Then the two men stopped another German force of fourteen, killing four and wounding three. The others fled. Still standing together, Ohata and Hasemoto repulsed another German attack on their flank, but Hasemoto was killed by artillery fire. Ohata lived through the war and always remembered his friend Hasemoto. "It hurt to see him die," he told me. "He was one of the best." Two more DSCs.

During the battle for Monte Marrone and adjacent hills, the 100th Battalion's casualty list soared. Snow was deep on the treacherous slopes and tops of the mountain range; hungry, thirsty GIs clung to precarious perches or dug into whatever mountain scrub they could find. To get supplies, men slipped and slid three miles down the mountain slopes— to where the mule trails ended. Captain George Grandstaff, the battalion supply officer, never waited for men to come begging for more supplies. He and his men made their way by night up the slippery trails as far as the mules could be coerced. Infantrymen packed supplies the rest of the way, carrying forty-five-pound boxes of C and K rations, clumsy five-gallon water cans, and ammunition. Sometimes they didn't make it back.

The C and K rations (when they were available) were dry, and the men sucked at snow and icicles to wet their tongues. Still, it wasn't enough. Water was precious, but if anyone had some and passed around his canteen, nobody would take more than a sip. And they were cold— mighty cold—wearing their summer uniforms and a ragtag collection of warm clothing scavenged from dead Germans. Then the snow changed to rain. The men licked water off shrubs and leaves, sucked it out of the dirt, and/or caught it in helmets and whatever else was available. There was almost no food left. They shared the bits they had. Shelter halves, which might have helped keep them dry and warm, were being used as stretchers.

Now another form of torment appeared: trench foot from prolonged exposure to the wet and cold. When a man with severely diseased feet was released from duty, he had to slide, crawl, or hobble down the mountain; there weren't even enough litter bearers for the wounded.

Still, the battalion attacked and counterattacked. More Silver Stars, more wounds, more deaths—until, at last, they were relieved by a detachment from the French 2nd Moroccan Division. Two officers and 43 enlisted men had been killed, 4 officers and 129 enlisted men wounded, and one officer and 6 enlisted men injured. Six enlisted men died of wounds and 2 more were missing in action.

When the men of the 100th Battalion finally came down from the mountains on December 9, they rode south—through areas in which they had fought and won—to Alife. Army engineers had resurrected the ancient walled village from its tomb of rubble to create a rest area. It wasn't an elaborate place, but there were movies and USO shows and American Red Cross girls (affectionately dubbed "Doughnut Dollies") who handed out coffee and doughnuts they had made themselves. The men luxuriated in warm showers. But for the 100th the best reward was the winter clothing in small sizes, which had finally arrived. It snowed Christmas Day and they loved that, too; it reminded them of Wisconsin, where they had left so many good friends.

At Alife the 100th got a new battalion commander, Maj. Caspar "Jim" Clough, Jr., to replace Major Gillespie, who was hospitalized with ulcers. Clough had formerly served with the 1st Infantry Division, which had fought in some of the most vicious battles in North Africa and Sicily. He had been through all of them. The 133rd Regiment also had a new commander, Col. Carley L. Marshall, who had been the executive officer and who had won the DSC in Tunisia.

Even at the rest camp, the men weren't idle. There was training and reorganization and new tactics to be learned. But no enemy was firing on them!

On December 30 they moved out, northward with the Red Bulls to relieve the 36th "Texas" Division and try, once more, to break through the German winter line. On New Year's Eve, they were still moving north, this time through a severe blizzard.

In that January of 1944, the 100th fought again above the timberline, along mountaintops and through gorges. Water froze in canteens, legs and hands and faces were numb with cold. Food was scarce. And, as far as the men could see, there was nothing but snow. With every advance, the battalion moved farther from its aid station; the battalion's journal comments that it sometimes required twenty-four hours to evacuate a man.

During one barrage in these frozen hills overlooking the Liri Valley, Sgt. Masaharu Takeba ran seventy-five yards in the open, through enemy fire, to rescue a seriously wounded companion and carry him to cover. For that he won an Oak Leaf Cluster to his Silver Star, awarded posthumously because a few days later enemy fire killed him as he tried to protect his platoon during a German counterattack.

On the night of January 7, three companies moved forward to take Hill 1109. In the dark, Company A, commanded by Capt. Mitsuyoshi Fukuda, and Company B, led by Capt. Sakae Takahashi, took the wrong trail. Without any landmarks to guide them in the snow-encrusted terrain, Company A descended the wrong slope and was bombarded by fire from an opposite hill. Fukuda faced a dilemma: his company couldn't retreat up the slope without being exposed to possible annihilation, and he couldn't communicate with his command post. Fukuda decided that the only way to save his company was for him to return alone to get help. It was a long, steep hill, and, against the snowy background, any figure would be an easy target. But it was a question of his company's survival.

He ordered his men to dig in where they were. Then, covered by their mortar and machine-gun fire, he started his run up the slope—zigzagging through knee-deep snow, his every move clearly visible to enemy gunners on the opposite hill. Bullets hit all around him, but the fountains of snow they threw up screened him. When he disappeared over the top of the hill, his men kept firing, not knowing whether he was dead or alive, and the enemy guns fell silent. Later in the war Fukuda was to lead his company through a minefield. Although repeatedly exposed to heavy fighting throughout the war, he was never wounded. His humorous, laconic explanation: "I learned to keep my head down."

The 100th withdrew that night but took Hill 1109 the next day. Next it faced Hill 1270. Three companies attacked it but were paralyzed by heavy enemy fire, until the 133rd Regiment sent another battalion along the ridge to break the Germans' grip. The Nisei then surged up and took the hill. From the amount of food and ammunition the Germans had stored in their bunkers, it was obvious they had been prepared to hold the hill against any odds; they hadn't counted on the strength and determination of the Nisei fighters.

Below Hill 1270 lay the hamlet of San Michele. The 100th took that on January 15. The winter line had been broken, and now they faced the Gustav line, one of the mightiest defenses the Germans would build anywhere during World War II. From the bluffs of Hill 1270 the men of the 100th could see a mountain rising precipitously above a long, flat plain and a river. This was their first sight of the Rapido River and Monte Cassino.

Back in the United States on November 4, the day after the 100th Battalion crossed the Volturno River for the third time, U.S. Army tanks moved into the Tule Lake internment camp in California to put down a mass demonstration protesting the death of a Japanese farmworker. A few weeks later, at Arizona's Gila River camp, an inmate was shot and wounded.

A rumor was going around the camps that the 100th men were being used as "shields" for the rest of the American army and that the men who had volunteered for the 442nd Regimental Combat Team would be used in the same way. Disheartened at their treatment by the American government, impoverished by quick, forced removal from their homes, families in the camps could believe any rumor about the Nisei troops. It wasn't until later, when wounded 100th Battalion men returned to the United States and visited the camps, that those incarcerated there learned the truth—that the battalion had shared its burden, shoulder to shoulder, with American troops of all nationalities.

CHAPTER 8

THE PURPLE HEART BATTALION OF CASSINO

The Battle of Cassino in early 1944 has been compared to the climax of a Greek tragedy: "Costly in human life and suffering . . . . deprived at the last of the full victory that would have made it worthwhile. . . . in the end little more than a victory of the human spirit; an elegy for the common soldier; a memorial to the definitive horror of war and the curiously perverse paradoxical nobility of battle."[1]

The tragedies of Allied infantrymen fighting at Cassino also have been likened to the Battle of Verdun in World War I and the blood-soaked siege of Stalingrad in World War II. Germans have described the Battle of Cassino as "far worse than anything they had encountered on the Russian Front."[2] It exemplified the neglectful treatment of the Italian campaign by U.S. War Department officials in Washington and by General Eisenhower as they gathered and hoarded men and materiel for the cross-Channel invasion of Normandy in France. Supplies for Italy were always short; fresh troops were never enough; adequate air support was not forthcoming—even in the most important and devastating situations. Italy was the stepchild of the war.

For the Nisei of the 100th Infantry Battalion, Cassino was the final, bloody proof they could give of their loyalty to America and the fulfillment of pledges to their families that they would, above all, fight with honor. Monte Cassino, commanding the route to Rome along the old Via Casilina (Route 6), would be the last great battle of the original 100th Battalion, which the U.S. Army had hastily shipped out of Hawaii in June 1942. After the Battle of Cassino, the 100th would be

so decimated that recruits from the 442nd Regimental Combat Team
would thenceforth fill the empty places.

Located in the angle between two valleys—the Liri and the Rapido—
Monte Cassino stands like an ominous sentinel. At the foot of the mountain,
Route 6 runs through the town of Cassino in the Rapido River Valley,
then rounds the corner of the mountain to enter the Liri Valley, which
leads to Rome, eighty miles to the northwest. There is a clear view of
Route 6 from the top of Monte Cassino, making it the guardian against
enemies approaching from any direction.

The ancient Via Casilina saw some of the greatest campaigns in history.
Roman legions marched it to stop Hannibal's attempt to invade their
capital. Belisarius used it, coming from the south to capture Rome.
Romans knew the town as Casinum, and it was a thriving market center.
But the town's fame was due to the huge building that rested on the
peak of Monte Cassino. There, St. Benedict founded the Benedictine
order and built its first monastery in A.D. 529 on the site of an ancient temple dedicated to the worship of Apollo.

In selecting a place for his monastery, St. Benedict looked for a location
safe from the marauding bands that roamed through early Italy. Monte
Cassino, rising fifteen hundred feet above the flat plain below, had
an unobstructed view in all directions and seemed easy to defend.
Nevertheless, the monastery St. Benedict built was destroyed four times
before World War II: by Lombards, Saracens, Normans, and, in 1349,
by an earthquake. When it was restored in the seventeenth century,
the monks built it like a fortress: a rectangle four stories high, 200
yards long, and 150 yards wide, with high stone walls ten to fifteen
feet thick. To reach their headquarters, the monks constructed a five-
mile road, with hairpin curves cut into rocks. This is what World War
II GIs saw looming above them on the crest of Monte Cassino. They
learned to hate it.

Through the ages, the monks had gathered one of the world's greatest collections of ancient manuscripts, books, and works of art. When
World War II began to ravage Italy, museums in Naples and Syracuse
sent their collections of art and archaeological treasures to the abbey
for safekeeping. Monte Cassino was believed to be so impregnable that
the Italian Military College had long used it as an example of proper

fortification. In fact, some military experts cited it as one of the world's greatest examples of a natural defense.

About twenty-five thousand people had lived in the town of Cassino in peaceful days, but by 1944 its women, children, and old men had joined the throngs of refugees walking Italian roads with whatever belongings they could carry. A few sought shelter within the compound of the great abbey. The Germans used hundreds of the men as forced labor to strengthen the area's defenses. The small stone houses perched on lower hillsides of the mountain were no longer homes. Nazi soldiers manning machine guns occupied them. Tunnels connected cellars on either side of roads. Larger buildings hid tanks. The whole town had been made part of the mighty Gustav line.

Germans announced that in order to protect the priceless Benedictine collections, they were not using the monastery building, or an area extending three-hundred meters on all sides. Later, they narrowed this zone to include only the monastery building itself. No public announcement was made of this, however, and Allied commanders continued to believe that a three hundred-meter neutral zone surrounded the entire building. The men fighting in the hills and plains below Monte Cassino found it hard to believe that Germans were not using the abbey as an observation post. The huge, spreading yellow building, its windows glinting as they caught the light, had a hypnotic effect on GIs looking up at them from their footholds and foxholes on the cold, rocky hillsides below. From time to time they saw—or imagined they saw— signs of German observation from monastery windows. Many men fighting below the abbey, including Catholics, thought the building should be bombed; preservationists throughout the world, however, argued that it must be spared, citing the inevitable destruction of irreplaceable manuscripts and works of art.

What they didn't know was that the abbey's greatest treasures had been moved to Spoleto, north of Rome.[3] The Germans never divulged this information, keeping up the guise of trying to preserve a sacred place, while using the surrounding area as the hub of their Gustav line. Sarcastic skeptics asked: "Do they think we should wait to fight them when they get on a mountain without an abbey?" But public pressure prevailed, and it was decided that the great Benedictine monastery would not be bombed.

For three months—since October 1943 when Hitler had ordered an all-out stand to be made south of Rome—the Todt Organization, Germany's supreme military engineering company, had been building the Gustav line, one of the strongest defense lines in all human warfare.[4] The topography itself presented a tough problem for attacking troops. The area's few roads and trails led into the mountains, making motorized vehicles virtually useless. To strengthen the natural defense that Monte Cassino provided, Hitler made unlimited supplies available to the Todt Organization. Huge quantities of concrete were hauled to Cassino to construct pillboxes. Some were complete with sleeping quarters. Others housed machine guns. Many were connected by underground passages. Todt engineers built steel-lined dugouts and armored pillboxes. If houses interfered with fields of fire, they were knocked down; if they could be used, they were reinforced with stone and logs. Mines guarded every path. Miles of barbed wire laced with explosives was strung in front of positions. Above everything, interlocking machine guns were aimed downward, ready to sweep the steep, rocky slopes clear of Allied attackers struggling up Monte Cassino.

The terrain below the mountain, which the 100th Battalion would have to cross in its initial battle, had been lush farmland before the Todt Organization began its work. German engineers had dammed the Rapido River, flooding the adjoining land to a depth of sometimes more than two feet. The inundated area confronting the 100th Battalion stretched to the road and the olive grove paralleling it on the other side of the farmland: two miles of mud and water.[5] In this stretch of marsh were four irrigation ditches that were also filled with water. The Germans built a concrete wall, seven to twelve feet high and topped by barbed wire, paralleling the Rapido River embankment. It served as a dike to retain water on the field. The river embankments were fourteen feet high and covered with double aprons of mined barbed wire, which also lined the seventy-five-foot width of the riverbed. It was obvious that ladders would have to be used to climb the wall and the riverbank.

All trees and brush had been cut from the inundated farmland to give the Germans on Monte Cassino unobstructed views of troops trying to cross the flooded terrain below. Tree stumps up to three feet high were left, however, to hinder the movement of tanks. Beneath the mud and water on all this flat stretch of land, the Todt Organization had planted mines every five feet with picket-type trip wires that ran in all directions.

Halfway up the mountain was "Castle Hill," named for its ruins of an old fort. The fortifications served as protection for Monastery Hill, looming above it, and the great Benedictine monastery on its peak. To get to the Liri Valley and Route 6 to Rome, the Americans would have to fight their way over or around Monastery Hill.

By the time the first of the four battles for Monte Cassino began, General Clark's troops already had suffered forty thousand casualties. Another fifty thousand men were sick. There was no chance of getting fresh troops or supplies, so most of the men who fought at Cassino had slogged half the length of Italy.

There was one Allied general who believed that there were other routes to Rome besides fighting over Monte Cassino. He recommended that troops bypass it and go through the nearby mountains instead. General Alphonse Juin commanded the Armée d'Afrique, which included 233,000 Moroccans, Algerians, and Tunisians, who had been joined by 15,000 Frenchmen opposing the German-dominated French government. One of Juin's first acts when he arrived in Italy in October 1943 was to study the terrain and roads and observe mechanized forces used by British and American forces. He determined that it was difficult for armored divisions to leave the roads and impossible for them to be deployed in the mountainous terrain that made up so much of Italy.[6] Juin's troops were experienced mountain fighters and not dependent on roads. To eliminate dependence on tanks and mechanized transport, the French general had collected hundreds of mules.

The first attempt to breach the German defenses around Cassino began in mid-January with Juin's French troops mounting a supporting attack in the mountains to the east and the British X Corps conducting a secondary effort in the west. The main effort fell on the 36th "Texas" Division, which was ordered to force a crossing of the Rapido River.

By January 20, the British had forced their way across the Garigliano River and opened up a considerable bridgehead. This attracted the attention of the German Tenth Army commander, who shifted all available reserves to that sector, leaving the British with their hands full.

In the east, General Juin's forces pushed the Germans back from their winter line, and Juin confidently predicted he could push through the vaunted Gustav line before the enemy could consolidate there if Clark would send him fresh troops with which to continue the chase.

Unfortunately, they simply weren't available. The debacle in II Corps's sector on January 20 saw to that. On that day, the ill-fated Texas Division attempted to force its way across the Rapido River at a point below San Angelo near the base of Monte Cassino. The Texans' boats—there were too few and many leaked—were shot out from under them. Some men, wounded during the crossing, drowned. The few who made it across were mowed down by waiting Germans. The operation was a bloody and complete failure.

But Juin refused to give up. He spent four days regrouping his forces after the initial assault and attacked again, without reinforcements. His troops pushed forward in night attacks, engaging in close-in fighting with bayonets and grenades. The battle at times degenerated into a hand-to-hand struggle in which it was sometimes impossible to distinguish between Germans and French. The situation became so critical for the Germans that, on January 23, the following order was passed among the troops:

> The Fuhrer orders that the Gustav position be held at all costs, bearing in mind that a completely successful defense will have political repercussions. The Fuhrer expects every yard of ground to be bitterly defended.[7]

Two days later the exhausted French had to abandon their attack. At that point the focus shifted back to the II Corps sector, where the Red Bull Division would follow the Texans' lead and try to force its way across the Rapido at a different point. The Allied command was still determined to fight its way through Monte Cassino.

After taking San Michele in mid-January, the 100th Battalion had remained there for a week, sending about fifteen combat-reconnaissance patrols to scout the terrain below Monte Cassino and try to find a point to cross the Rapido River. Patrols also went to St. Elia to consult with the French troops. On one reconnaissance, two Nisei who had gathered important enemy information became separated from their daylight patrol. Seven Germans attacked them, capturing one and throwing grenades at the other, Pfc. Sueyoshi Yamakawa. Yama-kawa hurled back two of his own grenades, scattering the Germans, then dove into the ice-cold water of a nearby irrigation ditch and swam three hundred yards before surfacing to rejoin his patrol at a prearranged rendezvous point. For the "extraordinary courage" he had shown in returning with critical information, Yamakawa was awarded a Silver Star.[8]

On January 22, Allied forces landed at Anzio on the west coast of Italy. Their hold on the beachhead was tenuous, and sufficient rein-forcements were not available. The idea behind the Anzio landing was twofold: (1) to provide another takeoff point for a drive to Rome, and (2) to relieve German pressure on Allied troops at Cassino by induc-ing the Germans to shift troops from there to Anzio. It didn't work. The Germans transferred troops from France, the Balkans, and north-ern Italy to contain the Allies at Anzio, making the beachhead like a huge holding pen. Instead of fighting German troops to keep them from reinforcing the Gustav line at Cassino, Allied troops at Anzio had to fight off repeated German attempts to drive them back into the sea.

On the night of January 24, the 100th Battalion left San Michele to head for its jump-off point: an olive grove that skirted the inun-dated fields. At 2330 the 133rd Regiment, with the 100th Battalion attached, launched its attack. Preceding it, massed division and corps artillery had laid down a rolling barrage on targets across the river.[9] It was totally ineffective. The Germans threw up colored flares, alerting their troops to an imminent attack, and let loose an earsplitting bar-rage, including the dreaded Nebelwerfers. The men of the 100th waited for the bombardment to end, knowing what they faced: the two-mile stretch of marsh with its picket mines; the four flooded irrigation ditches; the concrete wall rising seven to twelve feet above the riverbank; two fourteen-foot river embankments, sheathed in double aprons of barbed wire laced with mines; the Rapido River bed covered with mined barbed wire; a fifteen-hundred-foot mountain permeated with dug-in enemy weapons; the watchdog fort on Castle Hill protecting the monastery; and the monastery itself, looming high and huge in the light of bom-bardment flares.

Two companies of the 100th Battalion (A and C) jumped off with the 133rd Regiment's other two battalions, leaving B Company in reserve. Recalling that awful night, Captain Fukuda, commander of Company

A, told me: "As soon as we started across the flats we got machine-gun fire and mortar fire aimed at us. They knew we were jumping off and they were ready for us."

The 100th's Ammunition and Pioneer Platoon had begun clearing a ten-foot-wide path and marking it with white tape. Within a few yards the men reached the beginning of the minefields, and the infantry waited while the platoon groveled in mud and water, searching for trip wires to the mines. Again they marked a path with tape. The Pioneer Platoon then advanced a few feet, stopped, searched under mud and water for trip wires, and laid more tape. All night long it was move, stop, wait while mines and trip wires were located, mark the path with white tape, advance a few feet, then start the whole process again. And all this with enemy fire falling on them.

When mine detectors broke, the men used their bare, bleeding hands to find trip wires and mines in the muddy water. Three of the men received Silver Stars for the work they did that night: SSgt. Calvin E. Shimogaki, SSgt. Takeshi J. Miyagawa, and TSgt. Gary T. Hisaoka. Private Masanori Aoki won a Silver Star for administering first aid to a wounded man despite his own severe head wounds.

Men swore as they made their way through the mire. It was impossible to maintain silence. "I had a couple of officers with me and my whole company," Fukuda said, "and I recall one officer constantly calling out to me to be sure he didn't lose track of me. I kept reassuring him that I was right with him, to stick close and we'll get there. I recall another officer yelling to this first officer: 'Shut up. Don't make so much noise!'"

Nerves were taut. Tempers flared as the men struggled under fire to get off the muddy field of death. Uniforms and boots were slimy with mud and soaked by icy water as the men waded across the marshland and through one irrigation ditch after another. The shorter men had to swim the deepest ditch, holding their guns over their heads. It was the roughest battle they had yet encountered, with its combination of freezing weather and the tension of waiting on the flooded field for more tapes to be laid while enemy gunfire and artillery fell on them. All night long they struggled as the hated Nebelwerfers screamed and flares lighted the skies to reveal their position. As the hours passed, they pushed even harder to reach the concrete wall before dawn so they could have at least that scanty shelter from enemy fire. If they were caught on the open field in daylight, they knew they would be slaughtered.

It was nearly five o'clock the next morning when they finally reached the wall—exhausted, soaking wet, mud caked, glad for the few feet of safety at the base of the wall. Dawn was beginning to break, but gunfire from the mountain couldn't reach them there; it could only skim across the top of the wall to hit the wounded men lying in the mud and water beyond. Sometimes the cry "Okaasan" drifted through the gunfire. Sometimes the cry was "Mother." Whatever the language, the meaning was the same. Aid men couldn't get out to help without being shot themselves. The red cross on their helmets and sleeves wouldn't keep them from becoming another casualty of war.

But the 100th men weren't supposed to stop at the wall. The order was to climb the wall, cross the river with its mined barbed wire, then climb the other riverbank, cross the road skirting the top of the riverbank, then begin to climb Monte Cassino through shale and rocks and mud and ruts. According to the 100th's journal: "Their objective was to be the castle halfway up the hill to the famous Benedictine Monastery."[10]

Then the unbelievable happened. A smoke screen was thrown up, and men from Company B, carrying two long ladders, began crossing the flooded flats to the wall and the river. The ladders were for scaling the wall and the riverbanks. The smoke screen disappeared fast, however, and the Germans, spotting from the mountaintop, poured down machine-gun, mortar, and artillery fire. The men who were sheltered against the wall watched, horrified, then rushed out to grab any Company B men within reach and drag them to safety. Only 14 of the 187 men in Company B reached the wall. Some had managed to withdraw to the rear. The wounded lying on the muddy field were killed or wounded again, one by one, as they tried to crawl behind a tree stump or burrow into ditches or mud. For the Germans sitting high above on Monte Cassino, it must have been like shooting duckpins at a carnival. The wounded lay there all day and into the night before aid men could reach them or they could move back, if they were able, without being detected.

My friend, Charlie Nishimura, remembers crossing the flats that day:

That morning, after advancing under enemy fire, we were told to take cover as too many boys were getting shot. I sheltered behind a tree stump to avoid enemy fire. However, a sniper must have seen me and I was shot in my back, just above my spinal bone. We were pinned down all day until just about darkness when a medical aide came to help me transfer to a field hospital.[11]

Still the command continued trying to get the companies across the river and into the hills above the town of Cassino. On the night of January 25, Captain Fukuda was ordered to leave the riverbank and return across the muddy field to the command post to discuss the situation confronting the 100th Battalion. As he later explained to me: "I told them we could probably get a few men across the river but that they couldn't hold because there was nothing to back them up." Tanks stuck in mud and unable to reach the river were proof of his statement.

Even though officers at the command post argued vehemently against the plan, the verdict was that the order stood: the battalion must cross the river. Fukuda was now to lead Major Dewey, executive officer of the 133rd Regiment, and Maj. Jack Johnson, executive officer of the 100th, a messenger, wiremen, and litter crews back to the riverbank to establish a command post and survey the situation. As they started across the flats, enemy machine guns opened up. A mine went off, wounding Dewey and killing Johnson, who had been one of the great football players at the University of Hawaii and a favorite among the men of the battalion.

Here are Captain Kim's recollections:

During the first daylight hours our battalion observation post started with 26 individuals including the artillery liaison team, communication people and the intelligence section. By nightfall only four of us were left. Major Clough, our Battalion Commander, and myself in one location and Pfc Ginger Minami and Private Irving Akahoshi in another location, 20 yards away. Everyone else was either dead or wounded.

Major Jim Clough was ordered by Colonel Marshall, the 133rd Regiment Commander, to commit "B" Company across the open flats at daybreak. Jim protested that this was a suicide mission. Lieutenant Colonel Moses, the 1st Battalion Commander, to our right, had orders to also commit his reserve company. He protested and said he would personally lead his company because he could not issue such an order without sharing their danger. However, if he survived, he would prefer court martial charges against Colonel Marshall. . . . Here were three West Pointers at complete odds over battle orders. Jim continued to refuse to obey, so at midnight he was relieved of command.

Major Dewey, the Regimental Operations Officer, upon arriving to take command and after making an assessment of the situation, called Colonel Marshall and told him that their earlier evaluation was wrong. Clough should be restored to command and the daylight attack called off. Marshall stuck to his orders.[12]

The next day other elements of the 133rd tried to get across the river and onto the hills, but they were driven back. The 100th was then ordered into reserve at San Michele. By that time most of the men were sick from exposure or diarrhea. Doc Kometani dosed them with paregoric and other medications. Some bivouacked alongside a farmhouse that had a wine cellar. The men drank the wine, which probably helped cheer some spirits, although they complained that it tasted bitter.

At San Michele, Major Lovell finally rejoined the 100th. He had tried repeatedly to get released from the hospital in North Africa to return to the battalion, but doctors had refused permission. So he had simply left. When he arrived, the "coconut telegraph" took over and word spread throughout the ranks of the sick, tired men: "The Major is back, the Major is back." According to the battalion's journal: "There was hardly the need to mention the rest of his name for everybody in the battalion knew exactly who that meant."

On January 29, with Lovell in command, the 100th was ordered back on the line to relieve troops that had finally reached areas surrounding the town of Cassino. With each move the battalion was trying to climb higher on the slopes of Monte Cassino. On February 8, the 133rd Regiment (including the 100th) was ordered to take Castle Hill, while two other regiments of the 34th Division—the 135th and 168th—fought to take Monastery Hill. Captain Kim recalled that during this time a contingent of 100th men led by Major Lovell, and another led by Major Clough, reached the walls of the fort on Castle Hill below the monastery.

Warren Iwai tells of the action:

We were under the cover of smoke shots. I was the point at that time. As I approached towards the castle, I saw a silhouette of a soldier in front of me. I thought, "What the heck? Who's this soldier in front of me? There's not supposed to be anybody in front of me except for the enemy!" As I approached him, it was Major Lovell . . . and he was our battalion commander! What army in the world would you find the battalion commander in front of the point man in the attack? Let me tell you, you won't find anything like that in any other outfit, where you'll find the battalion commander out front like that, worrying about his men.[13]

In this attack, men of the 168th Regiment reached the walls of the monastery itself. If they had been able to take the monastery, they then could have swarmed over Monastery Hill to Route 6 and the Liri Valley. But there weren't sufficient fresh troops to back them up, and their attack was restricted. "This was the closest any Allied units came to capturing these two key structures until these buildings were captured later, despite many subsequent assaults," Kim told a postwar meeting of the 100th Battalion. "The 100th and the 168th did this without being permitted to either shell or bomb these defensive fortresses. Maybe we might have taken them if we could have shelled and bombed them."[14]

After withdrawing from the assault against the fort on Castle Hill, the 100th was ordered to consolidate on Hill 165, a position described by Captain Fukuda as "worse than crossing the muddy, flooded flatland in our first assault."

The Nisei would never forget Hill 165. It was steep and rocky with no chance for cover except behind crumbling sections of low terrace walls that had been used for grape growing in peaceful days. Exhausted, weighted down with ammunition and supplies, some men threw away their blankets as they climbed, crawled, and slipped along the rocky knobs of the hill. The smoke screen hiding them began to fade, and enemy machine guns and artillery picked them off as they rushed to find whatever shelter they could behind a rock or a mound of dirt or a piece of wall. One man, TSgt. Saburo Ishitani, stopped to retrieve the discarded blankets, stashing them where he could find them later. That night it was piercing cold, threatening to snow. Ishitani made his way back to retrieve the blankets and bring them back to the men in his command.[15] It was the kind of thing the Nisei did for one another.

The stories behind the Silver Stars might be forgotten, but the "Blanket Story" was to become part of the battalion's folklore.

Hill 165 lay in full view of enemy gunners on both Castle Hill and Monastery Hill. For the Nisei it was a nightmare. You couldn't move during daylight without getting shot at by guns above. If you had to urinate before dark, you did it into a ration container lying down. You waited until nighttime to defecate, and God help anyone with diarrhea. If you found some rocks or a piece of wall or a mound of dirt for shelter, you were lucky; if not, you could only hope for the best. If ammunition was low you hoped mule teams would reach the bottom of the hill at night, and then you hoped the men who climbed down in the dark to get it would live to climb back up. If you were wounded you hoped the medics could get to you without being killed.

Fukuda gave me this description:

> The Germans were 50 yards away with machine-guns, waiting for us to pop our heads up so that they could take a shot at us. . . . We figured that they would come charging down on us at any minute.
>
> It was an almost impossible task to get out there to treat any of the wounded because of the openness of the place and the German machine-guns trained down on this open area. . . . Some of our men who were wounded had to lie out there two or three nights before we could evacuate them.
>
> One time an American plane was going to bomb somewhere around the town of Cassino and a bomb fell and rolled down the hill into our area. . . . we watched it drop and roll toward us and waited for it to explode. Luckily it happened to be a dud.

Enemy tanks appeared above the 100th Battalion on Castle Hill; one tank, with a 75mm gun, moved into position a hundred yards from Company C and shelled the men below. To save the company, Pvt. Masao "Tankbuster" Awakuni crawled fifty yards across open ground with his bazooka until he reached a point about thirty yards from the enemy tank. He took aim. His first shot hit the track. His second hit the hull, but it was a dud. Now, under enemy fire, he aimed and fired a third rocket. The tank was engulfed in flames. All the German tankmen were killed, and a roar of cheers broke out from the 100th men sprawled on the hillside below. Enemy fire was now directed at Awakuni. He crawled behind a rock and was pinned down for ten hours, until it was dark. His arm was wounded as he crawled back across the hill, but "Tankbuster" lived to wear the Distinguished Service Cross he was awarded for his extraordinary heroism.[16]

Medics and their aides crawled up the hill because there weren't enough litter bearers to carry the wounded back to the aid station. Three aid men—Sgt. Irving T. Masumoto, T5g. Shigeru Inouye, and T4g. Isaac F. Akinaka—left their shelters to climb, under fire, all over the hill to help the seriously wounded who might otherwise have died. Silver Stars for all three.

When Major Lovell left the command post to climb Hill 165 he was wounded in the chest and right leg. He lay helpless in a gully, pinned down by enemy fire. Associated Press correspondent Lynn Heinzerling describes what happened next:

> Everyone knew he had been badly hurt but the nearest man to him had to cross 18 yards of open ground in the face of German snipers and a German tank which was on the road to the abbey.
>
> The nearest man happened to be Sergeant Gary Hisaoka from Hilo, Hawaii, who came into the army directly from the University of Hawaii. Hisaoka was almost beside himself with rage at the Germans. . . .
>
> Every time he raised his head to look at the major, a sniper would chip a rock a few inches from his head.
>
> Hisaoka began digging a shallow trench toward the major, hoping he would be able to slide through it and drag the major to safety. He dug a trench about eight yards long then suddenly he threw down his shovel. There still were ten yards to go.
>
> "Hell. I'm going now," he said. "I'm tired of shoveling. It's getting late and I won't get there till night at this rate."
>
> Hisaoka crouched, slid out of the end of his trench, then sprinted ten yards to the officer.
>
> "Major," he said, "I'm going to have to drag you in."
>
> "That's all right, boy," the major replied. "Get me back any old way."
>
> Hisaoka grabbed him by the arms, dragged him across open space to the trench and placed him on a litter.[17]

Hisaoka was recommended for an Oak Leaf Cluster to add to his Silver Star, but he was killed a few weeks later at Anzio and the award was made posthumously.

For four freezing days and nights the 100th stayed on Hill 165. Communication lines were shattered repeatedly. Wiremen crawled, under fire, to replace them. Medics and aid men crawled all over the hill under fire. But the Germans had every advantage. On February 11, through a violent snowstorm, engineers with flamethrowers tried to burn out enemy bunkers, with no success. Heavy fire beat them back. On February 12 the Nisei were finally ordered into regimental reserve, except for B Company, which was ordered into the town of Cassino.

The town was completely fortified by the Germans, its houses a series of machine-gun nests, its attics observation posts. Here it was not only house-to-house fighting but room-to-room combat. John Lardner, a correspondent for North American Newspaper Alliance, groped his way to the edge of Cassino and wrote:

> They fight for every pantry and every chest of drawers. American troops are clearly better at this in-fighting . . . but the going is very bloody indeed.
>
> The American forces include Japanese of Hawaiian birth, who have been in the thick of the Cassino fight. These old friends of your correspondent . . . have been outstanding in the matter of stamina since they went into the fighting line last September.
>
> Cassino needed stamina as well as the sacrifice of human life, and the Hawaiian Japanese gave it both.
>
> These Japanese are also handy with grenades. . . . I had collected a great deal of lore on Japanese (baseball) pitching. . . . A corporal who used to play a little baseball himself in Hawaii . . . had just had four days of house fighting.
>
> "You don't need a change of pace here," said the corporal. "Just throw straight and throw first. That's the main thing—throw first."
>
> In some cases of the indoor battle . . . it was literally a case of which soldier, German or American, could knock the first hole through a wall to drop his grenade into the next room. In one case when a German won the excavating race an American soldier dropped his grenade through the German's hole.

There are any number of variations of this parlor game, and they all are very rough.[18]

By this time the Fifth Army included units from as many as twenty-six nations. One of the most important of these to the British was the New Zealand Corps, commanded by Lt. Gen. Sir Bernard Freyberg. Since 1940 he had led his New Zealand Corps through combat in Egypt and North Africa. Freyberg, at the insistence of Maj. Gen. Francis Tuker, commander of the 4th Indian Division, which was attached to the New Zealand Corps, demanded that before his troops mounted an offensive against Monastery Hill, the Benedictine monastery must be bombed. It was poor judgment, he insisted, to allow this obstacle to remain. General Alexander, the British officer who succeeded Eisenhower as commander of Allied forces in the Mediterranean Theater, had no alternative but to agree; otherwise, the independent New Zealander might pull out his forces.

General Clark had adamantly and repeatedly objected to destruction of the abbey. The War Department's series on World War II states:

> Clark believed that no military necessity existed, that a bombardment would endanger the lives of civilian refugees in the building, and that bombardment would probably fail to destroy the abbey and would be more than likely to enhance its value as a fortification.[19]

But General Alexander instructed Clark to give the order to bomb the abbey. On February 12, Allied planes dropped hundreds of leaflets on Cassino, warning that the monastery would be bombed. The leaflets declared:

> The time has come when we must train our guns on the monastery itself. We give you warning so that you may save yourselves. We warn you urgently: Leave the monastery. Leave it at once. Respect this warning. It is for your benefit.[20]

No leaflet fell inside the abbey grounds. A civilian brought one to the abbot, who made arrangements with the Germans to help evacuate the abbey by mule path at 0500 on February 16. Because bad weather was predicted, however, the bombing was carried out earlier than planned. Beginning at 0945 on February 15, the monastery was hit by 255 planes, which dropped 576 tons of explosives on it.[21]

Most of the monks had been evacuated sometime before, but a couple hundred Italian civilians hiding in the monastery basement were killed. Indian troops on a nearby hill also had not gotten out in time and were wounded. Abbot Diamare led the remaining monks and civilians down the winding mountain path. Some had been wounded.

Word that the abbey would be bombed had been widespread, and hundreds gathered to witness it from distant hills. Cameramen and journalists came from as far away as Naples. The Nisei, watching from a nearby hill, felt the ground shake as wave after wave of bombers dropped their lethal loads. The only sound was the droning of bomber engines and explosions as their loads plowed into the mountaintop. There was no German antiaircraft fire. The bombers came in successive waves; by midafternoon the abbey, which had been a symbol of evil to thousands of GIs, was reduced to a heap of smoking rubble. A portion of the town of Cassino was also destroyed.

Throughout the United States, preservationists howled in anger, blaming General Clark for the destruction of the abbey. It was an accusation that would follow him the rest of his life, despite the fact that he had not thought it necessary to bomb the abbey and had repeatedly protested General Alexander's orders.

The second assault on Cassino began the same day as the bombing, February 15, with an attack by New Zealand, Maori, Indian, and Gurkha troops, fighting through deep snow on the rocky slopes. The air support they were counting on did not appear, however. It had been shifted to Anzio, where the enemy had started an all-out offensive. The Germans on Monastery Hill had not been dislodged, and they began to use the rubble of the monastery to shield men and weapons.

The 100th Battalion was ordered back into the line on February 18. The battalion made another attack on Castle Hill, with no results except for more men wounded. No Allied troops could break through the German stronghold on the mountain.

On February 22 the 100th turned over its sector to the 6th New Zealand Brigade and prepared to leave Cassino. Fatigued by day-and-night fighting, men fell down—exhausted. Those who could not limp or crawl were carried in litters down the mountainsides. To evacuate the wounded and the dead, every available man from the kitchen and rear areas was called to help. Strength in the 100th's rifle companies had dropped to approximately forty men, including those called in from kitchen areas.

The unofficial history of the 100th/442nd Regimental Combat Team, produced at the end of the war, includes this poignant description of the 100th's battle at Cassino:

> For the 100th Battalion and for the 34th Division, this was the end of the forty-day struggle against impossible odds, plus the cream of the German Army. Rest meant relief from cold, bitter weather that left men chilled to the bone and swelled their feet to the point where it was torture to take a step. The ranks were thin, so thin that when the medics carried a man out now, there was no one to take his place, only a gap in the line and an empty foxhole where he had been.
>
> This was the end of the 100th's fighting in Cassino itself, fighting that was never measured in yards or miles. It was measured instead in houses taken, in rooms of houses, and in cells of the jail wrested from the German paratroopers one by one.
>
> These men had seen all that there was to see, endured all that there was to endure. They had seen Cassino and the ancient Abbey crumble under the weight of thousands of tons of bombs and shells. They had attacked, only to find the German infantry risen from the rubble and the ashes to drive them back. They had learned that power was not enough.
>
> The attack on Cassino had failed, that much was clear. But history will record that when the line was finally broken and the enemy reeled back, five fresh divisions took on the job that one division (the 34th) so gallantly attempted and so nearly completed. History will also record that among the foremost in the ranks of that division were the men of the 100th Infantry Battalion. Among their ranks were fewer and fewer of the men who had started overseas with the battalion because casualties had again been heavy: four officers and 38 men killed; 15 officers and 130 men wounded or injured; six men died of wounds; two men missing; and one officer and one man, prisoners.[22]

When the 100th Battalion landed at Salerno on September 22, 1943, it had 1,300 men. Now—five months later—it could muster only 521 effectives. War correspondents had watched and admired and written about the 100th Battalion during this devastating campaign, and in the United States it had become known as the Purple Heart Battalion. For their endurance and pluck and bravery in the face of insurmountable odds, they were hailed as "the little iron men." It was a description that would also be given later to men of the 442nd Regimental Combat Team.

In summing up this phase of the Battle of Cassino, historian Fred Majdalany writes:

> The performance of the 34th Division at Cassino must rank with the finest feats of arms carried out by any soldiers during the war. . . .
>
> They had earned the praise which for soldiers is the best to receive—that of other soldiers who have moved in to relieve them and who alone can see at first hand what they have done, what they have endured. It was the British and Indian soldiers of the 4th Indian Division, moving in to relieve them, who proclaimed the achievement of the Americans the loudest.[23]

From Cassino the 100th went back to San Michele and then to Alife for rest and reorganization—a respite from the ugliness of war. On March 10 the men were trucked to San Giorgio, near Benevento, where the first group of reinforcements arrived from the 442nd Regimental Combat Team at Camp Shelby: 10 officers and 151 enlisted men.[24] Few were left of the Original 100th Battalion, which had sailed from Hawaii nearly two years before. From that point on the ranks of the 100th would be replenished by 442nd men.

As years pass, statistics of casualties and decorations may be forgotten, but the record of that Original 100th Infantry Battalion, and what it meant to the acceptance of Japanese Americans as loyal citizens, must be remembered. If the 100th had failed in its first months of fighting in Italy, other Americans of Japanese ancestry might never have had the chance to show their loyalty to the United States. By fighting for values and concepts of the United States, the Nisei set an example for people of all nations who seek sanctuary here.

Monte Cassino remained unconquered through nearly three more months of increasingly ferocious fighting. In the end, it took two more major assaults by five fresh divisions to conquer the infamous mountain. During the final battle, Polish Lancers, many with rags wrapped around their feet because they had no boots, broke through the last German defenses to hoist the Polish flag on the mountain's summit at 1020 on May 18. Ironically, the most important gains were made by Juin's French troops. Their deep penetration in the mountains to the west unhinged the German line, paving the way for the Poles' success.

A monument honoring the 100th Infantry Battalion now rests on the slopes of Monte Cassino at San Angelo. And, in the St. Martin of Tours Chapel of the new Benedictine monastery on Monte Cassino, a long, slender, stained glass window is dedicated to the 100th Infantry Battalion. Below its rounded top is the battalion's shield depicting a Hawaiian chieftain's helmet. The central figure is St. Scolastica, sister of St. Benedict, who founded the abbey. Dominating the window at its top is the Latin word for peace: *PAX*.

CHAPTER 9

SECRET WARRIORS IN BURMA

While the 100th Infantry Battalion was attacking the Gustav line on Monte Cassino, fourteen Nisei of the Military Intelligence Service who had sailed from San Francisco on September 21, 1943, were fighting through jungles in a battle that would become one of the most daring military campaigns of World War II: the struggle of Merrill's Marauders to reopen the Burma Road.

In July 1940 the British, complying with Japanese demands, closed the main land route through Burma for supplying arms to China. Threatened by a German invasion of the British Isles, England was unable to increase its forces in Asia, and within a month the Japanese had crossed the Chinese border into Indochina. With insufficient British troops to oppose them and with Chinese troops retreating, the Japanese drove deep into Burma, aiming ultimately to invade India, the prize colony of the British Empire.

The British tried to reopen the Burma Road but were beaten back, abandoning in Rangoon tons of supplies intended for Chiang Kai-shek's armies. To supply China with war materiel, the U.S. Air Transport Command began its spectacular five-hundred-mile flights over fifteen-thousand-foot Himalayan peaks (the "Hump"), threatened by violent winds, dense clouds, and Japanese attacks. But it was not enough. A ground route was urgently needed.

At the Quebec Conference in August 1943, Allied leaders agreed that an American special combat unit should be sent to the China-Burma-India (CBI) Theater. The American commander there was Lt. Gen. Joseph W. "Vinegar Joe" Stilwell. The force would be highly specialized, all volunteers, and trained in jungle warfare. Its immediate objective was the reconquest of northern Burma and the all-weather Myitkyina airfield for shipment of war materiel to China until the old Burma Road could be recaptured from the Japanese. The War Department projected a casualty rate of 85 percent for the operation; Gen. George Marshall, the U.S. Army chief of staff, requested volunteers "of a high rate of physical ruggedness and stamina." He described General Stilwell's mission as "one of the most difficult of the war," adding, "He faced an extremely difficult political problem, and his purely military problem of opposing large numbers of the enemy with few resources was unmatched in any theater."[1]

The commander of this special unit would be thirty-nine-year-old Brig. Gen. Frank D. Merrill, General Stilwell's assistant chief of staff for Plans and Operations (G-3) for the China-Burma-India Theater. Second in command would be Lt. Col. Charles Hunter, who headed the unit en route to India. It would become known as "Merrill's Marauders," and Nisei of the Military Intelligence Service would play a significant and unique role in its success. General Merrill was later to say: "As for the value of the Nisei, I couldn't have gotten along without them." He ordered the men of his special unit to protect the Nisei linguists with their own lives.

MISers had been offered the opportunity of volunteering for a hazardous mission; they were then screened and investigated to ascertain their qualifications. The men, selected from several hundred volunteers, were a mixture of Nisei from Hawaii and from the internment camps on the mainland:[2]

SSgt. Edward Mitsukado, in charge of the Nisei linguists, was a former Honolulu court recorder.

Thomas K. Tsubota, a former bank employee, was among the troops guarding Bellows Field on Oahu from further enemy attacks expected during the night of December 7, 1941.

Herbert Y. Miyasaki, who became Merrill's personal interpreter, was from the small town of Pauuilo on the Big Island (Hawaii).

Robert Y. Honda, of Wahiawa, Oahu, a University of Hawaii graduate, took a reduction in grade to accompany the team.

Roy K. Nakada, of Honolulu, was a University of Hawaii graduate whose diminutive size almost kept him out of the army.

Russell K. Kono, of Hilo, Hawaii, was the son of a World War I American veteran and a law student at the University of Michigan before volunteering for service.

Howard Furumoto, of Hilo, Hawaii, was a veterinary medicine student at Kansas State University when he volunteered for the Military Intelligence Service Language School (MISLS).

Roy Matsumoto, of Los Angeles, a graduate of middle school in Japan, was to become one of the heroes of the campaign.

Ben S. Sugeta, of Los Angeles, was a graduate of middle school in Japan.

Grant Hirabayashi, of Kent, Washington, graduated from high school in Japan and was one of the top MISLS linguists. After the war he was a teacher at the language school, a linguist during the war crimes trials in Japan, and served with the U.S. Department of State, the Library of Congress, and the National Security Agency.

Jimmy Yamaguchi, of Los Angeles, was a highly competent linguist as well as a spectacular orator in the Japanese language.

Henry Gosho, of Seattle, Washington, was highly skilled in both English and Japanese.

Calvin Kobata, of Sacramento, California, had attended middle school in Japan and junior college in California.

Akiji Yoshimura, of Colusa, California, one of the most articulate of the volunteers, regarded service in the U.S. Army as "a right and a duty" and, like the others in the group, was determined "to serve our country not just well but better than any other American."[3]

Mitsukado, Tsubota, Miyasaki, Honda, and Nakada had been members of the 100th Battalion when it sailed from Hawaii on June 5, 1942, but were transferred to the Military Intelligence Service Language School.

Gosho, Sugeta, Matsumoto, and Yoshimura were in West Coast internment camps when they volunteered to serve in the Military Intelligence Service.[4]

Hirabayashi joined the army three days before the Pearl Harbor bombing. His parents were in the Heart Mountain, Wyoming, internment camp.

Captain William Laffin, whose mother was Japanese, led the MIS group. Laffin had been an executive in Japan for the Ford Motor Company and was among those repatriated on the Swedish liner *Gripsholm* when American and Japanese nationals were exchanged shortly after the outbreak of war. He would become a unit intelligence officer (S-2) for Merrill's Marauders.

Sailing from San Francisco with the Nisei language team were two jungle-trained battalions: volunteers from the Army Ground Forces in the United States and from the Caribbean Defense Command. At New Caledonia and Brisbane, Australia, they would pick up a third battalion, all veterans of New Guinea, Guadalcanal, and other Pacific jungle warfare. At that time the group had a designation that meant nothing to anybody: 1688th Casual Detachment. Their mission was code-named Galahad.

When the MISers started their long voyage, many Caucasian veterans in the unit had never seen a Japanese; they suspected that the Nisei were former prisoners of war who had decided to fight for America. When the group boarded at San Francisco, one Caucasian asked Yoshimura: "Say, how're things in your country?"

Looking across San Francisco Bay to the California coast, Yoshimura replied: "It looks good from here."[5]

Before the journey was over, however, the Caucasians knew better. The Nisei lectured them about Japanese weapons, tactics, spiritual background, and physical training. The change in attitude toward the Japanese-American linguists can be gauged by a remark one of the Caucasians made to Grant Hirabayashi after the Marauders' campaign ended: "I'm glad we didn't throw you overboard," he said.

Their forty-day voyage through the Pacific, the Indian Ocean, and the Arabian Sea ended on October 31, 1943, at Bombay, India. From there they traveled 125 miles across India in ancient, insect-ridden, wooden coaches to a place near the town of Deolali, a hot, treeless tent city that would be their initial training area. When that was completed they rode the Indian Railway across the flat central plains for two days and three nights, then marched to a British camp near Deogarh, which was close to an area suitable for jungle training. It was here that Grant Hirabayashi discovered that he was allergic to K rations. He broke out in bumps, on his head and lips. To add to his suffering, he also fractured his arm.

"The doctor said I shouldn't continue with the group," he told me. "But I said: 'After all this training I'm not about to give up.'"

So he stayed, struggling to survive with the minimum of K rations, plus whatever else he could pick up to eat en route. Weakened by near starvation, he couldn't even carry his heavy infantryman's pack. "So

I put it on a mule, and going up the hills I'd hang onto the mule's tail and he'd look back at me as though to say: 'Hey, give me a break!'"

Hirabayashi could laugh about it as I talked with him, but every day of his long trek through Burma's jungles and mountains was a struggle to survive.

At Deogarh the outfit met General Merrill, was redesignated the 5307th Composite Unit (Provisional), and received its orders from General Stilwell: to reach, by February 7, the town of Ledo, in the Himalayan foothills of northeast India. From Ledo they were to proceed into northern Burma, where they would link up with Chinese divisions and fight south to capture the airfield at Myitkyina. Allied conquest of north Burma was necessary so that construction of the Ledo Road could continue, driving a new route from northeast India across north Burma, then tapping the Burma Road at the frontier of China.

The military situation facing the Marauders was this: General Shinichi Tanaka's 18th Division was advancing northward in the jungle-choked Hukawng Valley through which the Ledo Road was to continue, linking the India railhead at Ledo with the old Burma Road, to provide a land route to China. To complete the Ledo Road, it was necessary to clear the north Burma area of Japanese troops and capture the town of Myitkyina and its all-weather airstrip, which would provide an additional landing place for "over the Hump" flights and end Japanese use of the airstrip as a resupply center for their troops then fighting to subdue north Burma, preparatory to invading India.

The Marauders' orders were to conduct swift raids behind enemy lines, disrupting communications and destroying their strongholds so that two American-trained divisions of Chinese troops could then press the Japanese south with frontal attacks. Protected by the Chinese divisions, U.S. engineers had completed one hundred miles of the road. The main Japanese resistance and strongest positions were still to be met.

Troops would be supplied by airdrops containing medical supplies, ammunition, and a five-day supply of K rations for the men plus fodder for the pack animals. This problem was further complicated by the Marauders' organization for combat. The unit totaled 2,997 officers and men, who were divided into three battalions; each battalion was divided into two columns, which operated independently in simultaneous attacks on separate targets. Finding a suitable area for the drops was a constant problem. For each drop zone the troops had to hack clear several acres of jungle growth.

Following the Marauders were road construction gangs that would continue building the Ledo Road to Myitkyina. Because of the nature of the mission, no prisoners were to be taken.

Before the regiment left Deogarh, a bevy of reporters descended to gather material for stories, although they would have to put them on hold until the secrecy ban on this outfit was lifted. Among the reporters was James Shepley of *Time* and *Life*. He thought the regiment's bland name, 5307th Composite Unit (Provisional), would not arouse reader interest, so he thought of the more interesting "Merrill's Marauders." The nickname stuck.

From Deogarh to Margherita, the men traveled a thousand miles on the strange variety of conveyances known in India: on a train—ten days this time—through flat plains along the Ganges River, then via a ferry, a paddle wheeler, and the wooden coaches of another train. This one lumbered through more hot, flat country until it reached the staging area at Margherita, on the edge of jungles through which the men would have to fight to reach their objective.

Complying with General Stilwell's orders, the Marauders reached Ledo, the jump-off point of their expedition, on February 7, having marched the final fourteen miles from Margherita with their newly acquired herd of seven hundred mules and horses. From there, laden with packs and weapons and driving their animals, they marched more than a hundred miles along the steep, partially completed Ledo Road to the village of Ningam Sakan. There they left the road and traveled through jungle to Ningbyen, the rendezvous point of the three battalions. By February 21 the Marauders were prepared to drive south through jungles bordered by mountains rising to more than ten thousand feet. It was the same route along which thousands of refugees had fled from Burma (many of whom died) when the Japanese marched into their country.

Stilwell's plan was for the Marauders to circle the Japanese troops, disrupting their communications and plans so that the Chinese troops could then move in and destroy them. Between Ningbyen and Myitkyina, with its critical all-weather airport, was the Japanese 18th Division, steadily pushing northward. Nearly three hundred air miles separated Ledo, where the road started, from the point near the Burma-China border where it would link up with the old Burma Road leading into China. To aid the Marauders, an OSS force called Detachment (Det) 101 would work its way through the jungle and send Kachins, natives recruited from Burmese mountain areas, to ambush Japanese troops. Another team of Nisei linguists from the Military Intelligence Service was attached to Det 101.

Below Ningbyen the entire valley was heavily forested, filled with sharp-edged elephant (*kunai*) grass four to six feet high, and tree growth so thick it sometimes took a battalion an entire day to push forward one mile. The valley was crisscrossed by rivers, streams, and mountainous areas. The Marauders were dependent on airdrops for food, supplies, and grain for their animals. Sometimes the drops were delayed or couldn't be completed because of enemy interference. The men went with little—sometimes no—food for days, hacking their way through tropical undergrowth three to four feet deep, wading through streams—often neck deep and infested with leeches—struggling through mountains so steep that mules and horses sometimes fell to their death. And in the hot, humid climate, malaria, dysentery, and typhus were endemic.

The three battalions now started working as individual units—sometimes alone in circling enemy patrols, sometimes together in fighting the Japanese. The Marauders also began sending out reconnaissance patrols accompanied by Nisei linguists. Maneuvering beyond their own lines, the MISers crawled near Japanese soldiers and listened to their conversations. As protection, each MISer was assigned a security guard.

"We'd crawl out between the lines," Hirabayashi remembers. "You could hear the enemy's conversation and we'd crawl up to listen. There'd be an escort following me, and as we crawled closer to the enemy line he's telling me: 'Come on back! Come on back!'"

Sometimes the enemy talk included commands during attacks, and the MISers relayed their interpretations back to Marauder troops. If they had been detected they would have been caught between the enemy firing on them and their own forces shooting back to protect them. If the Marauders found an enemy telephone wire and could tap it, the Nisei listened in to learn about Japanese plans and

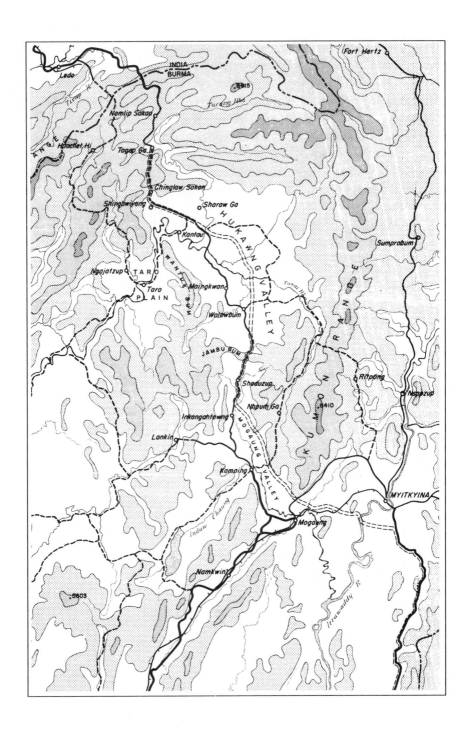

troop dispositions. If Japanese battle orders, diaries, or other documents were found, MISers gleaned tactical information from them.

The Marauders' mission was to cut the chief Japanese supply route, the Kamaing Road. Their first objective was a Japanese force near the village of Walawbum. To reach it they marched with their pack animals for eight days through sixty miles of jungle, only to find that General Tanaka had concentrated his main force all around Walawbum. The Marauders were forced to beat off one bayonet charge after another. One unit, cut off on a hilltop for two days without food or water, repelled repeated Japanese assaults. It was there that Henry Gosho doubled as linguist and rifleman, interpreting the commands the Japanese officers shouted to their troops to pinpoint the area they would attack, thus enabling his platoon to shift automatic weapons to meet each assault successfully.

Hirabayashi, starved because of his allergic reaction to K rations, had a lucky break at Walawbum. The Japanese, surprised by the Marauders' attack, retreated in a hurry and couldn't take their rice with them. They tore open the sacks and poured the rice on the ground. Hirabayashi managed to fill a water bag "grain by grain—enough for one good meal" before he had to run to catch up with the 1st Battalion, to which he was assigned.

The Japanese 18th Division's telephone communications from the front to headquarters at Kamaing ran along the road and passed through the perimeter of the roadblock established by the Marauders' 2nd Battalion. Roy Matsumoto—helped by Roy Nakada, Bob Honda, and Ben Sugeta—tapped the enemy phone line and heard a Japanese sergeant in charge of an ammunition dump begging "help and advice" from his commanding officer because he had learned of the enemy's arrival on the road. In reporting the location of the Marauders' 2nd Battalion, the Japanese also revealed his own position. When American planes appeared for a supply drop, the 2nd Battalion signaled the crews to send fighters or bombers over the enemy dump with "help and advice" of an unexpected kind.[6] Other messages intercepted by the 2nd Battalion indicated that the enemy was planning to attack at 2300 that night. Because the battalion had fought for thirty-six hours without food or water, it was ordered to withdraw, rather than meet the attack.

Their next mission called for two deep penetrations of thirty to forty miles behind enemy lines. As the Marauders moved they were unaware that they were receiving assistance from a group of irregular Kachin guerrillas, led by a Det 101 officer, who ambushed and harassed the rear of the Japanese forces. By this time the long marches through the jungle had begun to thin Marauder ranks; among those hospitalized were two Nisei: Roy Nakada had contracted a tropical disease and Tom Tsubota had a fever and a severe hernia.

General Merrill's orders were to fight the Japanese south and establish a block on the road leading toward Myitkyina. While the 2nd Battalion established the block, the 3rd Battalion remained behind to fight off Japanese movements. The Kachin guerrillas of Det 101 continued to protect the rear of the battalions from Japanese patrols. And fight they did—not only the enemy but also the jungle: twelve hours a day on the trail, hacking through dense jungle growth of twisted, intertwined bamboo, soaked to the skin by rains, fording streams and rivers where leech bites left their uniforms caked with blood. In one five-day period, the 2nd Battalion marched seventy miles and made more than a hundred river crossings.[7] And on one of those days, they fought off continual Japanese attacks at point-blank range.

It was during this long march south that Hank Gosho, working with the 3rd Battalion, earned his nickname, "Horizontal Hank," because so much of the time he was pinned down, flat on his stomach, between enemy and Marauder fire, while listening to and interpreting enemy commands and actions. He had attended school in Japan and knew the "everyday" speech of Japanese, which made it easier to understand conversations among Japanese soldiers.

Near the end of the second phase of the Marauders' mission, the 2nd Battalion was blocking the route that a Japanese counteroffensive force was using. Three miles behind the 2nd Battalion lines, more than a hundred sick and wounded Marauders lay on a newly constructed airstrip awaiting evacuation. It was vital for the 2nd Battalion, now surrounded, to delay the Japanese force, and there were no Marauder reinforcements available. The 1st Battalion had just finished a successful battle at Shaduzup and was fighting off attacks as it marched to relieve the 2nd Battalion. The 3rd Battalion, separated from the 2nd Battalion by enemy troops, was also trying to fight its way through, with air and artillery support.

So the 2nd Battalion stood alone in a battle that raged for fifteen days at Nhpum Ga Hill, which became known as "Maggot Hill." A Military Intelligence report describes the conditions there:

> Since the first day enemy artillery had played havoc with the Marauders' animals, which could not be dug in . . . Of 200 horses and mules, about 75 had been killed, and their carcasses after lying for 2 days on the ground had begun to putrefy. From beyond the perimeter the wind brought the smell of Japanese corpses which were already decomposing. The stench was almost insufferable.[8]

The battalion ran out of food, and the only water hole, near the base of a hill, changed hands repeatedly until the Marauders finally lost it. The shortage of water was so grave that doctors had none for making plaster casts and had to give patients sulfadiazine dry. But the men fought on, hungry and thirsty, until they received a supply drop of food and water. The Japanese troops were also running out of food and supplies, and they were continually harassed by the Kachin guerrillas of Det 101, who cut Japanese phone lines and ambushed supply columns.

Excerpts from a diary kept by Bob Honda describe the 2nd Battalion's hazardous situation:

> There are Japs all around us. . . . They seem to sleep all day and crawl all nite, harassing us and keeping us from sleeping. . . . It's hell!
>
> At 11:30 they hit us with everything they got. . . . I fire and fire in sheer self-preservation. Kill, or they will kill me. My whole body shakes, uncontrollably. Scared? I don't know. I cannot stop shaking. Stupid thing to do, but I counted 64 rounds of artillery.[9]

It was Roy Matsumoto, a slightly built, quiet man, who pulled off one of the most spectacular feats of the campaign. An intelligence report of April 2, 1944, from north Burma to CBI headquarters in New Delhi tells the story:

> Sergeant Matsumoto crawled out close to the Jap perimeter every night and sniped at Japs. He listened to them talk and secured

information. He normally returned just before dawn. Last night however he returned about 2300 hours and reported to Lt. Edward A. McLogan that the Japs were going to attempt to cut off a part of the perimeter that Lt. McLogan was occupying. Lt. McLogan's perimeter stuck way out on a nose of ground that sloped down hill. It was difficult to defend but so far they had held it mainly because they wanted to deny the defilade it would offer the Japs if we pulled back to the crest of the little ridge.

Sergeant Matsumoto said the Jap plan was to creep up as close as possible to the perimeter before dawn, then rush the little nose, which about twenty men were holding. Lt. McLogan figured that it might be possible to give them a surprise. He decided to pull his men back to the crest of the ridge, concentrate tommy guns and BARs along that side of the rise, booby trap the foxholes they were leaving and let the Japs attack the nose of ground, take it and then be annihilated by his automatic weapons.

At dawn everybody was set. Sergeant Matsumoto was in a two-man foxhole overlooking the nose of ground with a tommy gun. Suddenly there were shouts of Banzai! Death to the Americans! Die! and a hail of hand grenades hit around the nose of ground as a reinforced platoon swept up the hill. A moment later they were sticking bayonets in foxholes, firing wildly, shouting and grenading everything that looked like a gun emplacement.

Their sudden occupation of the nose startled them. They charged up the hill, an officer leading them carrying a sword (which later proved to be a beauty). Lt. McLogan held his fire till they got within fifteen yards of his perimeter. Then tommy guns, Browning automatic rifles, grenades—everything—opened at once. The Japs were falling like flies. Another platoon or part of a platoon was following the first platoon and they started hitting the ground— jumping in our booby trapped foxholes. Then Sergeant Matsumoto shouted in Japanese "Charge! Charge!" and they charged. Thirty minutes later fifty-four dead bodies were counted on that slope including two officers.

Sergeant Matsumoto became a legendary character overnight.

When the 3rd Battalion reached Nhpum Ga, its artillery helped finish off the Japanese. It was here that Gosho really merited his name

Horizontal Hank. He, Honda, Matsumoto, and Sugeta crawled beyond the perimeter repeatedly to listen to enemy commands and conversation. The information they gathered allowed the Marauders to shift forces to meet enemy attacks. And, listening to the battlefield cries of Japanese troops calling for medics, Gosho could tell if American guns were aiming correctly. It was about this time that General Merrill suffered a heart attack and was temporarily replaced as the Marauders' leader by Colonel Hunter.

After this battle, the final, most important job faced the Marauders: Operation End Run, the capture of the vital airfield near Myitkyina, a hundred miles away, through some of the worst jungle and mountainous areas yet encountered. It *had* to be taken: besides lying astride the proposed path of the Ledo Road, Myitkyina was the principal Japanese base for defense of Burma from the north; it was at the head of the Irrawaddy River, which was being used as a water transport route for Japanese supplies; and it was the principal air base from which Japanese aircraft menaced American transport planes flying supplies to China. This would be a race against time: the monsoon season was approaching and the stamina of the Marauders was deteriorating.

Since February 9, the Marauders had marched and fought through five hundred miles of perilous terrain, living on K rations and suffering from diseases, leech bites, fevers, and sheer fatigue. They were down to "less than a third of their original strength."[10] General Stilwell now added Kachins and Chinese troops to the Marauders' ranks, bringing their strength to about seven thousand. Two Chinese regiments were to follow the Marauders. Also helping were some of Brigadier Orde C. Wingate's Chindits, specially trained guerrilla raiders who savaged Japanese facilities and supplies. Other MISers accompanied the Chindits.

With detachments of Kachin guerrillas from Det 101 to serve as guides over hidden trails, the Marauders began their drive for the Myitkyina airfield on April 28, after Merrill had discharged himself from the hospital. Four days later the monsoon rains began. The effects of forced marches, through difficult terrain in torrential downpours, began to thin the Nisei ranks. Hirabayashi, Honda, and Sugeta were evacuated because of fever and fatigue; in Hirabayashi's case, these conditions were accompanied by extreme weakness from hunger caused by his allergy to K rations. He remembers being evacuated in a Piper Cub, which, because the enemy surrounded the place, had to wait until sundown to take off on its flight ("just above tree-top level") to the hospital at Ledo.

On the way to Myitkyina the Marauders faced fifteen days of climbing—sometimes crawling on hands and knees—over steep, slippery trails and scaling mountains, including Naura Hkyat, the 6,100-foot pass of the Kumon Range. It was a killing march under monsoon rains so heavy that litters on which wounded and sick men were carried had to be drained constantly. Mules fell to their death off mud-drenched, slick mountainsides. Some mules died of sheer exhaustion; others were abandoned. Supplies were also abandoned. Anything that was not absolutely necessary was left behind. Men struggled against fatigue and diseases: malaria, amoebic dysentery, and typhus. A few died from mite typhus, for which there were no inoculations. But the Marauder forces kept pushing on toward the vital airfield, while Kachin guerrillas continued to protect them from enemy attack.

The trail they took through the hills had not been used in ten years, and reports said it was impassable. Captain William A. Laffin, who had headed the MISer group when it left the language school, was now serving as intelligence officer of the Marauders. With another Marauder officer, he moved ahead of the troops with thirty Kachin soldiers and thirty Chinese workmen to repair the worst sections of road.

At one point their guide was bitten by a poisonous snake. His foot swelled badly, and he became too sick to move. Without him, the Marauders faced an almost impossible task of finding their way through a maze of paths. Laffin and the other Marauder officer slashed the spot where the guide's foot had been bitten and sucked poison from the wound for two hours—until the Kachin was well enough to mount a horse and resume leading the column. Shortly afterward, Laffin was killed.

On May 15, Merrill signaled Stilwell: "We have a fair chance."

Stilwell replied: "Roll on in and swing on 'em!"[11]

Somehow, they made it.

Just before 11 A.M. on May 17, the Marauders launched their attack on the airfield, which the unsuspecting Japanese had left lightly guarded. By midafternoon Colonel Hunter signaled General Stilwell that the field had been captured. But the fight was not yet over. Japanese forces stationed at Myitkyina began threatening the airfield, determined to recapture it or fight to the death. The situation became so critical that Marauders still recuperating in hospitals were returned to the line if they were able to stand and hold a weapon. In this desperate effort to retain the airstrip, the Nisei continued to serve as interrogators and translators.

By the end of May, only two hundred of the men who had started with Merrill's Marauders were considered fit to remain at Myitkyina, and the unit was disbanded.[12] The stubborn Japanese defense of the city disheartened the Chinese divisions, which had arrived belatedly; but, by sheer persistence, they finally wore down the enemy. On August 3 the Japanese commander at Myitkyina, General Mizukami, committed suicide.

The Marauders' mission was completed. The unit had fought through five major and thirty minor engagements, marched through almost seven hunded miles of seemingly impossible terrain, and cleared the north Burma area of the seasoned troops of the crack 18th Japanese Division.[13]

From then on supplies could be flown into China from the Myitkyina airfield instead of over the Hump. Soon a new Burma Road would be finished. But, as General Stilwell wrote in his diary: "Galahad is just shot."[14]

Merrill's Marauders were dropped from the War Department's roster on August 10, a week after the capture of Myitkyina. The unit had won a Distinguished Unit Citation for its work in Burma. The Japanese-American linguists were awarded Combat Infantryman's Badges, a Legion of Merit, and fourteen Bronze Star medals and clusters; and seven of the fourteen men were commissioned.

Forty-nine years later (on July 19, 1993), Matsumoto was inducted into the Ranger Hall of Fame for his service at Nhpum Ga and for subsequent service during and following World War II, including intelligence work for the Chinese Nationalist Army guerrilla forces behind enemy lines near the French Indochina border; postwar work for Headquarters, China Command at Shanghai, China; and undercover missions for the general headquarters of the Allied forces in Japan. General Merrill's evaluation of the Nisei:

As for the value of the Nisei group, I couldn't have gotten along without them. Probably few realized that these boys did everything that an infantryman normally does plus the extra work of translating, interrogating, etc. Also they were in a most un-enviable position as to identity as almost everyone from the Japanese to the Chinese shot first and identified later.[15]

Charlton Ogburn, a Marauder officer, had this to say in his book *The Marauders* about the Nisei who served in his outfit:

All of us, I suppose, when we are moved to reflect upon what human beings are capable of, find that certain images come to mind as illustrations of surpassing achievement. One that will always leap to mine is a composite recollection of Nhpum Ga, and of no part of it more than the heroism, moral as well as physical, of those Nisei . . . their persistent volunteering to go forward to intercept the commands of the enemy when the lead units were engaged by trailblocks. What was unspeakably hard for the others can only have been harder still for them. Some had close relatives living in Japan, all had acquaintances, if not relatives held in concentration camps in the United States on the grounds that persons of Japanese descent and feature must be presumed disloyal. . . . What were their thoughts in the solitude of soul that jungle warfare enforces? I have no way of knowing. But in the case of Sergeant Roy A. Matsumoto, whose mother was living in Japan, we may perhaps justifiably surmise that he took some comfort from the reflection that she was not in one of the major cities but in a smaller one less likely to attract attack by American bombers—Hiroshima.[16]

An officer writing about the Nisei with Merrill's Marauders stated:

Throughout, whenever and wherever there was need for any of the boys, they never hesitated. They were not only interpreters, but soldiers at the front. They faced danger willingly, whenever called upon. They faced the enemy, fought against him. Roy Matsumoto, Ben Sugeta, Robert Honda and Henry Gosho are credited with about 30 Nips.[17]

And a letter sent by a Caucasian soldier with the Marauders to the *Seattle* (Washington) *Times* in March 1945 stated:

The men of our platoon owe their lives to Sergeant Henry Gosho, a Japanese American of Seattle. Hank (we call him Horizontal Hank because he's been pinned down so many times by Jap machine-gun fire) guided the machine-gun fire on our side which killed every Jap on that side. The boys who fought alongside Hank agree that they never have seen a more calm, cool and collected man under fire. He was always so eager to be where he could be of the most use and effectiveness, and that was most always the hot spot.[18]

And here is what one of the Nisei Marauders, Akiji Yoshimura, had to say about the group:

For the most part, we came together as strangers. We shared, however, a common commitment to what we perceived to be a right and a duty. Perhaps most important, each of us in our way looked beyond the "barbed wires" [of the War Relocation Camps] to a better America.[19]

When the Marauders were disbanded, the Nisei scattered. Henry Gosho served for a while in the Office of War Information (OWI), then was returned to the United States for medical care. Tsubota was shipped to the United States for further hospitalization. Nakada, Furumoto, Hirabayashi, Matsumoto, Yamaguchi, Kobata, Sugeta, and Yoshimura were transferred to China to the Sino Translation and Interrogation Center (SINTIC). Several participated in the Japanese surrender negotiations in Chinkiang and Nanking, China.

A few Marauders, including two of the Nisei linguists—Ed Mitsukado and Robert Honda—joined Det 101 to continue the battle to free Burma of Japanese troops. One Nisei, T3g. Shigeto Mazawa of Det 101, parachuted into the Burmese jungle to serve with the Kachin Rangers in raids behind Japanese lines, even becoming a temporary captain in the British army when he commanded a company of the Kachins.[20]

When Merrill's Marauders closed out operations at Myitkyina, another group moved in to continue their jungle warfare to push the Japanese south to Lashio, the southern terminus of the Burma Road. This was the 5332nd Brigade (Task Force Mars) composed of the 124th Cavalry and the 475th Infantry Regiments, with twelve MISers attached to each outfit. Like Japanese-American linguists with the

Marauders, the Nisei of Task Force Mars went beyond their own perimeters and overheard conversations that disclosed enemy positions and movements and the locations of enemy ammunition dumps. During almost seven months of operations—from July 26, 1944, to February 16, 1945—they moved, with their pack animals, through more than three hundred miles of jungles and across mountains up to seven thousand feet high. When the Nisei finished that assignment, the old Burma Road had been recaptured. The MISers then hitch-hiked their way by plane to New Delhi, India, for reassignment by the Southeast Asia Translation and Interrogation Center (SEATIC).

Among the outfits that had arrived during the battle for Myitkyina was a crew from the Office of War Information, including Nisei linguists. They wrote pamphlets that were dropped to Japanese troops, urging them to surrender. In the mopping-up operations at Myitkyina, a Nisei interpreter with the OWI pulled off one of the most spectacular triumphs in MISer history and became known as the "Nisei Sergeant York."

Sergeant Kenji Yasui, a graduate of high school and college in Tokyo, was fluent in Japanese and had been working on OWI propaganda. At Myitkyina, he and two comrades volunteered to round up a bunch of Japanese soldiers who were holding out on an island in the Irrawaddy River. Halfway across the river, Yasui got a cramp and almost drowned, but he managed to get to land and shout to the Japanese to come out. Two of the holdouts attacked and had to be killed, and one tried unsuccessfully to blow up himself and Yasui with grenades. Then Yasui had an idea. He assumed the identity of a well-known Japanese officer, Colonel Yamamoto, and commanded the Japanese to line up and execute close-order drill. The enemy soldiers filed out. After they had performed to his satisfaction, he ordered them to swim across the river to the mainland, pushing ahead of them a raft on which Yasui stood with his carbine aimed at them. The thirteen Japanese who obeyed without question ended up as POWs.[21]

By this time Japanese-American linguists of the MIS had spread throughout the CBI with British, American, Burmese, and Chinese units—none of them household names in America. As fast as MISers arrived in the CBI, the Southeast Asia Translation and Interrogation Center handed out assignments.

Henry H. Kuwabara, who served as a linguist with the British 36th Division, won a British medal when he obtained information that led to the capture of Japanese strongholds at Hopin and Pinbaw in Burma.

Eiichi Sakauye, serving with the Chindits in India, received a Silver Star for saving the life of a British army officer while under fire. The Chindits, a long-range British penetration unit that included British and Gurkha troops, landed by gliders in areas behind Japanese lines. They had their own bevy of MISers to deal with the enemy and his language.

A five-man team of MISers arrived in Yenan, the wartime capital of Communist China, in July 1944. Chiang Kai-shek's Kuomintang Party held southern China, but the rest of the country was split between Japanese, in control of urban areas, and Chinese Communists, who controlled rural areas of northern and central China. General Stilwell, needing political and military intelligence, had repeatedly requested that an American observer group be sent to Communist China. Finally he got what he wanted: a team of State Department officials, military tacticians, weather experts, navy personnel, propaganda experts from OWI, OSS officers, economic experts, and intelligence personnel. Most of them were fluent in Mandarin Chinese; it fell to the MISers to ferret out intelligence information about Japanese units from Japanese prisoners of war. These MISers nicknamed themselves the "Dixie Team" because they were in rebel territory, living among China's Communist leaders, including Mao Tse-tung. The five Nisei linguists were Shoso Nomura, George I. Nakamura, Koji Ariyoshi, Tosh Uesato, and Jack Ishii. Among their duties: interrogating Japanese POWs and writing propaganda leaflets to be distributed among the prisoners. Nakamura was also sent on several missions into areas from which messengers frequently did not return; one of these missions was to rescue a wounded U.S. pilot who had been shot down. The U.S. observer team tried to get Chiang Kai-shek and Mao Tse-tung working together, but the mission failed, with the later result of civil war in China.

Akiji Yoshimura, who had been with Merrill's Marauders, and Joe Ikeguchi worked in intelligence activities. Nobu Tanabe, one of six Nisei with Gen. Claire Chennault's Fourteenth Air Force, made four parachute jumps, completed infantry training, and served overseas with the OSS—all the while classified as 4-F.

John Morozumi, with Chiang Kai-shek's troops as a tactical adviser, became involved in combat numerous times. He later worked on war crimes investigations in Shanghai.[22]

Ted Tsukiyama, who had volunteered for the 442nd Regimental Combat Team but was transferred to the Military Intelligence Service, was attached to the Tenth Air Force in the CBI, intercepting communications that detailed Japanese air force traffic in Burma. As with most intelligence work, there was no public glory in this type of assignment: it was a tedious job of listening, day and night, hour upon hour, to Japanese conversations and orders, so that Allied forces would know where and when to shoot down Japanese planes or intercept the enemy's troop and supply movements.

Don Kuwaye headed a radio interception team in northeast India.

And in Calcutta, Nisei linguists worked around the clock, monitoring Japanese radio conversations, working to help break Japanese codes.

Writing from the China-Burma-India Theater, Capt. Barton Lloyd gave this evaluation of the work Japanese Americans of the MIS did in the CBI:

> I cannot overstate the value that Colonel Stilwell [son of General Stilwell] and his headquarters place on Nisei language men. As far as everyone who had contact with the Nisei is concerned, they are tops.[23]

In January 1944, while the Marauders were still training for their jungle maneuvers and the 100th Battalion was fighting at Cassino, the War Department announced a new policy governing Nisei military service. Whereas Japanese-American men had been allowed to *volunteer* for the 442nd Regimental Combat Team, the War Department now reinstated the *draft* for Japanese-American men, putting them on the same basis as all other Americans—except that their families would remain behind the barbed wire of internment camps. Thousands of Japanese Americans reported for the draft. They would be ready for overseas duty with the 100th/442nd Regimental Combat Team at a time when Nisei troops already there were being decimated by German forces.

And the fighting went on.

CHAPTER 10

ANZIO TO ROME—AND BEYOND

Thirty-five days after the survivors of the Battle of Cassino left the slopes of Monte Cassino, the 100th Battalion landed at Anzio, where the Germans were threatening to push Allied troops back into the sea.

It was the same day (March 26, 1944) that the second battalion of Merrill's Marauders in Burma headed toward Nhpum Ga, and the same day that U.S. forces were poised to defeat the Japanese in the Solomon Islands—with MISer linguists playing a key role.

Nine days after the 100th Battalion reached the Anzio beachhead, a second contingent of reinforcements from the 442nd Regimental Combat Team landed there: ten officers and two hundred enlisted men.[1] On April 2, Lt. Col. Gordon Singles became the 100th's commander. (The battalion had more than a dozen changes of command during the war.)

Anzio was a new experience for the 100th Battalion: there were no mountains to climb. But the flat plains were almost as deadly. Since the January 22 landing, American, French, Canadian, and British forces had been hemmed in, with German guns pointed down at them from surrounding hills. By the time the Nisei climbed off landing craft at Anzio, the invasion was threatening to become a replica of the World War I Gallipoli campaign (like Anzio, also conceived by Churchill), when Australian and New Zealander troops were almost annihilated on a beachhead in Turkey.

Until Allied troops made their amphibious assault at Anzio, the place was unknown to the rest of the world, except for a few historians who recognized it as Antium, the birthplace of Emperor Nero. The nearby

Pontine Marshes, a malarial swamp, had been the subject of several reclamation projects through the ages, but none was completed until Benito Mussolini established a workable drainage system there. In honor of his accomplishment, the largest drainage ditch was named Mussolini Canal. After the Allied landings, it became part of the no-man's-land separating German and Allied forces. The 100th Battalion's sector of the Anzio beachhead was seven miles from the seacoast, strung along this canal. Other drainage canals and ditches, twenty to fifty feet wide, cut the flat plain into a grid pattern. The entire area around Anzio and Nettuno had been devastated. Seaside villas where the rich had vacationed were piles of rubble. Bombed tanks and the debris of war were everywhere. The area's farmhouses had become the prized headquarters of whoever occupied them first. Civilians had fled the area, although a few hardy souls remained nearby to take their chances.

Following the initial landing, two battalions of American Rangers had tried to break through the German lines. Only 6 of the 767 troops involved returned.[2] In another effort, only 650 of the 800 men from a U.S. 3rd Division contingent returned. By the time the Nisei arrived, both sides had dug in and were planning for a spring offensive. Anzio had become another stalemate: the Allies couldn't break out for a run to Rome via Route 7, and the Germans had been unable to eliminate the Allied beachhead. Axis Sally, the German radio propagandist, dubbed the place "the largest self-supporting prisoner of war camp in the world."[3]

Any Allied plan to break out of Anzio hinged on the Battle of Cassino, still raging. So did two other Allied assaults on the planning books: the cross-Channel invasion from England to the Normandy coast, which was scheduled to begin after the Allies took Rome, and Operation Dragoon, an attack through southern France, which was being planned to draw troops away from the Normandy beaches. In short, Anzio and Cassino governed the future timetable of the war in Europe.

Anzio was a rare battlefield: everything was "on the line" night and day. It was a front with neither a forward nor a rear. Hospitals and rear-echelon offices along the coast were as vulnerable as any other area. Amphibious craft ferrying supplies from ship to shore, and the Quartermaster Corps troops unloading them at the dock, suffered as many enemy hits as the infantrymen dug in along the Mussolini Canal. At night, bombs rained down and ack-ack sounded all over the place.

German tank attacks to penetrate the beachhead perimeter were a constant threat. Luftwaffe airstrikes occurred almost daily. Snipers from hills overlooking the beachhead would fire at anything that moved on the flat plain below. And huge rounds from the railroad gun nicknamed "Anzio Express" (sometimes dubbed "Anzio Annie") threatened the entire area.

The 100th men, who had been used to mountains, rivers, and rock-strewn fields, were forced to live like moles—underground in foxholes during the day, coming out at night. Even when wounded they stayed hidden.

Night patrols were the most dangerous. The Germans frequently sent out motorized units trying to capture prisoners from whom they might get information. Firefights and motorized chases through the grid pattern of the canals were extremely hazardous.

After living in the cold and snowy weather of mountainous Italy, the 100th now faced Anzio's warm, humid climate. It seemed that wherever one fought in Italy, weather was also an enemy. A few men who were quick, or just lucky, inherited farmhouses—a luxury, even though none had indoor toilets and most, by then, were without roofs and were full of rubble and, usually, rats. Unlucky GIs had to dig foxholes. They lined them with grass or newspapers or scrap wood to keep out dampness, surrounded them with sandbags for added protection, and decorated them with pictures of movie stars (Rita Hayworth was a favorite). They passed the time by shooting craps, playing cards, strumming their ukuleles, and making coffee and snacks on Coleman stoves. For the most part, the holes were safe, unless they took a direct hit.

Stanley Nakamoto could testify that foxholes weren't always a safe refuge. Stanley was one of the 442nd replacements sent to the 100th Battalion. He had been among the thousands of Nisei who streamed into army depots in Hawaii when the call went out for volunteers. Stan and another Nisei were in their foxhole when a German plane dropped a bomb close by. The two men were blown out of the hole, and when Stan landed on the ground, blood was trickling from his mouth. He hurried off to the aid station, where Doc Kometani noticed that Stan's teeth were loose and promptly pulled them all out. Holed up in Anzio, Stan couldn't get a GI issue of false teeth, and his friends began teasing him about his toothless state. To camouflage his loss, Stan did the next best thing: he grew a mustache.

After nightfall, when the Nisei weren't on patrol, they could crawl out of their foxholes and lounge outdoors, enjoying the starlight. They sang their Island songs, gossiped and smoked (under cover of blankets to hide the light from watching Germans), or listened to Axis Sally's broadcasts from Rome. Their "radios" were a concoction of safety razor blades, scraps of wire, and dry batteries, which battalion communications men had taught them to fashion.

Axis Sally seemed to know where the Nisei were, even before censors allowed correspondents to file stories about them. She played Hawaiian melodies and told the men to go back to their beautiful beaches and enjoy life. They particularly liked her jokes because they were so corny, and they thought her mispronunciation of American city names was hilarious.

So the troops sat and waited, though always with rifles at the ready, hoping to get off the beachhead someday soon. Sometimes their boredom was relieved when German shells burst in the air and spewed propaganda pamphlets urging the boys to go home. The men, grateful for souvenirs, picked them up and laughed.

All GIs complain about food, but the Nisei battalion had a special complaint: they were always short of rice. Throughout the war various army commanders, General Ryder included, tried to remedy this, boasting that they had gotten an increase in the outfit's rice ration. The kitchen crews also did their bit by making sharp trades with Caucasian outfits: potatoes for rice. Their white officers got sick of eating rice, but the Nisei paid no attention to them. So the Caucasians ate rice camouflaged with whatever was handy: catsup, gravy, salt, sugar, fruit—anything that might give flavor to what they decided was the most unpalatable, bland food they had ever swallowed.

One night a barrage of gunfire startled the battalion's command post. Officers grabbed their guns and rushed toward the noise. They saw a group of excited Nisei huddled over something on the ground. It turned out to be a cow that the men had carefully stalked and shot. It was an old cow and, therefore, pretty tough, but the kitchen crew managed to produce its own unique *hekka* (a Japanese stewlike dish): a blend of the tough beef, GI rations, bouillon cubes, and other unidentified ingredients. In time, legend increased the number of cows caught that night to the size of a Texas herd.

May Day arrived and the stalemate had not eased. To celebrate the first day of May, Lei Day in the Islands, the men gathered flowers from nearby fields and made leis. It was a brief respite; for the next two days the Luftwaffe dropped bombs near the battalion command post.

In May, as fighting at Cassino continued and as increasing numbers of troops and supplies were unloaded onto the Anzio docks, plans were being laid for a breakout from the beachhead and the run for Rome. It was vital for the 34th Division to know what German troops were in its immediate area, particularly if any Panzer outfits might be encountered. German captives were needed for interrogation about the identification, disposition, and estimated strength of troops in the sector. So far, all attempts to capture prisoners had failed. Captain Kim spent days training his binoculars on enemy troop and sentry movements, trying to figure out a way to capture some Germans. By this time, Captain Kim had become the most admired officer in the battalion. Historic, feudal differences between Japan and Korea didn't matter to Japanese-American GIs. The California-born officer was simply a damn good soldier—the smartest, the best. The Nisei GIs never questioned his commands.

Step by crafty step, Kim made his plans, then presented them to the battalion staff. They thought he was crazy, but they bucked the proposal up the line for review. Ultimately, Kim got permission to try his scheme. According to the 100th's unofficial history, here's what happened:

Leaving the forward lines of Company B in the afternoon, the five men selected a route along a drain ditch, waist to shoulder deep, and succeeded in infiltrating through enemy lines and outposts. After working their way for an hour they could hear troops talking, singing and digging. At this point, knowing that the enemy at the outposts were extremely cautious at night, Captain Kim and his party decided to rest until dawn. When it was light enough to be able to avoid mines, wires and other obstacles, the patrol headed forward, cutting through entwined briar brush, and bypassed many enemy strongpoints. Later, around 0900, after they had covered only a few hundred yards more, Captain Kim ordered a halt, moving his men to an advantageous position to observe the enemy defenses.

Remaining here, the patrol gathered valuable information and decided on the next move. They would have to go through a wheat field and hit the suspected strongpoint from the rear. While the three riflemen were posted to cover, Captain Kim and Pfc

Akahoshi crawled forward through eight to eighteen inch wheat stalks and after two hours of stop-and-go had advanced only 250 yards. Finally they neared a draw from where there could be heard the chatter of Germans and the sounds of someone cleaning a gun. Several more yards were gained where they silently parted the wheat stalks. Directly to the front were two Germans, presumably security guards, sitting in their slit trenches.

Quickly Captain Kim and Pfc Akahoshi brandished their tommy guns, completely surprising the two, and ordered them to remain silent. The startled guards raised their hands and were quickly disarmed while not far away other Germans were talking and laughing unaware of the stealth in their midst.

The two prisoners were led back through a different route barely missing other strongpoints. Captain Kim and Pfc Akahoshi found the rest of the group waiting and the party headed back for friendly lines. At 1330 hours, the next day, the battalion CP was reached and an outstanding but dangerous mission behind enemy lines was concluded. Upon questioning, the prisoners were found to be members of the 7th Company, 955th Regiment, 362nd Infantry Division. They talked freely and so intelligence was able to find out all the necessary information not previously known.[4]

It was another mission that further enhanced the reputation for tough fighting that the Nisei already had among both German and American forces throughout Italy.

General Ryder was so delighted with this successful and highly original maneuver that he passed the word up to Fifth Army headquarters, and General Clark personally awarded Kim and Akahoshi Distinguished Service Crosses.

On May 18, the day after Kim and Akahoshi returned with the two prisoners, Polish Lancers raised their flag on top of Monte Cassino and British troops began moving into the Liri Valley. Five days later Plan Buffalo went into effect and, at dawn, 150,000 troops in seven Allied divisions began bursting out of Anzio to head for Rome along Route 7. It quickly became a race to determine who would get to Rome first—the British or the Americans. General Clark, having stomached enough of British claims for conquests in Italy, was determined that his Fifth Army had earned the right to be the first to enter the Eternal

City. Clark had one other goal: to enter Rome before the Allied invasion of Normandy, planned for June 5. (It was delayed until June 6 by weather.)

For a week the Fifth Army drive northward gained ground against a tough, determined German line. But on June 2, the 34th Division was stopped around La Torretto and Lanuvio, the final enemy stronghold before Rome. The same enemy defenses were holding up the 1st Armored Division, veterans of the fierce North African campaign. The Germans had created an intricate roadblock of overlapping machine-gun positions, which had to be eliminated before the Allied push to Rome could continue. Already General Ryder had received an order "to crack this Lanuvio. It's holding up the whole thing."[5] Two battalions from the 135th Regiment had tried to break through, but failed. Now the Fifth Army command was asking one battalion of Japanese Americans to do the job that twice its number had found impossible.

The 100th attacked on June 2, with Companies B and C in the lead (and Company A passing through), but ran into strong machine-gun lanes guarded by numerous minefields. After a thirty-six-hour fight, they had cleared the minefields and knocked out close to a dozen machine guns. No one in the Allied command had anticipated the power of the 100th's drive, and when it smashed through the bulge the Germans had created, it was mistaken for enemy troops and fired on by Allied artillery. Technical Sergeant Yasuo Takata, leading a B Company platoon, was finally able to get word to an aerial artillery observer to stop the fire. He saved his own platoon but, as it moved through the crossroad, the men saw dead and wounded comrades in the woods. The battalion's journal states that "the 100th suffered 15 killed and 63 wounded and one missing in action."

The determination of the Nisei never to turn back, to win at any cost, was graphically illustrated in this short, fierce confrontation. They fought like fiends. After the engagement, B and C Company riflemen were awarded six DSCs, a Silver Star, and three Bronze Stars.

Private 1st Class Robert Yasutake, serving as an automatic rifleman for his squad, wiped out two machine-gun nests; he killed six enemy and wounded seven more. A DSC.

Private Shinyei Nakamine, Sgt. (later Lt.) Yeiki Kobashigawa, Sgt. Yukio Yokota, Pfc. Thomas Ono, and Pfc. Haruto Kuroda in three hours neutralized eight German machine-gun nests and five machine-pistol

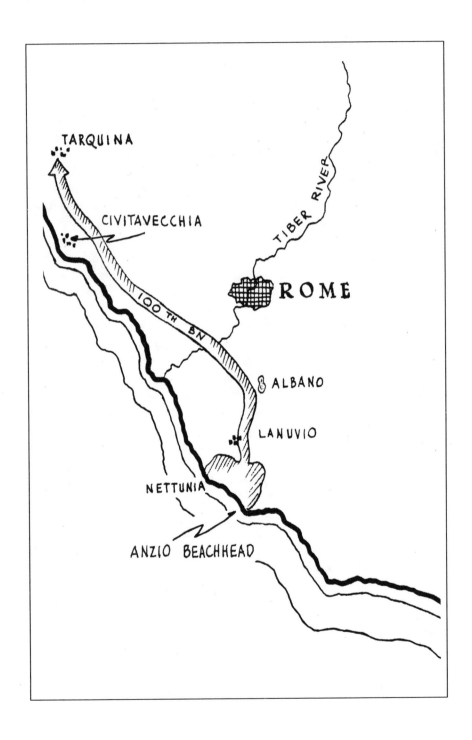

nests; they killed or captured twenty-four enemy and routed many more. Five more DSCs.

First Lieutenant Bert Tanaka rescued his pinned-down platoon and led two of his men to knock out an enemy dugout under heavy artillery and small-arms fire. A Silver Star.

The next day the Nisei cleared a road junction and a German stronghold near Genzano, wiping out enemy observation posts and machine-gun emplacements, capturing fifty prisoners, and routing the final elements of the German 29th Panzer Division.

The 100th had wiped out the final enemy stronghold on the road to Rome, but there is no reference to this vital small-unit action involving the 100th Infantry Battalion at Lanuvio in the official U.S. Army history of the campaign. But Americans who fought with the Nisei didn't forget. After the battle at Lanuvio, one Caucasian officer wrote to the Auburn (California) *Journal:*

We had been sitting and living in foxholes at Anzio some 63 days. Then the big push out and the capture of Rome. They (100th Battalion) wiped out the last heavy German resistance we met some 12 miles south of Rome and then it was practically a walk into the city.

Meanwhile, General Clark had ordered Lt. Gen. Lucian K. Truscott to send the bulk of his corps toward Rome. The initial plan had been to send Truscott's corps to try to surround the German forces being pursued by the British. The change was General Clark's final effort to win for his Fifth Army the credit for entering Rome before the British Eighth Army, which, in his opinion, had done little fighting.[6]

On June 4, as the 100th Battalion pursued the Germans along Route 7, the Nisei saw what they had been looking for—a road sign reading: Roma, 10 Kilometers. The prize was almost in sight. Then the 100th was ordered to the roadside to await truck transportation. While they waited, tanks, motorized infantry, and what seemed like the rest of the Fifth Army passed them by. As Yasuo Takata remembered it: "Every vehicle on wheels was rushing by at great speed. It seemed we were in greater danger from the traffic than the enemy."

That night the Fifth Army began filtering into the city. General Clark waited on the outskirts until the next morning to make his triumphant entrance, becoming the first general since Belasarius to enter Rome from the south. The 100th men had also wanted to be among the first to enter Rome, and their disappointment grew as they watched the Fifth Army whirl past them. Rumors flew through the ranks, one of them that racial prejudice had denied them the prize. Given the tremendous esteem in which General Clark and other officers of the Fifth Army held the 100th Infantry Battalion, such prejudicial treatment seems improbable. As *Puka Puka Parade,* the 100th Battalion veterans' publication, explains:

> It was finally ascertained that the 100th had been halted by battalion order, so that the battalion officers could attend a meeting relating to the impending pull-out of the 100th from the 34th Division for a link-up with the 442nd Regimental Combat Team which had just arrived in this area.[7]

Some 100th veterans, however, have continued to believe that racial prejudice prevented them from being among the first troops to enter Rome.

The 100th Battalion's official wartime journal tells the rest of this story:

> The battalion was finally put on trucks and at 2200 hours on the night of the 5th the 100th passed through the outskirts of Rome heading northwards in pursuit of the enemy. The city's celebration, from being freed from Nazi rule, was centered in the area around St. Peter's Church and, on the outskirts as the trucks then rolled by, there were few people to greet the men. But the cheers of the few were loud and long and certainly it could be marked as a famous day. Two years previously (to the day) the *Maui* had slipped out of Honolulu Harbor and the 100th Battalion was then starting on the road to Rome.

Significantly and poignantly, this is the last entry in the 100th Battalion's journal, "Salerno to Rome." Along the way the battalion had suffered nine hundred casualties. It had also won acclaim in newspapers throughout the United States and the admiration of the military units with which it served.

The day after General Clark entered Rome, Allied forces landed in Normandy. Although General Eisenhower had refused to accept the 100th Battalion in his command, the Nisei made a contribution anyway. Nisei linguists of the Military Intelligence Service helped provide detailed descriptions of Germany's western defenses (the Atlantic Wall), which Eisenhower's invading Allied troops would have to breach in order to get a foothold in Europe. The Japanese ambassador to Berlin, Maj. Gen. Hiroshi Oshima, had been given an extensive tour of Germany's defenses along the western French coast, and he sent the description to Tokyo. However, his messages were being intercepted in Turkey and relayed to Vint Hill Farm Station, a remote army camp, hidden by tall trees in a farming area between Warrenton and Manassas, Virginia. Japanese diplomatic codes had been broken early in the war, and their communications were monitored continuously. Working with the decoders were teams of Nisei linguists, and their English translations were dispersed among top army officials. Therefore Eisenhower knew about the Germans' Atlantic Wall about the same time that Tokyo did.[8]

On June 11, in a valley north of Civitavecchia, the ancient port of Rome, the 100th Battalion was attached to the 442nd Regimental Combat Team (RCT), which had just arrived in Italy, and the Nisei RCT was attached to the 34th Infantry Division (General Orders No. 44 Headquarters 34th Infantry Division). By then the 442nd had sent almost all of its 1st Infantry Battalion to Italy as replacements for the 100th. The 442nd units that landed in Italy consisted of the 2nd and 3rd Infantry Battalions, Antitank Company, Cannon Company, Medical Detachment, Service Company, 522nd Field Artillery Battalion, 232nd Combat Engineer Company, and the 206th Army Band. The 442nd was a self-sustaining force, and all its units were to play highly significant roles.

Because of its distinguished record through nearly nine months of bitter fighting, the 100th Battalion was allowed to retain its original designation in this new combination. The Nisei fighting unit was officially known as 100th/442nd Regimental Combat Team. Of this new combination, the 34th Division history states:

The brilliantly successful performance of the 100th Battalion, Nisei troops, had persuaded Higher Command at home that more

Japanese Americans should be committed to battle. Accordingly, the 442nd Infantry Combat Team was sent over from the States to join the Division. The battle-tired 100th, still maintaining its identity, joined the 442nd. The 34th was now again a square Division, consisting of four combat infantry regiments.

As men of the 34th observed the battle conduct of the Nisei, they grew to resent the treatment accorded the parents and relatives of these little, brown American fighters. They resented the confiscation of their property and the herding of their families into concentration camps at home, while their sons were dying by the hundreds in the cause of human liberty. They determined then to raise their voices in protest and to demand justice and recompense for the wrongs inflicted upon these people. The Nisei became true buddies of the 34th.[9]

As the 100th and the 442nd began working together, animosities again flared between the two outfits. It took a while for the men to resolve these problems and become a cohesive unit. Added to old feuds, men of the 442nd were angry about unit loyalties. It seems that many of the replacements they had sent to the 100th Battalion after the Battle of Cassino preferred, like the 100th, to wear the Red Bull insignia of the 34th Division rather than the regiment's "Go For Broke" insignia. For their part, the 100th men felt that their record in training and in combat had inspired formation of the 442nd and given its men the chance to see combat, but that now the 100th would become swallowed up by this larger group. And the 442nd men were proud of being volunteers, whereas men of the original 100th Battalion had been draftees—even though they had been stationed throughout Hawaii that unforgettable night of December 7, 1941, and had proven themselves ready to fight any attempted enemy invasion.

In Italy the controversies reached a climax on June 26 when the 2nd and 3rd Battalions of the 442nd were stopped in their drive up the west coast by heavy German fire from high ground at Belvedere, which was held by a crack SS motorized battalion. Dominating a vital highway, it was impeding the advance of an American infantry unit. General Ryder, furious at the failure of the two 442nd battalions to surround the Germans, stormed into 100th Battalion headquarters and ordered it on the line. Without time for reconnaissance, the battalion's officers hurriedly worked out a plan: they would cut Nazi phone lines, send one Nisei company to block the entrance to the town, send another company to block exit from the town, and send its remaining company to attack the town itself. They destroyed the entire SS battalion, killing 178 Germans, wounding 20, and capturing 73, and destroying or capturing tanks, trucks, jeeps, and heavy weapons. The enemy remnants fled before the 100th's assault. The Germans' right flank positions had been destroyed, cutting their progress on the road leading north to Florence.

A few days later, in a Fourth of July review honoring Secretary of War Henry Stimson, General Clark requested that representatives of the 100th Battalion be present. Captain Sakae Takahashi, who had planned much of the battalion's assault at Belvedere, and his B Company, were selected. As the dignitaries stopped in front of the company, General Ryder patted Takahashi's shoulder and told Stimson: "Mr. Secretary, this is my best outfit."[10]

For its brilliant performance at Belvedere, the 100th received the Presidential Unit Citation, the first of three it would be awarded:

> All three companies went into action boldly facing murderous fire from all types of weapons and tanks and at times fighting without artillery support. Doggedly the members of the 100th Infantry Battalion fought their way into the strongly defended positions. The stubborn desire of the men to close with a numerically superior enemy and the rapidity with which they fought enabled the 100th Infantry Battalion to destroy completely the right flank positions of a German Army . . . forcing the remainder of a completely disrupted battalion to surrender approximately 10 kilometers of ground. In addition large quantities of enemy weapons, vehicles and equipment were either captured or destroyed, while the American infantry division operating in the sector was able to continue its rapid advance. The fortitude and intrepidity displayed by the officers and men of the 100th Infantry Battalion reflects the finest traditions of the Army of the United States.

From Belvedere the 100th/442nd Regimental Combat Team swept up Italy's west coast and crossed the Cecina River, aiming for Livorno

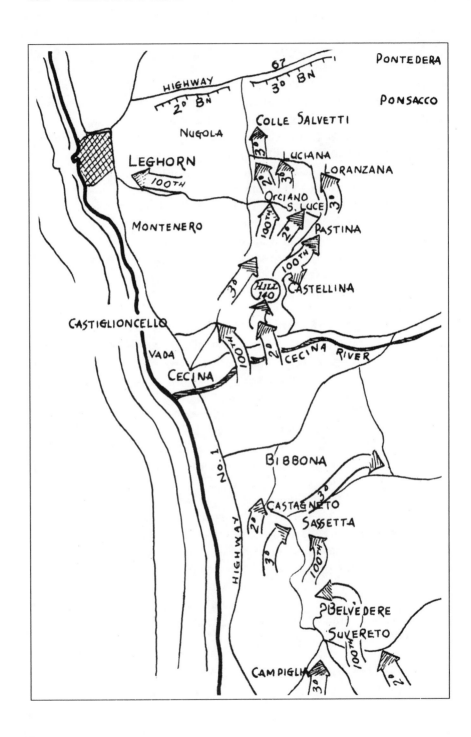

(Leghorn), the most important seaport in the area, through which supplies were reaching the Germans. On the way, they hit Hill 140, where they were pinned down below the enemy's hilltop observation posts. It was here, during a five-day battle so fierce the men dubbed it "Little Cassino," that the men of the 442nd began to reap citations for their valor, including one man who had almost been rejected when he volunteered for U.S. Army service.

At four feet nine inches, twenty-four-year-old Pfc. Takeshi Kazumura (nicknamed, of course, "Shorty") was probably the shortest man in the army. In the fifty years after I wrote about Shorty for the *Honolulu Star-Bulletin,* no one else came forward to claim the title of "shortest"—not even after the Smithsonian Institution included Shorty's measurements in its exhibit about Japanese Americans during World War II. Not only was Shorty at Pearl Harbor when it was bombed, but he was in the *middle* of the harbor when the planes with the Rising Sun emblem dropped their first lethal loads on America's Pacific Fleet. Ford Island is a small dot in the harbor, and that's where he was—loading lumber onto a ferry. He saw all of it—the bombs dropping, the ships exploding, the dogfights in the smoke-filled sky. And then he began picking up bodies—and parts of bodies. It comes as no surprise that when the War Department called for Japanese Americans to form the 442nd Regimental Combat Team, Shorty was in line, along with thousands of Island Nisei.

How did he get into the army? I asked him, since it was obvious he didn't measure up to any minimum height. He replied:

> The officer who was in charge just looked at me and said: "Son, you're too small. Go home."
>
> Well, since the line was so long, they didn't check as they usually do, measuring everybody, weighing everybody. Too many in line. So I sneaked into line again and waited. When I got to where they were checking, another fellow, a sergeant, was at the desk and he said: "How tall?"
>
> "Five feet two."
>
> "Weight?"
>
> "115 pounds."
>
> "Next," the officer said.
>
> And that's how I got in.

From that time on, there was a continuing battle with the Quartermaster Corps to get clothes and boots small enough to fit him. His shoe size was 2½ EEE; the smallest combat boots the Quartermaster Corps sent him were size 8.

"I had to pad the toes," he told me. "The hardest part was walking in the pine forest [in the Vosges Mountains]. I slid a lot and it was very hard to take a step. As for my clothes, the sleeves were too long, the shirt reached to the floor and the trousers reached to my neck and the in-seam was so long the trousers dragged on the floor."

When the 442nd was training at Camp Shelby, Mississippi, Earl Finch, the white rancher who became a sort of godfather to the regiment, finally got Shorty to a local tailor to have the GI clothing altered.

Despite his size, Shorty passed all the hiking and obstacle tests and fought in Italy until he sustained four wounds on the cheek and forehead. Along with his Purple Heart, he was awarded the Bronze Star for saving a white officer's life, under fire on Hill 140. The officer was 1st Lt. Mike Kreskosky, a Pennsylvanian, and he tells the story:

> I was hit July 7, 1944. . . . We were on the military crest of Hill 140 and our right flank was exposed. The Germans threw artillery fire at us and I was hit on my right arm at the elbow. It was hanging by about one inch of skin. I yelled out: "I'm hit. I need a medic."
>
> Another officer replied: "Can't you wait till the artillery stops?"
>
> I held my upper arm to try and stop the bleeding and that is when Shorty crawled up to me and put a tourniquet on my arm. When he raised his head to put the tourniquet on he was hit in the face by artillery fire. I do not know if Shorty was unconscious or not. That's the last I remember seeing Shorty. My arm was amputated at the elbow.

Lieutenant Kreskosky, who was transferred from Fort McClellan, Alabama, to the 442nd after becoming a first lieutenant, became a great admirer of the Nisei:

> The first thought I had when joining the 442 was: Did the Japanese already invade America? Later on, I found out how loyal they were to the United States. As fighting men, they were outstanding

and wanted to get the war over with to return to their homes and families—some of whom were in concentration camps. In combat, when we were stopped waiting for our units on our right and left flank, the men would yell: "Let's get this over with."

The Unit and I became very close friends. In 1953, I went to the first reunion of the 442 in Hawaii and I've attended every reunion since then. Some of the men and their wives have also visited me . . . and I still correspond with some of them. . . .

Shorty was our company runner and his sense of direction was unbelievable.

One of the men awarded a DSC for his courage on Hill 140 was SSgt. Kazuo Masuda of the 2nd Battalion. He crawled two hundred yards through enemy fire from his observation post, secured a 60mm mortar tube and ammunition, and dragged it back to his post. Needing a base plate for the mortar tube, he used his helmet. For the next twelve hours he fired single-handed, never leaving his post except to run for more ammunition. During that time, he repulsed two counterattacks. Masuda was later killed patrolling along the Arno River when he deliberately sacrificed himself so the men with him could deliver vital information to their headquarters.[11]

At the end of the war in Europe, Masuda's family was warned by night-riding vigilantes not to return from the Gila River internment camp to their farm in Talbert, California, near Santa Ana. But they did. It was at a special ceremony there that Gen. Joseph Stilwell presented Kazuo Masuda's Distinguished Service Cross to his family.

On Stilwell's return from the China-Burma-India Theater, he became commander of the Sixth Army at the Presidio of San Francisco and a dedicated defender of Japanese Americans in their struggle against discrimination. Outraged at threats the Masuda family had received, he told them: "We ought to take a pick-axe handle after such people."[12]

And, of Japanese-American soldiers in World War II, Stilwell said:

> They bought an awful hunk of America with their blood. . . . You're damn right those Nisei boys have a place in the American heart, now and forever. We cannot allow a single injustice to be done to the Nisei without defeating the purposes for which we fought.[13]

Three years later, when the Masuda family brought Kazuo's body back to the United States, a cemetery near their home denied him a burial plot, citing "restrictive covenants" (which meant whites only). This time Gen. Mark Clark, who succeeded Stilwell as Sixth Army commander, interceded, and a burial plot in the cemetery was finally found for Kazuo Masuda.

There were other DSCs won in that spectacular battle on Hill 140:

Private 1st Class Frank H. Ono drove the enemy back with grenades when his rifle was shot from his hands. He took a weapon from a wounded comrade but, under heavy fire, he deliberately stopped to give first aid to two men who had been hit. Then, in an exposed position, he made himself a target until his platoon could withdraw safely.

Private 1st Class William K. Nakamura silenced an enemy machine gun that had pinned down his platoon. He killed its crew and fired continuously at other enemy machine guns until the GIs reached cover. He himself was killed.

Staff Sergeant George S. Iida knocked out one machine-gun position, directed fire to knock out another, then took command of his platoon when its leader was wounded. He advanced alone to within a few yards of enemy guns and destroyed them with hand grenades.

And on the west slope of Hill 140, TSgt. Ted T. Tanouye, a Company K platoon leader, kept fighting after his left arm was hit and paralyzed. He crawled twenty yards to get more ammunition, then silenced a German position with a hand grenade, knocked out a machine-gun nest with fire from his tommy gun, wounded three more of the enemy, and finally seized his platoon's objective before permitting himself to be evacuated. He later died at the Arno River.

Fighting toward the town of Castellina, Pfc. Kaoru Moto shot a gunner firing on his platoon and dispersed a machine-gun squad. He was then wounded but dressed his injury and continued to deny Germans the use of a house as an observation post. He also forced a German machine-gun crew to surrender. After that, 1st Lt. Takeichi T. Miyashiro led a squad to take over the house and repulse a counterattack and, when heavy fire began falling in his area, ordered his men to the rear and remained in observation himself to obtain information. He then led an attack to beat back the enemy. Both Moto and Miyashiro were awarded Distinguished Service Crosses.

In an assault on the town of Pastina, Sgt. Togo S. Sugiyama of the 2nd Battalion spotted two German machine-gun squads, crawled to a closer observation point, and killed five men, forcing the rest to withdraw. But as he crawled back to his squad, a hidden machine gun fired at him; he was killed as he stood to return the fire. Another DSC, this time posthumously.

When the 100th was stopped along the Castellina-Rosignano Road by Germans holed up in an old castle, Pfc. Kiichi Koda volunteered to lead a squad to take the building. He threw grenades through open windows, then led the way into the castle, but he was killed by an enemy grenade. His comrades killed ten Germans and took three prisoners. Another DSC awarded for courageous leadership.

As the Nisei raced through the small towns of Italy toward Livorno, the Germans, as before, were always on the top of hills. North of Orciano, SSgt. Kazuo Otani of the 2nd Battalion fired his tommy gun to attract enemy attention to himself, organized his men against a counterattack, and directed fire at the enemy so that the rest of his platoon could reach safety. When one of the men was wounded, Otani crawled to him, dragged him to cover, and was dressing his wounds when he himself was killed by machine-gun fire. Another posthumous DSC.[14]

At Luciana, vital to the capture of Livorno, the 3rd Battalion had a two-day fight, during which Pfc. Harry F. Madokoro won a DSC. He deliberately exposed himself to an enemy machine gun and silenced it with a burst from his Browning automatic rifle (BAR).

By the time the 100th/442nd finished with Luciana, it "resembled something a man might imagine in one of his worst nightmares," according to Maj. Orville C. Shirey, historian of the 442nd Regimental Combat Team. But Luciano was taken, along with a shaggy, squint-eyed but loving mongrel pup that 3rd Battalion medics adopted and named Lucy.

The next day, July 18, Livorno fell, and the 100th Battalion moved in to protect key installations. Most of the unit was placed where the main highway entered the city because General Clark wanted to prevent looting. An incident occurred here that has become part of the 100th Battalion's folklore; no story about that battalion would be complete without it.

A private, just topping five feet tall, was standing guard at his post when a long line of army trucks stopped in front of him and a colonel stepped out. This is the conversation that followed, starting with the colonel:

"We are from the Engineer Corps. We are here to secure the port and make it ready for the ships to come in with the supplies. Let us through."

"May I see your orders, sir?"

"I don't have orders. I must get through."

"Colonel, nobody gets through without orders."

"I can kill you right here and take my convoy through."

The private drew a line with his foot and said: "Colonel, you cross this line, you *ma-ke*."

"*Ma-ke?* What is *ma-ke?*" the colonel demanded.

"*Ma-ke* means you're dead."

"We can take you; you are only one," the colonel threatened.

"You think me stupid? I am a combat soldier. You are now covered by many machine guns. Cross the line and you *ma-ke!*"

The colonel and his convoy withdrew.

The story went all the way to the top of the Fifth Army—to Gen. Mark Clark—and he came to Livorno with a bevy of newsmen and staff.

"Bring this private to me," he demanded. "I want to meet him."

As the five-foot private stood beside the six-foot four-inch general, Clark put his arm around him and turned to the press corps. "I commend this soldier to you," he said. "I personally selected the 100th to guard Leghorn because I knew my order would be obeyed and carried out. I can depend on the 100th to successfully carry out any mission. I have absolute faith in every soldier in the 100th. This private is an example of my trust."[15]

By July 21, patrols from the 2nd Battalion had penetrated Pisa, where Italian partisans, working with Allied troops to drive the Germans from Italy, provided information about enemy minefields and crossings along the Arno River. From now on, help from partisans would be invaluable to the Combat Team.

In late August the 100th Battalion was assigned to IV Corps to cross the Arno River near Pisa; the 442nd RCT was assigned to II Corps to cross the river near Florence. The 100th's crossing was unique in the annals of warfare. As Captain Kim described it:

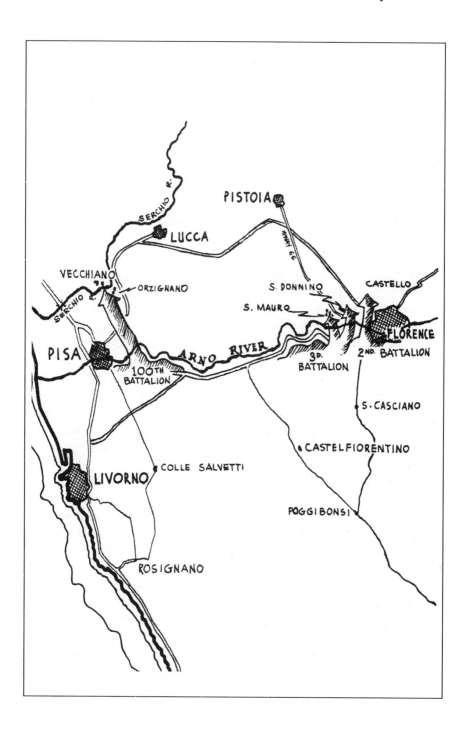

The 100th faked the Germans out of their socks and crossed literally unopposed. It was the craziest river crossing to witness—everywhere were discarded brand new, just issued, gas masks that were so poorly designed that to wear one endangered a soldier's life. The 100th soldiers were decked out in colorful Italian sport shirts, worn Hawaiian style, with numerous colorful summer parasols waving in the bright early morning sunlight. These items were just liberated the night before from abandoned factories that were in the middle of No Man's Land.[16]

The 2nd and 3rd Battalions ran into concentrated opposition and suffered numerous casualties from German troops determined to hold their line south of the Arno. But the Nisei succeeded in establishing a bridgehead on the north side of the river and began probing the periphery of the Germans' newest bastion, the Gothic line, which was being strung across the Apennine Mountains. The Germans, in their retreat, had blown all the bridges on the Arno except one: the ancient Ponte Vecchio in Florence. The reason: Hitler liked the bridge and ordered that it must not be harmed.

Just as the Fifth Army was about to tackle the Gothic line, the 100th/442nd was pulled back, destined for another front. Troops taken from Italy were being used in Operation Dragoon, the invasion of southern France. The 442nd's Antitank Company had been pulled out of the Nisei unit on July 14 for that assault and had landed along the Mediterranean coast.

One biographer of General Clark states:

He was sad when he learned that he was about to lose his Japanese Americans. . . . Their departure was a great blow to him, for they were among his ablest soldiers.[17]

Interruption of the Allied push into the Apennines at this point became one of the most controversial decisions of the war. The summer offensive had brought Allied troops 270 miles in sixty-four days—to the edge of complete victory in Italy. The Nazis were still regrouping, following their rout at Cassino and Anzio. Some military observers believe that the weakened German armies could have been driven back to the Alps at that time and that, with the success of the cross-channel invasion at Normandy, the time was ripe to knock out Hitler's armies in Italy and push Allied troops into the Balkans. But at the Teheran Conference in November 1943, Roosevelt, Churchill, and Stalin had decided instead to invade southern France after the Normandy landing.

Generals Eisenhower and Marshall were insistent that this plan be followed and that the Allied command in Italy provide the forces for that invasion. American and British commanders in Italy protested, but the U.S. chiefs of staff were adamant about carrying out the proposed southern France invasion. So, on the verge of pushing the war in Italy to a victorious conclusion, seven of the best Fifth Army divisions were shifted to the new front.

For one brief moment in World War II the Italian campaign had reaped world acclaim when it freed Rome from Nazi control. But it soon reverted to being a tragic secondary theater, which Congresswoman Clare Boothe Luce aptly described, during a visit there, as "the forgotten front." Allied forces in Italy, weakened by the transfer of troops to France, were left at the foot of the Apennines to begin trying to breach the German Gothic line while the Germans were building even more defenses farther north, including the Genghis Khan line. The decision to send troops into southern France at this juncture ultimately resulted in battles that brought the Nisei the worst casualties they would ever suffer.

That summer of 1944, while the 100th/442nd Regimental Combat Team was fighting up the west coast of Italy, Nisei of the Military Intelligence Service were landing with assault troops on a string of islands in the Pacific, the Marianas, one of which would be the base for the planes destined to carry atomic bombs to Hiroshima and Nagasaki.

Flags of the 100th Infantry Battalion and the 442nd Regimental Combat Team, with the MIS Gopher, mascot of the Military Intelligence Service Language School.

PFC Takeshi (Larry) Kazumura, believed to be the shortest man (4'9") to serve in the U.S. Army. His boots, specially ordered for him by the Quartermaster Corps, were size 2 1/2 EEE. "Shorty" salutes 1st Lt. (later Captain) Joseph L. Byrne, at 6' 3" one of the tallest men in the 442nd Regimental Combat Team. *U.S. Army Signal Corps.*

Nice, France, November 1944. The l00th/442nd was probably the only infantry unit to capture an enemy minisubmarine. *U.S. Army Signal Corps.*

Maj. John Alfred Burden (*right*) and a Nisei of the 25th Division Language Section, G-2, interrogate a Japanese prisoner on Vella Lavella, Solomon Islands. *U.S. Army Signal Corps.*

Rendova landing, Solomon Islands, 30 June 1943. Attacking at daybreak during a heavy rainstorm, the first troops to land, accompanied by Japanese Americans of the MIS, find cover behind palm trees. *Kneeling at base of tree:* Mamoru Noji. *Kneeling at left:* Kiyoto Nishimoto. *National Archives.*

Brig. Gen. Frank Merrill and Japanese Americans of the Military Intelligence Service. *Left*: Herbert Miyasaki; *right*: Akiji Yoshimura. Fourteen Nisei of the MIS fought through more than 500 miles of Burma's jungles with Merrill's Marauders. *U.S. Army Signal Corps.*

George Harada, Arthur Morimitsu, and Tom Tsunoda (*left to right*) were among the Nisei serving in Burma with the Mars Task Force, which relieved Merrill's Marauders. *U.S. Army Signal Corps.*

Shigeya Kihara, one of the first MIS language instructors.

Richard Sakakida, CIC agent.

Minoru Hara, MIS.

Sadao Munemori of the 100th Infantry Battalion, awarded the Medal of Honor.

Maj. Mitsuyoshi Fukuda, first Japanese American to command a U.S. Army battalion.

Yoshinao "Turtle" Omiya and his beloved seeing-eye dog, Audrey. Turtle was blinded on Hill 600 after the 100th Battalion's third crossing of Italy's Volturno River. *Honolulu Star-Bulletin.*

Hoichi Kubo, linguist with the MIS, comforts a Japanese child found alone in a field on Saipan. Kubo was awarded a Distinguished Service Cross for entering a cave to confront armed enemy soldiers. *U.S. Army.*

Capt. Young Oak Kim (*left*), the most decorated member of the 100th/442nd, reviews the honor guard with Lt. Gen. Mark Clark and Under Secretary of War Robert Patterson in Livorno, Italy. *U.S. Army Signal Corps.*

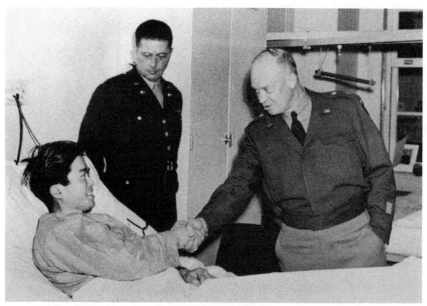

Sagie Nishioka is greeted by Gen. Dwight Eisenhower in a Colorado hospital. While in a foxhole in Italy, Nishioka received word that his name had been removed from the municipal honor roll in his hometown, Hood River, Oregon. *Courtesy Sagie Nishioka.*

Col. Kai Rasmussen, commandant of the MIS Language School, pins major's leaves on John F. Aiso. The library at the Defense Language Institute in Monterey, California, is named in Aiso's honor; he is also enshrined in the MIS Hall of Fame. *U.S. Army Signal Corps.*

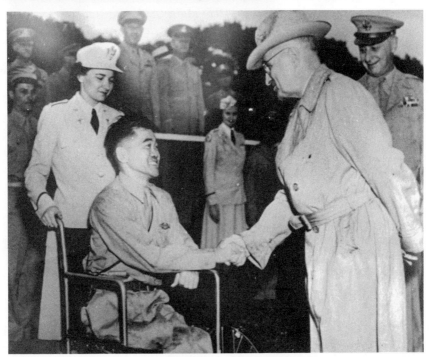

President Truman greets Wilson Makabe of the 100th Battalion after reviewing the 100th/442nd on its return from Italy in July 1946. *U.S. Army Signal Corps.*

CHAPTER 11

AN OCEAN RED WITH BLOOD

The beginning of the end for Japan was the American victory at Saipan. The island was one of the Marianas, which straddled Japanese communication lines in the Central Pacific and provided the first line of defense for the Japanese homeland. Equally important, the islands protected air and sea communications between Japan and its Pacific island holdings. Saipan, Guam, Tinian, and Rota were large enough to support air bases. They were, in effect, "stationary aircraft carriers" from which Japan could launch planes to repel American advances throughout this Pacific area. These islands and the Philippines were a vital part of Japan's overall defense strategy in the Pacific.

The American conquest of Saipan was significantly aided by the work of Nisei and Caucasian translators in Australia when a twist of fate landed secret Japanese plans in the hands of the Allied Translator and Interpreter Service. This document, known as the "Z Plan," was authored by Adm. Mineichi Koga. At the death of Adm. Isoroku Yamamoto, architect of the Pearl Harbor attack, Admiral Koga became commander in chief of the Japanese Combined Fleet. With this new command, Koga inherited Yamamoto's plans for protecting Japanese possessions in the Pacific. When this strategy brought increasing failure, Koga devised a plan for an all-out counterattack by almost the entire Japanese naval and air strength against Allied naval forces moving westward across the Central Pacific. The attack's basic objective was to destroy the U.S. Fifth Fleet and protect Japanese-held islands in the Philippines and the Marianas.

When American planes began attacks near the Palau Islands, where Koga was temporarily based, he decided to move his headquarters to Tawitawi, an island west of the Philippines, to prevent being cut off from his forces and to be nearer to Borneo's oil fields, which could provide high-grade crude oil for his ships. In planning his flight to this new command post, Koga ordered his chief of staff, Adm. Shigeru Fukudome, to board a different plane, in case of accident to his own, and gave Fukudome his copy of the Z Plan. It was bound in a red cover that bore the letter Z.

Koga's plane was lost in a tropical storm. Fukudome's plane ditched off Cebu, in the Philippines, and he was captured by Filipino fishermen who salvaged his briefcase. There was Koga's plan, wrapped in a waterproof container. Filipino guerrillas rushed it to the coast, where it was picked up by an American submarine and taken to a shore base on New Guinea. From there it was flown to MacArthur's headquarters in Brisbane, Australia. Under the direction of Colonel Mashbir, chief of ATIS, five men went to work on it. Two were Nisei: Yoshikazu Yamada (the medic who had been evacuated from Del Monte when the Philippines fell) and Koyoshi George Yamashiro, an American counterintelligence agent who had been picked up in Hawaii a few days before the Pearl Harbor attack and rushed to Australia.

The two Nisei made the final check on the twenty-two-page translation. When Yamashiro differed with everybody else on a major translation point, he implored Colonel Mashbir to have it checked with the highest authority he could find in Washington. The answer came back: Yamashiro's translation was correct. Twenty copies were made on a mimeograph machine, then flown to Admiral Nimitz's headquarters at Pearl Harbor and distributed to every flag officer in the Pacific Fleet. The document was the Japanese navy's Combined Fleet Secret Operations Order No. 73, dated March 8, 1944. Military historians have termed it one of the most significant enemy documents seized during the war.

Operation Forager was the name Americans gave the Marianas campaign. Even before it began, Koga's basic strategy had been undermined: American planes had systematically bombed Japanese air bases that, according to Koga's Z Plan, Japan would use to protect the Philippines and the Mariana Islands. At the same time, American submarines were sinking ships that carried much needed supplies and reinforcements to strengthen defenses in Saipan, leaving the Japanese command there without air defenses and adequate bulwarks and shelters to repel an invasion. A Japanese regiment bound for that island lost most of its men and weapons when ships in its convoy were sunk. Lieutenant General Yoshitsugu Saito, the Japanese commander on Saipan, had to plan his defense with 29,662 troops.

When the Americans landed on Saipan on June 15, 1944, the Japanese triggered the Z Plan, leading to one of the greatest naval battles of World War II. It was a battle for supremacy of the Philippine Sea, and its outcome would dictate the future of both the Marianas and the Philippines, as well as, ultimately, Japan itself. For three days the two fleets maneuvered closer to each other. On the morning of June 19, American radar discovered a Japanese attack group 150 miles distant, the first of four Japanese raids launched from carriers. The fighting went on all that day, with the Japanese losing 475 planes and three carriers to American attacks.[1] "The Great Marianas Turkey Shoot" was over, but the next day the American fleet chased the Japanese fleet, shot down 65 more planes, sank two carriers, three cruisers, and other ships, then headed for Saipan to cover the American invasion there. The Battle of the Philippine Sea, which Japan had long and meticulously planned, became one of the most decisive battles of the war: it resulted in a lack of reinforcements for Saipan and weakened Japan's ability to repel an American invasion of the Philippines.

At 0542 on June 15, two marine divisions began landing on Saipan, followed by the army's 27th Division with its teams of Nisei linguists.

With the 27th Division was Tim Ohta's team, which he had led from the MIS Language School to Hawaii in 1943. (Prior to Saipan, the team had been through the Marshall Islands campaign, where they had studied captured documents that proved a strong Japanese force existed on nearby Parry and Eniwetok Islands. Based on this information, the American forces revised their plans and were able to capture Eniwetok in a two-and-a-half-day assault.[2])

Naval gunfire had swept Saipan's beaches to clear landing areas, smothering the island in a cloud of smoke and dust. But through the haze, 1,554-foot Mount Tapotchau loomed clear in the center of the island, giving Japanese observers an unobstructed view in all directions. Every side of the mountain was sheer cliff, embedded with lava caves. In areas to its north there were more cliffs, ending in 833-foot Mount Marpi at the most northerly point. Along the plain on the edge of the island were Saipan's villages. The terrain would make an American victory difficult, and Japanese soldiers were still confident they would defeat this invasion.

Japan had spread anti-American propaganda throughout Saipan, frightening both soldiers and civilians with tales of American torture—to the extent that they would rather die than be captured. At one point civilians joined Japanese troops in an effort to push the Americans back into the sea, rushing at them with knives and daggers tied to the ends of bamboo sticks, climbing over dead bodies to attack the invaders. The suicidal effort ended with piles of Japanese civilians and soldiers dead.

In another catastrophic fight, Americans, trying to take well-fortified Hill 500, stormed through the valley and charged up the mountainsides. The enemy soldiers were well hidden in the caves that honeycombed the slopes. At night, Japanese civilians and soldiers would creep out of the caves to attack the Americans. Pushing north on the island, Americans suffered devastating losses as they tackled Mount Tapotchau and its adjacent areas, which marines aptly named Death Valley and Purple Heart Ridge.

As the Nisei moved with the troops across Saipan, intelligence men looked for diaries, battle orders—anything that would give clues to the enemy's welfare and plans. It was not surprising to learn that the Japanese soldiers had no thought of retreating or surrendering. The Nisei also uncovered a box of documents, which they sent on to Pearl Harbor. When the box arrived, a mistake was made. It was mistakenly marked "routine" and forwarded to the Pacific Military Intelligence Research Station at Camp Ritchie, Maryland. Fortunately, a Nisei linguist, Kazuo Yamane, discovered the box and took a look inside. The documents turned out to be a prize of inestimable future value—the National Inventory of the Japanese Arsenal, listing specific weapons in the highly classified Imperial Army Ordnance Inventory.

As the MISers worked with the troops, they were always in danger of being mistaken for the enemy. Japanese soldiers were known to dress in American uniforms in order to infiltrate U.S. lines. In fact, any brown skin could provoke a reaction. A Puerto Rican GI on Saipan was mistakenly identified as a Japanese soldier by a Caucasian GI, but was rescued in time.

Some of the Nisei moved across the island with invading American troops; others worked in camps established by the American military government for POWs and civilians. There Jesse Miyao and a team of linguists interrogated Japanese soldiers to get information about the conditions in, and the plans of, the Japanese military. It was a tough job: the captured Japanese soldiers preferred to kill themselves rather than remain prisoners.

Nisei linguists faced another task that was both difficult and pathetic: trying to reason with the civilians and enemy soldiers who had retreated into caves deep in the mountains and shoreline cliffs and save their lives. The Nisei pleaded over loudspeakers, urging people to come out before the caves were torched by flamethrowers. It was necessary to clear the caves to ensure that American soldiers wouldn't be ambushed.

One of the most spectacular feats of the Saipan invasion occurred on July 23, when a platoon from the 27th Infantry Division discovered a cave in the cliffs south of Marpi Point. The platoon, accompanied by TSgt. Hoichi Kubo, was mopping up enemy stragglers when two civilian men appeared at the edge of a cliff and stood motionless with their hands upraised. Questioning by Kubo revealed that the men had lived on the island since being brought there from Okinawa several years before by the South Seas Development Company. They and more than a hundred civilians—men, women, and children—had been held captive for ten days by eight Japanese soldiers in a large cave at the base of the cliff. The two men had escaped by climbing up a rope. After reporting the situation to his platoon commander and longtime friend, 1st Lt. Roger Pyre, Kubo returned to the Okinawans. He urged them to return to the cave and try to convince the Japanese soldiers to free the civilian captives. The men refused, fearing that they would again face captivity and, probably, death because they had escaped.

Finally, Kubo told Lieutenant Pyre: "I'm going down!" He slipped a pistol under his shirt and slid down the hundred-foot cliff via the rope the two civilians had used in their escape. It was 1000 hours when Kubo disappeared from sight. He was beyond the protection of friendly troops.

From the base of the cliff he walked about seventy-five yards through light jungle growth. Rounding a point, he found himself facing a cave. Eight Japanese soldiers were aiming their rifles at him. Their surprise at seeing someone of their own race wearing an American uniform was probably the reason they didn't fire. Kubo took off his helmet, placed it under his arm, and began talking with them.

"You're a spy!" the Japanese sergeant yelled at him.

"I am an American!" Kubo shouted back. "My grandfathers fought with the 5th and 6th [Japanese] Divisions! I am here to take out the non-combatants."

After learning that Kubo's ancestors had fought with Hiroshima and Kumamoto units, the Japanese soldiers allowed him to enter the cave to sit down and talk with them. Grenades, conspicuously placed beside the Japanese soldiers, had replaced the rifles, but Kubo paid no attention to them. Noticing that a pot of rice was being prepared, Kubo handed over his K rations as a contribution to the meal. ("I always kept about a half-dozen K's stashed away in my pockets," Kubo explained.) At the rear of the cave more than a hundred captive civilian men, women, and children huddled, listening as Kubo joined the Japanese soldiers in their meal and talked with them.

Three of the civilian prisoners later gave this report of the conversation that followed. The Japanese soldiers wanted to know how Kubo, of Japanese descent, could serve with Japan's enemy, the United States. "You are the sons of Japanese parents," Kubo replied. "You were born in Japan and fight for your country, Japan. I am also the son of Japanese parents but I was born in the United States. The United States is my country and I fight for it. The United States has honored me by making me a sergeant. I do not come here to discuss that you give yourselves up. I wish that you devote your considerations to releasing the civilians whom you are holding captive."[3]

Kubo also quoted a lesson that young Japanese students learned from their schoolbooks. Nearly eight hundred years before, in Japan, Shigemori Taira was urged by his father to lead forces against an Imperial faction. His quandary resulted in a palindrome, which Kubo repeated in Japanese; translated it reads: "If I am filial I cannot serve the Emperor. If I serve the Emperor, I cannot be filial." It was a quotation well known among Japanese, meaning that a man's loyalty goes to the higher authority: Taira must serve the Emperor and disregard his father.

Therefore, said Kubo, a Nisei must choose his native land, the United States, which was a higher authority to him than Japan.[4]

For more than an hour Kubo presented his views, pleading for the release of the civilians. Finally, the Japanese soldier in charge told Kubo to return to his platoon, promising they would discuss the question. If they reached an agreement, he said, the civilians would be allowed to climb the rope, starting at 1400.

At exactly that hour, the first of the hostages emerged over the edge of the cliff. Eventually, 122 men, women, and children came out. At the tail end of the column, the eight Japanese soldiers appeared, without their weapons, prepared to surrender.

A high-ranking regimental staff officer rushed to the scene to find out what had happened; Lieutenant Pyre gave him a report. Then a shot rang out from a nearby jungle area. Japanese soldiers hiding in the jungle, who knew nothing about what had happened in the cave, had seen the American officers and shot at the group. Lieutenant Pyre was killed instantly. His body rolled down the cliff.

When Kubo found out what had happened, he was furious. He shouted to the Japanese who had come out of the cave: "Someone shot that man who saved all of your lives! Is there not a samurai among you?" In answer, four of the Okinawans who had been held hostage climbed back down the cliff to recover Pyre's body.

"For a couple of days after that I had no desire to save anyone," Kubo, still deeply disturbed, told me. "However, when we saw those ill-nourished women and children we [Kubo and his bodyguard, Pfc. Lyle Nelson] went in again to many other caves."

The military's request to award a Distinguished Service Cross to Kubo was supported by affidavits from enemy civilians who had been held hostage in the cave. A few months later, Kubo was decorated with the DSC for "extraordinary heroism" on Saipan.

Despite his medal, Kubo does not consider himself a hero. Still regretting that he wasn't allowed to remain with the original 100th Infantry Battalion, he maintains: "They are the heroes. Not me. They left their arms, legs, eyes, life in Europe. What I did was nothing in comparison. They would have fought just as hard against Japan in the Pacific as they did against Germany in Europe. They never got that chance but it was what they—all of us in the 100th—wanted. We had to show, somehow, that America was our home, our country, the country we loved. Not Japan. There were so many lies, so much propaganda, spread against us."

Kubo had been training at Camp McCoy when the Military Intelligence Service started rounding up 100th Battalion men who could speak Japanese for intensive training at its language school. Although he had had twelve years of Japanese-language training in Hawaii, he didn't want to be shifted to any school. So he tried to pretend he didn't understand Japanese. Like the other 100th men, outraged by the bombing of their islands, he wanted to get into the shooting war. But even his appeal to the commander of the 100th Battalion couldn't stop the MIS from taking him to its language school at Camp Savage, Minnesota.

From there he had been sent back to Hawaii to work on captured documents. After that he was attached to the "Fighting 69th," the "Shamrock Battalion" of New York's 165th Infantry, and was pitched into the maelstrom of war on Makin Atoll in the Gilbert Islands. As Kubo remembered it: "We had three bodyguards and soon found out they were more to watch us than guard us."[5] Three months later Kubo was on Majoro Atoll in the Marshall Islands, followed by the invasion of Saipan.

Although Kubo's was the most spectacular of the Nisei efforts to get civilians and Japanese soldiers out of Saipan's caves, there were others. Ben Honda and George Matsui also saved many lives and won the Bronze Star. Ben Honda's award states:

> When it was ascertained that large groups consisting of both Japanese soldiers and civilian residents of Saipan were hiding in caves, he voluntarily offered to enter the caves in an effort to induce the civilians to peacefully submit to the protection of U.S. troops. On 2 July 1944 he stood at the entrance of a cave in a position where he was exposed to hostile fire, well knowing that ten armed Japanese soldiers were located in the cave. It became necessary for a patrol to kill two of the soldiers as they attempted to use their weapons. Notwithstanding his dangerous situation, he continued to perform his duty and succeeded, with the assistance of Technician 3rd Grade Matsui, in separating a large number of non-combatants from Japanese soldiers. His continued successful performance of this type of

duty has resulted in the separation of many hostile groups from non-combatants, thereby saving unnecessary bloodshed.

The desperate efforts of the Nisei sometimes failed, however, and the caves then had to be firebombed. And often the Japanese took their own lives.

On July 6, General Saito had issued a final order to his troops, commanding each man to take "seven lives to repay our country."[6] Saito had then committed seppuku, slashing an artery with a sword and commanding his adjutant to shoot him. The next day Japanese troops tried to carry out Saito's order, hurling themselves en masse against American troops and machine-gun fire, trampling over mounds of dead bodies. On the following day Americans were forced to watch the most stupendous horror they had yet witnessed. Japanese women, many with children in their arms, emerged from the caves at Marpi Point and hurled themselves into the sea from eight-hundred-foot, boulder-strewn precipices. The surviving Japanese soldiers followed them, pulling pins on their grenades as they jumped off the cliffs into the ocean until the waves were red with blood.

Nisei, calling through loudspeakers, were among those trying to prevent this disaster. According to a Marine Corps account:

> Interpreters, using public address systems, pleaded with people in caves to come out. The device was not only attempted from land but from sea as well. LCI gunboats moved close inshore and broadcast promises of good treatment, for which they were answered with fire from Japanese soldiers in the caves. Even some of Saipan's leading citizens, who had surrendered and received good treatment, talked to those in the caves, urging them to yield. But, for the effort expended, the results were not encouraging. The primary reason for this failure was that the people had been saturated with Japanese propaganda to the effect that the Americans intended to torture and kill them. This had been repeated so often that the people came to believe it.
>
> At this time the very zenith of horror occurred. Hundreds of civilians, believing that the end had come, embarked on a ghastly exhibition of self-destruction. Casting their children ahead of them,

or embracing them in death, parents flung themselves from the cliffs onto the jagged rocks below. Some waded into the surf to drown or employed other gruesome means of destroying themselves. How many civilians died in this orgy of mass hysteria is not known. A commander of a patrol craft said that progress of his boat around Marpi Point at this time was slow and tedious because of the hundreds of corpses floating in the water.[7]

Saipan was declared secure on July 9, 1944, and final mopping-up operations began. The Japanese garrison of nearly thirty thousand men had been virtually destroyed. The island was to become a base for B-29s and for broadcasts directly to Japan by Japanese Americans of the Office of Strategic Services. There were more far-reaching results, however, than just American occupation of a major Japanese base; it precipitated the downfall of Gen. Hideki Tojo, Japan's prime minister and wartime dictator, who resigned on July 20. The outcome of the battle of Saipan was the first inkling Japanese people had that their country faced defeat.

Capture of Tinian, the island four miles south of Saipan, was next in the American advance. The marines landed on July 24, and by August 1 they had rolled over the flat sugarcane fields to end Japanese resistance. Don Oka, a member of one of the Nisei intelligence teams sent there, learned after the war that his brother died participating in a kamikaze attack on the island.[8] Tinian, too, became an important base for B-29 bombers, two of which carried atomic bombs from there to Hiroshima and Nagasaki.

American naval bombardment of Guam began while Saipan was still under siege, and on July 21 two teams of Nisei linguists hit the beaches with the 1st Marine Provisional Brigade and the 3rd Marine Division. A third Nisei team went in with the 77th Infantry Division. Its leader was Shigeo Ito, an old-timer whose work with MIS dated from 1942 when he was put ashore on the Aleutian island of Attu to interview a Japanese officer. On the way across that island he sometimes had to find shelter under ledges among the dead bodies of Japanese soldiers.[9]

The MISer team that went in with the 3rd Marine Division was led by Lincoln Taira and included one of the most remarkable of the Nisei linguists, Stanley S. Shimabukuro.[10] (Five months later in the Philippines, Shimabukuro's translations of captured Japanese documents and battle orders would help determine the timing of a major shift of American troop strength from Leyte to Luzon to retake Manila.)

As soon as Nisei of the Military Intelligence Service finished their battles in the Marianas, they would join in more Pacific invasions: Iwo Jima and the Philippines; some, ultimately, would land on Okinawa.

On the other side of the world the newly combined 100th/442nd Regimental Combat Team had been fighting up Italy's west coast to cross the Arno River. Soon the unit would be shifted to France, where it would wage its most tragic battle: the fight to save the Lost Battalion of the 36th Infantry Division.

CHAPTER 12

FORESTS OF DEATH

When the 100th/442nd Regimental Combat Team was transferred from the Arno River to bivouac outside of Naples, the men knew they would be leaving Italy. They arrived in Naples Harbor about midnight on September 11, were assigned to Seventh Army, and began guessing their next destination. Most hoped they would get to Paris, the goal of every GI. Some figured they'd be sent to the Pacific, or maybe hit both places.

During the wait for shipment to "somewhere," a few men got passes to see the ruins of Pompeii. Others went into Naples. The city was a catastrophe. Streets teemed with impoverished, homeless people, with begging children, with prostitutes and their pimps. Some men visited the big army hospitals where wounded comrades had been taken for treatment before a trip to stateside hospitals—or back to the lines.

Another group of Nisei arrived to join the 100th/442nd. But most of them differed from earlier replacements in one important way: they were draftees, the first such to arrive since the army reinstated the draft for Japanese Americans.

Finally, on September 27, 1944, the 100th/442nd sailed for Marseilles to be attached to the 36th "Texas" Division, operating with the U.S. Seventh Army in southern France. The 36th was still called "Texas Division" despite the fact that men from almost every state of the union were in it. Many who initially made up this National Guard unit had been killed or wounded in North Africa and the hard push through Italy, including the Rapido River crossing, which had been catastrophic for them.

A number of war correspondents reached southern France in mid-August after the Seventh Army landed, and a group of them, including Frank Gervasi of *Colliers* and Eric Sevareid of CBS, were trying to make their way north when they stumbled on the 36th Division's command post, which had been surrounded. As Gervasi described the situation:

> We asked to see the general, but our hearts sank when he stepped out of his trailer. The man who had replaced General Walker . . . appeared in trousers and undershirt, and "flop sweat" beaded his brow. His decidedly unmilitary appearance, manner, and what he said were almost as disturbing as the prospect of capture. . . . He . . . counted us off, and grunted: "Well five more men might help. You may have rifles in your hands before morning."[1]

(Journalists were never armed. If they were captured carrying weapons, Germans were entitled to shoot them.)

Gervasi's estimate of the new commander of the 36th Division, Maj. Gen. John E. Dahlquist, presaged the fate of the Nisei assigned to his command.

The Seventh Army's advance up the Rhone Valley had been rapid until autumn, when it reached the Vosges Mountains in northeast France, near the German border. There the Germans used mountains and dense evergreen forests to bolster their advantage. They hoped to hold the Vosges as long as possible before retreating into Germany itself.

The mission of the Allied armies in eastern France was to seize passes through the Vosges Mountains and launch an offensive that would carry them to Strasbourg and across the Rhine River into Germany. The focal point of the U.S. Seventh Army's autumn drive was Saint-Dié, an industrial, commercial, and communications center and the key to three important Vosges Mountain passes, one of which led northward to the Sélestat/Strasbourg area. Guarding a vital approach to Saint-Dié was the town of Bruyères, a rail center and road intersection of approximately five thousand people. German troops had been concentrated in the area to prevent Allied capture of Bruyères. And so far they had. The 100th/442nd Regimental Combat Team was ordered to take the town.

The Combat Team was now fighting in the Alsace-Lorraine area, which for centuries had been a battleground for the Germans and French. It was an area where French patriotism ran high and hatred for the "Boche" was deep. A U.S. Army Intelligence report stated:

> It is evident that the enemy is fighting where he can, and with what troops he can lay hands upon, and shows all signs of attempting to prevent the battle from reaching into Germany. The enemy does not yet show any signs of admitting defeat, and it should be expected that he will continue to hold every piece of ground until he has been forced to surrender it.[2]

Further emphasizing the importance of the Vosges Mountains was a report by German prisoners that a Fuehrer *Befehl* (Hitler edict) commanded that the area be held at all costs.[3]

At 0800 on October 15, the Nisei shouldered their packs, hefted weapons, and moved with Seventh Army infantry and support groups to begin the fight to free Bruyeres. The town lay in a valley bordered on three sides by four conical hills. For easy reference the hills had been named A, B, C, and D: Hill A, the highest, was eighteen hundred feet. All were seeded with mines and protected by felled trees, roadblocks, machine guns, sniper fire, tanks, rocket launchers, and a determined enemy. Intermittent fog and dense pine growth hid the enemy. The few roads and trails were soon tramped into swamps. Artillery barrages and screeching Nebelwerfers pounded continuously. Slit trenches had to be roofed with logs as protection against tree bursts. The rain was constant and heavy, filling slit trenches, turning to ice. The Nisei tried to ignore the cold, drenching rain, but uniforms, socks, and boots were soaked. Numbed feet began to swell.

It was a new kind of terrain for the Nisei, vastly different from Italy, where the land was hilly and sparse. Italy was M1 country—the three-hundred-yard (open) range of M1s came in handy there. France, on the other hand, was Thompson machine-gun country. Unable to get tanks and tank destroyers through the thick forests, the Nisei formed bazooka teams and successfully beat back the German tanks they encountered.

On and between the hills the enemy held fortified farmhouses. Two of these, about twenty feet apart, were near the foot of Hill A, and a detachment from Company C rushed across open plowed land to investigate them. Sergeant Mike Tokunaga, with three men, headed toward the first house, but they were driven back by machine-gun fire and took cover behind a nearby stone wall. Lieutenant Masanao Otake, with one man, went to the second house and fought until he was wounded by machine-pistol fire. His body lay in the open and his buddy rushed to get help. While Otake's partner distracted the Germans by firing, Tokunaga ran across the open space and dragged Otake's body to the side of the house, where enemy fire could not reach them. In spite of their efforts, Otake died without regaining consciousness. Another DSC, posthumous.

Working up the slopes, dodging between trees, the Nisei rooted Germans out of their machine-gun nests. The 522nd Field Artillery Battalion and the 36th Division's 131st Field Artillery Battalion laid down heavy barrages. But the Germans surged again to retake positions, and more German troops were being poured into the area. The hellish fighting went on through heavy rain.

The 100th Battalion finally took Hill A on October 18. By then the 2nd Battalion had a tenuous hold on Hill B, and the 3rd Battalion had pushed through a valley that led into Bruyeres and had begun creeping along the narrow streets, fighting house to house. At 1830 the 3rd Battalion met up with the 36th Division's 143rd Infantry Regiment, which had fought its way into the town from the south. After four years of brutal Nazi occupation, Bruyeres was in Allied hands.

The two units began mop-up operations to rout the remaining enemy. Colonel Pence, commander of the 100th/442nd, rode into town in a jeep while the 3rd Battalion's K Company was still fighting to clear a roadblock. A group of Germans had taken refuge behind two massive concrete barricades, and it took the combined force of infantry and the Nisei 232nd Engineer Company to dig them out.

The two other hills, C and D, and the nearby railroad embankment remained in German hands. General Dahlquist raced around the battlefield, giving orders to officers who knew the enemy strength and conditions and had infinitely more combat experience. Dahlquist had held prestigious desk positions but had little time in combat. The result was a growing dislike for the general, in addition to confusion and consternation. Despite this, the two remaining hills were taken. But the 100th/442nd officers felt that many casualties could have been avoided if

Dahlquist had not interfered with plans they had made on the basis of intelligence reports and personal knowledge.

More DSCs were awarded to the Nisei for this action:

On Hill D, SSgt. Yoshimi Fujiwara, leading a squad that was threatened by German tanks, tried to stop the tanks with antitank grenades. When that didn't work he got a bazooka and fired at them. He damaged one tank, but it continued to advance. He kept firing rockets, even though their flash exposed his position, and finally knocked out the lead tank. The second tank withdrew. He had stopped a breakthrough in his sector.[4]

Technical Sergeant Abraham Ohama of F Company was wounded on Hill D when he went to aid a man from his platoon who had been hit. Both men were on stretchers when the Germans opened fire, killing Ohama. Nisei retribution for this violation of the Geneva Convention was swift and devastating. Without any command, they charged up the hill, fighting hand to hand, tree to tree, killing fifty Germans and refusing to take any prisoners.[5] At the end of two days of fighting, more than a hundred German bodies were counted on Hill D. (This was not typical behavior for the Nisei: the Combat Team reeled in hundreds of prisoners during fighting in the valleys and farmhouses and the men were known for their considerate treatment of these captives.)

In another incident on Hill D, the Germans shot again at a carrying party. To stop the carnage, SSgt. Robert Kuroda led an attack on a machine-gun nest, killing the crew. When he saw a 442nd lieutenant hit, he ran to help him, but the officer was dead. Kuroda picked up the lieutenant's tommy gun and knocked out another machine-gun emplacement. As he turned to fire on enemy riflemen, a sniper killed him. But the carrying party had been rescued. Another posthumous DSC.[6]

The prayers of the Bruyeres people were not only for their own safety but also for the Americans fighting to free their town. The people hid in cellars, without electricity and with diminishing supplies of food and water, listening to the sounds of war. In his book *Bridge of Love,* John Tsukano, a member of the 100th Battalion, describes the chaotic conditions in the beleaguered town. He tells the story of a fifteen-year-old boy, Serge Carlesso, who was wounded by shrapnel when he left his family's cellar to search for food.

At the field hospital, the doctors are barely able to save Carlesso's right leg, but his left leg had to be amputated. . . . The first person he sees after the gruelling operation is a 442nd soldier who had also lost a leg, smiling at him. This, Carlesso remembers most of all.[7]

A young doctor, Raymond Collin, was with his family in their cellar when he heard noises in his upstairs hallway and went to investigate. In the darkness the figures were indistinct. He thought they were Germans until one called out: "Don't be frightened. We're from Hawaii."

It was what he and the rest of Bruyeres had waited so long to hear. His wife had secretly made an American flag. Now she hoisted it from a second-story window. Her sister, oblivious to the danger, ran into the street to kiss and welcome these strange, Asian-looking American soldiers.[8]

Appalled by the condition of the Bruyeres people, the Nisei dug deep in their backpacks for whatever they could share with these new friends: cigarettes, candy bars, snacks from their own meals. In sign language and smiles they spoke to each other through the curtain of alien languages. From the Hawaii Nisei, the children of Bruyeres learned "Hawaii Ponoi," the anthem of the Territory of Hawaii. And they learned what "aloha" meant in both words and deeds. The friendships grew into a mutual admiration that neither the people of Bruyeres nor the Japanese-American soldiers would ever forget.

On October 19 the last Germans were captured. Bruyeres was free, though German gunfire from hills to the north could still be heard.

The next day, at 1930, the following message was telephoned from 36th Division headquarters to 442nd headquarters:

> General wants you to know the 442nd is not getting publicity in *Beachhead News* due to censorship. Please tell men and S-6 [Colonel Pence] that the General appreciates their efforts and regrets censorship does not permit mention of the 442nd.

There is no record of any 442nd reply to this message; the next communication was about plans for a "flanking attack" outside Bruyeres.

The operations in the Vosges were in fact being carried out under a cloud of secrecy. Because the Germans knew the Nisei had been fighting in Italy, public acknowledgment of their presence in southern France, or the presence of other units shifted from the Italian front, would have provided the Germans valuable intelligence information. But the Nisei still felt their role in the capture of Bruyeres should have been acknowledged.

Another irritant to the men of the 100th/442nd was the fact that all of the Combat Team's recommendations for award of the Medal of Honor up to that time were downgraded to the lesser Distinguished Service Cross.

Although Bruyeres had been taken, fighting for hills around the city continued. On October 20, a German armored column began moving south toward Bruyeres. P-47 Thunderbolt fighter-bombers and a special task force of armor and infantry turned it back.

After the 100th/442nd had taken the hills, the men secured a railroad embankment at the edge of town and began pushing the Germans north toward the forested area of Belmont. Aided by defense plans found on a dead German officer, a task force commanded by Maj. Emmet L. O'Connor and consisting of one company each from the Nisei 2nd and 3rd Battalions struck the enemy rear and cleared the ridge dominating the village of Belmont. The action earned a Presidential Citation for F and L Companies of the 100th/442nd.

At this point, General Dahlquist gave the command that would threaten the 100th Battalion with annihilation. While the 2nd and 3rd Battalions continued fighting to free areas immediately around Bruyeres, Dahlquist ordered the 100th to take the high ground overlooking the village of Biffontaine, northeast of Bruyeres. Max-Henri Moulin, leader of a group of thirty French underground patriots serving with the Freedom Fighters of the Interior (FFI), assigned his men, led by Jean Drahon, to guide the 100th Battalion through the thick forests. Before they reached the hills, the men had to tramp through exposed areas where they were strafed by enemy planes. When the men finally reached the high ground above Biffontaine, German lines closed in on three sides. A young Nisei from Hawaii later wrote:

We wait for the inevitable. The Germans have us just where they want us. My gunner and I dig a deep hole under a big rock, afraid of what is in store for us. We exchange worried looks but say nothing. Night is fast approaching. Everybody is quiet, except our sergeant who reminds us to go easy on our rations and water. We receive an order to fire five rounds of heavy explosive mortar shells. We don't know what the target is. We only know the range, deflection and instructions. As soon as we fire the first shell we know what is going to happen. . . .

We await the onslaught of powder and steel which is sure to follow. Then the slaughter begins. It starts from the forward position. Like a slithery snake, it weaves to the right, then to the left, each time moving closer to where we are. . . . and as it comes nearer and nearer our slit trench, my gunner and I are grateful that we dug our hole under a large rock. . . . After the barrage, there is silence, an eerie kind of silence . . . As expected, many are wounded seriously, a few are buried in their slit trenches. A grotesque sight catches my eyes. A shattered hand and arm is embedded on a shattered branch halfway up a tall pine tree and it's waving at me. It sends chills up my spine and makes me want to vomit. Our worst imaginations when we first entered the Vosges forests have come true. Trees with human parts. Humans with tree parts. . . .

One of the recent replacements who is seriously wounded is placed in an open slit trench next to us. There is nothing more the medics could do for him. We are now surrounded by the enemy so he cannot be evacuated. Both of his eyes are swollen so much that he can no longer see. We don't know him. He is not from our company. . . . He and most of the others in that replacement group were "kotonks" from the mainland. Most of them had been drafted prior to or immediately after Pearl Harbor before all Japanese Americans were declared ineligible for the draft. . . .

We look at the replacement now lying in the shallow slit trench and wish that he had not volunteered. . . . If he dies, as he surely will, how will his death affect his parents, brothers and sisters who are still locked up behind barbed wires? Will they understand his death? Will they believe that the death of their son and brother will contribute something positive?

The dawn confirms what we had feared all along. The young replacement died in the night. . . . For us from Hawaii, the tears are genuine and sincere. By now we have come to know our mainland "kotonks" very well. We have identified with them and they with us. We are united in a common cause.[9]

The 100th had advanced more than a mile from the nearest friendly troops; the forest trail over which it had come was patrolled by the enemy, and Germans had tapped its phone line. Ammunition was nearly exhausted and the men were using captured German supplies. Water and food couldn't get through. An armored force carrying water, food, and ammunition, with a platoon of Nisei soldiers riding the tanks, fought to break through German lines. It was ambushed by enemy fire, but Sgt. Itsumu Sasaoka stayed on top of his tank and kept firing his machine gun. Critically wounded, he continued shooting until the convoy passed the Germans. Then, weakened by loss of blood, he fell from his perch. Although the tanks were finally forced to retreat, friends went back to search for Sasaoka. He was never found. Later he was sighted at a German POW camp but was killed by invading Russian forces. His DSC was another posthumous award.

On October 22, the 100th messaged headquarters: "The 100th will have to be throwing stones if they don't get any ammo."

Later that day another message from the 100th: "We are getting enemy action from the rear. Will probably have to use the cooks pretty soon. . . . Colonel Singles wants you to know that the area is too big. Being hit from three sides."

And in midafternoon: "Colonel Singles wants me to tell you we are being hit from the rear, we have no supplies."

When supplies finally reached the 100th Battalion they were carried on men's backs. Jeeps couldn't maneuver on sodden trails, blocked by debris and shattered trees. Finding the way was also a problem. Trails shown on the maps no longer existed or had been intertwined with other trails carved by Germans in their long occupation of the area. It was men from the FFI who finally guided a supply party to relieve the beleaguered 100th Battalion.

In a surprise move to cut off the 100th, the Germans moved up bicycle troops, but the Nisei 2nd Battalion pushed the Germans back. Then the 100th received an order from General Dahlquist that no one in the unit understood the rationale behind: descend from the ridge overlooking Biffontaine and take the town itself. The move would place the battalion beyond range of artillery support and radio communications, to capture an objective that battalion leaders believed was tactically worthless. Biffontaine was a small farming community of a few hundred souls without any rail line passing through it.

The battalion swarmed down the steep hills from three sides. By sundown it held the town but was surrounded by Germans. The other two Nisei infantry battalions were fighting to break through to it. That night the Germans regrouped and descended on the town, swarming among the houses, shouting: "Surrender! You are surrounded."

"Go to hell!" the Nisei yelled back, plus other obscenities, shouted in Japanese, English, and pidgin.

In house-to-house, room-to-room fighting, the 100th beat the Germans back. When houses collapsed from enemy shelling, the Nisei went into cellars. When Germans entered ruined houses, the Nisei rushed from cellars to fight them again.

The villagers helped the Japanese Americans when they could. The French from this and other villages in the Alsace-Lorraine area had fought Germans in World War I. One of those severely injured in that war was a man named Voirin. He and his wife, Josephine, and their small son lived in a Biffontaine farmhouse where approximately thirty wounded Nisei were brought. Other Nisei soldiers prepared to defend the home from enemy tanks, which were now shooting point-blank at village houses. Madame Voirin placed the most seriously wounded on mattresses; others lay on the bare floor. One, so badly hurt that his stomach and bowels were exposed, could not hold the cup of water she offered, so she spoon-fed him. He managed to grasp her hand and whisper to her, but the only word she understood was "Mama." He died a few minutes later.[10]

At dawn on October 23, a German patrol intercepted a group of soldiers struggling from Biffontaine toward Belmont; they were moving wounded Nisei soldiers using captured Germans as litter bearers. Captain Kim spotted the enemy soldiers before they reached the litter train, and he flashed a signal to T4g. Richard Chinen, a medic, that he would attempt an escape. Kim, though wounded and under sedation, jumped off his litter and, followed by Chinen, disappeared into the surrounding woods. The two men finally made their way back to regimental headquarters.

One of the 100th men taken prisoner that morning was Pfc. Stanley Akita, who was among the guards accompanying the litter-bearing detail. Akita and both of his parents had been born on the Island of Hawaii, where his father had been a first sergeant in the Hawaii National Guard. Akita was with the first 442nd replacements sent to the 100th Battalion following the devastating Battle of Cassino, and he had fought all the way up the boot of Italy before being sent with the 100th to France.

After his capture, Akita was taken to a prison camp in Germany, Stalag 7A, near Landshut. His first German interrogator inferred that because Akita was of Japanese descent he should be fighting for Germany, the Axis partner of Japan.

The German asked him: "How come you're fighting for America?"

"Because I'm an American," Akita answered.

"What makes you feel like an American?"

"Because I was born in America," Akita replied.[11]

In midmorning of October 23, General Dahlquist sent a message to the 100th, telling it to hold out. Relief was pushing through, he said. By dusk, reinforcements from the 3rd Battalion had arrived and the last German attack was beaten back.

At 1715 that night the message went out to division headquarters: "Biffontaine now belongs to the 36th."

The Nisei were relieved by elements of the 36th Division, and by nightfall of October 24, the 100th and 3rd Battalions arrived at the rest area around Belmont. The 2nd Battalion got there the previous day. They were bone-tired, and many had swollen feet from exposure to rain and cold. After nearly two weeks of living on the ground, the men welcomed the shelter of pup tents or slit trenches, despite the enemy shells still falling around them. They received their pay for the month of September, and mail caught up with them. They showered, ate square meals, slept, and settled down to various pastimes—playing cards, shooting craps, reading, writing home, attending church services. And the Quartermaster Corps had a surprise for the Nisei: a huge lot of Women's Auxiliary Corps (WAC) clothing, proudly displayed at Belmont.

Ever since the Japanese-American soldiers had become part of the armed forces, the Quartermaster Corps had been deluged with demands for clothes and boots that would fit them. The corps had done its best, but small sizes simply weren't available. It was tough to fit troops whose average height was 5 feet 4 inches; average weight, 125 pounds; neck size 13 1/2 inches; sleeves, 27 inches; trousers, 26-inch waists and 25-inch inseams. The solution: WAC clothing!

The men and officers were skeptical. They looked the ladies' apparel over carefully, snorting disdainfully at the female underwear. They did gladly accept the WAC raincoats, however. But there were still no boots, the most basic necessity for infantry.

While at Belmont the 100th/442nd received some good news: the Combat Team's Antitank Company had completed its assignment in southern France and would be rejoining them. None too soon, for urgent messages began arriving on October 24. The 36th Division's 141st Regiment was in a firefight and needed help.

At 0845 on October 24, the 141st Regiment, following General Dahlquist's orders, had begun moving along the ridge north of the village of La Houssiere to reach the highway running to Saint-Dié. When Lt. William Bird of the 141st asked General Dahlquist if the rear flank would be protected, the general replied that no Germans were there.[12]

Less than an hour after taking off, the 141st was in trouble. The following communication is recorded in the 442nd Infantry journal:

The 141st is having trouble up there. What they thought were Maquis are not Maquis but Miliciens. So warn all your outfits if they (Frenchmen) should make any act of hostility, just shoot, and try to get prisoners because we'd like to get some information. . . . The 100th had reported some Frenchmen being not so civil. . . . These Milicien are French collaborators, and very dangerous. There are no Maquis now. They have all been called back and disbanded.

After covering about seven kilometers along the ridge, the 141st Regiment was attacked again, and its Headquarters Company, along with part of its 1st Battalion, was trapped by Germans moving in on all sides. The battalion tried to fight its way free but failed. The other two battalions of the 141st Regiment fought to reach it. They couldn't. The trapped Texas battalion had only radio communication to connect it with the outside world. For two days the unit was isolated on a hilltop north of La Houssiere.

General Dahlquist next ordered the 100th/442nd Nisei, still exhausted after their battles to free Bruyeres and Biffontaine, to rescue the trapped Texas battalion.

On October 26, at 0300, the Nisei 2nd Battalion slogged through the freezing rain to reach its jump-off point. How far would the Nisei have to fight before they reached the Lost Battalion? "As the crow flies," it was something like four miles. But circling enemy strong points made it more like nine miles, climbing ridges and hills and circumventing mined paths and dense evergreen woods. German observation posts, hidden in the forest, directed artillery fire on every vehicle and troop movement.

The 2nd Battalion advanced a couple hundred yards. Faced with an enemy perched on overlooking hills with heavy artillery, and threatening to swarm down and surround them, the Nisei battalion dug in and waited for help.

Before dawn the next day the 442nd's 100th and 3rd Battalions were called from reserve to join the battle. They sloshed through the mud in the darkness, squares of white toilet paper fastened on the men's backs, to help those following keep the line of march.

On October 27, as they pushed to rescue the surrounded Texas battalion, the Nisei were pitted against the most densely packed and determined enemy forces they had ever faced. The three Japanese-American infantry battalions started off abreast, with the 2nd on the left, the 3rd in the center, and the 100th on the right. With them was the largest support group they had ever known: their own 522nd Field Artillery Battalion, 232nd Engineer Company, and Cannon Company, plus tank, chemical, and mortar battalions from the 36th Division and other Seventh Army units. They knew what they were up against. German prisoners had told interrogators that Hitler was watching this fight and had commanded that the trapped battalion be held at any cost. No prisoners were to be taken; the stranded Texans would be killed.

Combat in the dense woods of the Vosges was like jungle fighting, with soldiers dodging from tree to tree, trying to shoot the enemy or escape from him. Heavy fog shrouded the mountains. The temperature was down to freezing. If they were lucky, soldiers could see twenty feet ahead through the forest. Squad leaders often could see only two or three of their men. Sometimes it was so dark they could hardly see anything. A message at 0710 read: "It's so dark you can't see your hand in front of your face. I don't want to walk blindly into them."

German machine guns had been dug in, then camouflaged with dense forest growth. The Germans would wait until the GIs passed, then spring the trap, shooting them from behind as they faced firepower ahead. Enemy machine guns on hilltops fired down on infantry approaching from below, shooting with mathematical precision—one gun taking over to rake territory where the previous gun left off, with mortars covering any open space between. Nebelwerfers screamed at all hours of the day and night. Tanks were of limited use on the narrow roads that topped steep ridges. Captain Pershing Nakada's Nisei engineers built corduroy roads of logs, then rebuilt them after the tanks splintered them. There was little, sometimes no, cover for engineers. Too often, they had to throw down their tools and take up guns to defend themselves. The ridges were too narrow to accommodate infantry companies, so men fought on hillsides and in the ravines below.

The physical suffering was excruciating: pain from trench foot, sickness from exposure to cold and rain, fatigue from lack of sleep. But the men staggered on, without a break. Joe Itagaki and other mess sergeants tried to get hot meals to the men, but it was often impossible. And when food did reach them, they were often too tired to eat. At night—if they could stop—they dug holes and roofed them with logs as protection against the deadly shards of metal and tree parts that were thrown on them when shells burst overhead. When they were just too tired to dig holes they rested under the trees and hoped for the best.

Even if they dug holes, they weren't always safe. Sergeant Mike Tokunaga remembers the night he dug a shallow hole, settled in to rest, and then discovered he didn't have any cigarettes. Looking through the darkness, he couldn't see anything except trees, so he waited for an artillery barrage to end, then shouted: "Hey, anyone got a cigarette?"

"Yeah," someone yelled.

"Okay, I come bum one."

He crawled out of his hole and ran, crouching, toward the voice. Hidden by a shelter half, he smoked a cigarette with the other fellow. As he started to return to his hole, the Germans began another systematic barrage of the area. He waited until it was over, then ran to find his own hole. It wasn't there. He knelt down and felt cloth under his hands—remnants of his backpack. They smelled of gunpowder. He shuddered and crawled away. He remembers thinking: If I were here, I'd be dead. Thank the Lord I wasn't here. It doesn't matter whether He's a Christian or a Buddhist Lord. I'll thank whichever Lord saved me.[13]

Sergeant Stanley Nakamoto of the 100th Battalion remembers the night he and his men were on a hill, trying to get some much-needed rest:

> It was so quiet! And the Germans were letting us alone so my men dozed off. Suddenly I heard Germans talking! I crawled and saw them coming up the hill and I grabbed my tommy gun and began shooting. A German almost got one of my boys, Takeshi Teshima, but I unloosened all the hand grenades I had and unloaded them on the Jerries and opened up with my tommy. When my boys began shooting, the Jerries must have thought it was a whole company there so they took off.

The Japanese Americans had begun to make an impression on the Germans, Nakamoto told me:

> When we first came up to the front we saw the American soldiers of the 36th Division who tried to rescue that battalion, all dead in their foxholes. They were all over the place. They couldn't do it so we had to go in. As we approached closer we saw German soldiers. Allan Ohata and I went from tree to tree. The Germans didn't see us.
>
> Then an American tank began coming up from the rear and it made a lot of noise and the Germans opened fire with mortar barrages. Our boys started throwing grenades, one after the other. Fast! I think the Germans knew then that the Japanese soldiers were on the line. They were afraid of us, you know. They didn't counterattack that time.[14]

As the three battalions moved forward, the 2nd Battalion, commanded by Lt. Col. James Hanley, left the other two units and veered northeast toward Hill 617. The German guns on the heights could rake the area in which the rest of the 442nd was fighting. Hanley maneuvered his battalion until it reached Hill 617. Then he placed one of his companies along the bottom of the west side, stringing it out so that it looked like a whole battalion; he led his other two companies farther north until they reached a ridge occupied by U.S. Seventh Army infantry. He was setting a trap that, if successful, would weaken German firepower aimed at the other two battalions.

Meanwhile, as the 100th and 3rd Battalions continued on, they found out from captured Germans that reinforcements were being packed in north of Biffontaine. The surrounded Texas battalion was in a desperate situation. It had lost more men in repeated attempts to break out of its encirclement. Its wounded needed medical help. The battalion's only remaining radio was short on batteries. In every message to regimental headquarters the stranded men asked for batteries but they had yet to receive any. Most air-dropped supplies had landed in trees or in ravines below them. With fog making visibility near zero, it was hard for reconnaissance planes to fly, but one was able to make it over the Lost Battalion's hill and reported that the Texans were crowded into a space a little more than four hundred yards across on the top of the hill.

Communications from 36th Division headquarters to the Japanese Americans were constant and demanding. On October 28 the Nisei 100th and 3rd Battalions, fighting on and alongside a ridge, were stopped by roadblocks. Under heavy fire, engineers tried frantically to clear the area for the waiting battalions. General Dahlquist's order to the 442nd's Colonel Pence: "Get the men out there crawling and get the Krauts out of the holes."

By day's end on October 28, the 2nd Battalion had completed its preparations at Hill 617. The trap was set. Colonel Hanley was ready to launch a surprise attack on Hill 617.

It was none too soon. The isolated Texas battalion had beaten back five enemy assaults, with mounting deaths and casualties. They had covered their foxholes with branches from trees and bushes, pooled and rationed their food, and collected rainwater to alleviate their water shortage. Attempts to break out only meant more deaths, so they sat and waited, listening to the sounds of battle as men tried to reach them.

October 29 was the worst day. At 0830 General Dahlquist was on the phone, ordering officers at 442nd headquarters: "Keep them [the Nisei] going and don't let them stop. There's a battalion about to die up there and we've got to reach them."

Sixteen minutes later the general was on the phone again: "Let's keep them going. Even against opposition."

Captain Pershing Nakada, commander of the 232nd Engineer Company, was up front supervising removal of a roadblock when he heard that order. Nakada—whose first name was given in honor of Gen. John J. Pershing, under whom his father had served as an orderly in World War I—later recalled that nobody in the 442nd respected Dahlquist. "He didn't give a damn how many people we killed as long as we just got up there."[15]

When the general wasn't up front giving orders, he was on the phones until harassed regimental staff officers, who knew the situation firsthand, ignored his commands. On one of his many trips to the front, General Dahlquist began giving orders to Lt. Allan Ohata, a much-decorated veteran of the Italian campaign. Ohata listened politely. Stan Nakamoto, who heard the exchange, remembers it this way:

> Dahlquist: "How many men do you have here?"
>
> Ohata: "One company, sir."
>
> Dahlquist: "That's enough. Here's what you do. We've got to get onto that hill and across it. You get all the men you have and charge straight up that hill with fixed bayonets. That's the only way we can get the Krauts off it."
>
> Ohata: "You want my men to charge up that hill, sir?"
>
> Dahlquist: "Straight up. It's the quickest way. There's a battalion going to die if we don't get to it."
>
> Ohata: "You realize what this means for our men, sir? They'll be slaughtered climbing a hill in the face of heavy fire in full daylight."
>
> Dahlquist: "It's *got* to be done."
>
> Ohata: "I refuse to accept your order. You can court-martial me. You can strip me of my rank and decorations but I refuse to accept your order."
>
> Dahlquist: "You REFUSE? I'm ORDERING you: take your men and make a bayonet charge up that hill and get those Krauts off it quick."
>
> Ohata: "We'll get them off it OUR way and try to save as many of our men as possible."[16]

The general walked away from this exchange without another word, and Ohata and his men knocked the Germans off the hill—but they did it their way. Ohata was never reprimanded and his decorations were never taken away.

Rudi Tokiwa remembers a similar incident involving Lt. Col. Alfred Pursall, a hefty midwesterner who was commander of the Nisei 3rd Battalion:

> General Dahlquist came up to Colonel Pursall and I heard him say: "Order your men to fix bayonets and charge." Pursall got real angry, . . . [and] told the general, "Those are my boys you're trying to kill. You're not going to kill my boys. I won't let you kill my boys. If there's any orders to be given for my boys to attack, I'll give the orders personally and I'll lead them."[17]

Shortly afterward, the Lost Battalion had a very close call. The 522nd Field Artillery Battalion received a startling request from Capt. Moyer Harris, one of its forward observers: he was checking on an order from the general to fire artillery:

> Captain Harris: "345573. I want clearance from 1st Battalion 141st [the Lost Battalion] on that hill."
> 522nd Field Artillery Battalion reply: "We'll have to check with them. That plots right in the middle of the Lost Battalion."
> 522nd Field Artillery Battalion to Regimental Headquarters: "We had a call from forward observer that General Dahlquist wanted some [fire] on Hill 345573. Isn't that right in the middle of the Lost Battalion?"
> Regimental Headquarters: "Yes, it's in the middle of the Lost Battalion."[18]

So the firing coordinates were changed. The Texans were "saved" for the first time by the alert Nisei.

Captain Billy Taylor of the 522nd Field Artillery Battalion remembers October 29 as one of the most active days in the battle to rescue the Lost Battalion. It was the sixth day the Texans had been isolated and the fourth day the Nisei spent fighting to reach them. It was crucial to get artillery onto the German forces that separated the isolated Texans from their rescuers. Taylor explains their problem:

In order to comply with the General's order and give support to the 3rd Battalion's I and K companies and not fire on them or on the 141st Battalion [the Lost Battalion], we had to know their exact locations and coordinate on our firing map. The 3rd Battalion headquarters and companies couldn't give us this information as the platoons had moved and dug in close to the enemy. This was when we were sent to the 3rd Battalion headquarters and company areas to tie in and locate their positions by map coordinates. We were successful in identifying their positions on our maps by means of using "aiming circles," roads and other landmarks—"mosaics" as well as overlays and maps.[19]

Sergeant Don Shimazu of the 522nd Field Artillery Battalion's survey section led a seven-man team through German minefields that day to locate infantry units of the 100th/442nd and pinpoint their positions to protect them against fire from their own artillery battalion. Before beginning the task he asked if any men wanted to be excused. None did. It wasn't until they saw signs warning "Actung Minen" (Attention Mines) that they knew they were going through minefields. But they got through without tripping any booby traps. They reached the infantry and figured out on the map exactly where they were. Then they radioed their locations back to headquarters.

On this day the 3rd Battalion faced the most crucial fight of its history as it tried to advance along a narrow ridge with precipitous slopes on each side. Weakened by the loss of men and officers, it called up rear-echelon personnel: kitchen crews, mail workers, anyone who could hold a gun. Only two companies could attack along the ridge. K and I Companies were there. On top of the hill ahead, the men faced one of the most astounding concentrations of weapons they had ever seen: machine guns with interlocking fields of fire, mortars, and grenadiers covering any gaps. Colonel Pursall first tried a flank attack up the left side of the enemy-held hill, but it was heavily defended and too steep. His K Company took heavy losses.

An artillery attack failed because tall trees made it impossible to adjust fire properly. Pursall then called for a tank attack. K and I Companies had advanced slightly but were pinned down by machine guns. Unable to maneuver on the narrow road, the tanks had to withdraw.

When all the weapons of modern warfare couldn't break through the firepower up there, Pursall was left with only his men. He drew his pearl-handled .45s. Chet Tanaka describes what happened next:

> I remember that final attack by Company K. There was no yelling of "Banzai." We did not fix bayonets. K Company was pinned down by small arms fire and rifle grenades [little grenades, concussion type]. Colonel Pursall came striding up to where K was pinned down. He looked down at me and said: "Let's get going, Sergeant."
>
> I looked up at him from my prone position and thought: My God! If that dumb son-of-a-bitch is going to walk up into that fire, I guess we better, too!
>
> I called to the some 16 men of K (all that were left) to get up and get going. I was the first up (slowly). All the others got up. We fired from our hips. No yelling. Didn't want the enemy to hear us. Pursall led the way.[20]

Then Pvt. Barney Hajiro of I Company, a BAR man, was on his feet and starting up the hill. He fired as he went, killing Germans in their foxholes, destroying single-handedly two machine-gun nests and killing the gunners, killing two snipers who fired at him. It was like spontaneous combustion: K and I Companies came charging out of their covers, running up the hill, shooting from the hip. When men fell, others took their places. When wounded, they staggered on, shooting, always advancing. Dead and wounded Nisei lay in enemy holes beside dead Germans, outside enemy dugouts, across enemy gun barrels. German forces that had been so confident just thirty minutes before threw down their weapons and fled, scattering guns, ammunition, and clothes as they sought to escape the onslaught. There was no counterattack. Someone later named the area "Banzai Hill." For the Nisei it was a hill of death.

Hajiro was recommended for the Medal of Honor. It was downgraded to a DSC, like every other such recommendation the 100th/442nd had submitted. British officers, however, didn't forget what they had witnessed Hajiro do, not only that day but also in actions that had led to the capture of Bruyeres. Four years later, on Novem-

ber 1, 1948, in a formal ceremony, Hajiro was awarded the British
Military Medal for "three separate actions in Eastern France in which
he showed gallantry under fire." His citation, in part, read:

> On security duty, Private Hajiro killed or wounded two snipers
> with BAR fire. Again on outpost duty he ambushed an enemy
> patrol, killing two, wounding one and capturing sixteen. Later,
> when enemy machine guns killed eight and wounded twenty-
> one comrades, he went after the enemy alone. Duelling fully
> exposed, with BAR fire he killed three at the first nest twenty
> yards distant and killed one sniper protecting the nest. Duel-
> ling as he walked slowly into machine-gun fire from the sec-
> ond nest twenty-five yards away, he killed two, plus the one
> sniper protecting the nest. Private Hajiro was riddled in the side
> and arm by the third machine gun.[21]

Hajiro's DSC was not the only one earned on Banzai Hill. Two others
were earned that day by men of K Company: SSgt. Fujio Miyamoto
and Pfc. Jim Y. Tazoi were both wounded in the attack but kept firing
as they moved toward the concentrated, incredibly strong German defense
until it was broken and the enemy was fleeing from its hilltop stronghold.

All over the hill there were cries of wounded and dying men—Germans and Japanese Americans. In the charge up Banzai Hill, Company I suffered five killed and forty wounded. Company K was left
with seventeen riflemen. All its officers had been killed or wounded,
and a sergeant, Tanaka, was in command. The 100th Battalion strength
was down to about two platoons, with sixty-five in A Company, eighty-
five in B Company, and seventy-two in C Company.

Throughout the 100th and 3rd Battalion areas, trucks were being
loaded with dead and wounded Nisei GIs like stacked cordwood.

Colonel Pence also went up on a ridge and was wounded and evacuated.
The man who had commanded the 442nd since its beginnings in Camp
Shelby, Mississippi, then the combined 100th/442nd as it liberated town
after town in Italy, was out of this battle. He was promoted to brigadier
general and given less strenuous duties after his recovery. Lt. Col. Virgil
R. Miller, next in command, succeeded him. And the battle went on.

While the 100th and 3rd Battalions were smashing their way toward the Lost Battalion's hill, Colonel Hanley completed his push toward Hill 617. More than a hundred Germans, including newly arrived mountain troops, died on Hill 617 when Hanley led his two companies onto it from the north. The Germans still had their guns trained on the company he had left strung out along the west side of the hill as a decoy and were caught in a pincers movement. When one Nisei platoon was temporarily stopped, SSgt. Tsuneo Takemoto ran thirty yards straight into enemy fire, shouting as he fired at enemy positions. His platoon charged with him and, later, checked a counterattack. In another attack, Takemoto ran thirty yards toward enemy fire, giving his platoon a chance to close in on the enemy position and capture thirty-four prisoners. Takemoto was awarded a DSC.

By the end of the day the Combat Team was down to half strength, but the remnants of the 3rd and 100th Battalions were preparing to move again. And the 2nd Battalion was also ready to drive south through the valley toward the Lost Battalion, clearing the enemy from farmhouses as it went.

Planes finally had made a successful drop to the isolated battalion. It had medicines and a three-day food supply, but it was still threatened by enemy troops surrounding it.

The dawn of October 30 was cold, with rain threatening to turn to snow. Heartsick at the death and suffering he had seen in this brutal battle, Chaplain Masao Yamada wrote that morning to his old friend Col. Sherwood Dixon:

> After four days of fierce fighting, we are still pushing to get to the trapped battalion. . . .
>
> The cost has been high. I admire the courage and the discipline of our loyal men. They take their orders in stride without complaint and go into the volley of fire, with one spirit and one mind. Actually, those that saw the charge (our men call it the "banzai" charge) came home with a vivid and stirring account of our men unflinchingly charging on the double, falling under machine gun fire, yet moving on as the ceaseless waves beating on a sea shore.
>
> I am spiritually low for once. My heart weeps with our men, especially with those who gave all. Never has any combat affected

me so deeply as has this emergency mission. I am probably getting soft, but to me the price is too costly for our men. I feel this way more because the burden is laid on the combat team when the rest of the 141st [Battalion, 36th Division] is not forced to take the same responsibility.[22]

Dense fog and heavy forest growth made it seem like night. Mortar and firing from the 522nd Field Artillery Battalion blanketed the remaining ridge separating the 100th and 3rd Battalions from the Lost Battalion. When the barrage ceased, the infantry began their approach. Yard by yard, the two battalions neared Hill 345573, where the Texans waited. A patrol from Company I, 3rd Battalion, started up the hill, examining every bush and tree and lump of ground as it went. In command was TSgt. Takeo Senzaki, a Nisei from California.

The Texans, in their cold, muddy holes, knew somebody was climbing their hill, but they had orders not to shoot until they could identify who was approaching. So they listened and waited—and some prayed.

As the 3rd and 100th Battalions were approaching the Lost Battalion's hill, the Nisei 2nd Battalion was smashing into the Germans in the valley leading toward the hill, preventing the enemy from surging up to the stranded Texans.

At 1420 Colonel Miller advised division headquarters: "Unconfirmed, they think they have the first traces of the Lost Battalion. They have passed the road block and are going up the slope."

At 1610 came the message: "Just got word over the radio from the 141st Infantry that patrols from the 442nd Infantry have reached them, the 1st Battalion 141st Infantry."

From their hilltop, scouts of the Lost Battalion had been watching every move of Sergeant Senzaki's patrol as it slowly climbed the hill. By then it was afternoon, and in the growing darkness it was hard to tell who they were. Perhaps it was a glimpse of olive-drab uniforms or a GI helmet, or the momentary sight of a Japanese face, but suddenly the watchers on the hilltop knew: it was the Nisei.

Word flashed back to their command post and to the men who had waited so long for help. Then all who could walk were on their feet, running to meet the men who had fought so long and so hard to reach them. For all their joy, it was hard to talk: throats were choked; eyes were filled with tears. They hugged the men who had saved them. One of the Nisei pulled out a pack of cigarettes and passed it around. Others did the same. And the Texans, out of cigarettes for most of that week, lit up and smoked—some in silence. Moments later the 100th Battalion broke through and the Texans were surrounded by the small men with the Japanese faces.

But the celebration lasted only a few minutes. The Nisei had to post guards to watch for an enemy attack.

The 100th/442nd Regimental Combat Team had rescued the Texas Division's Lost Battalion after five days of continuous night-and-day battles. It suffered more than 800 casualties to rescue 211 Texans—all that were left of the 275 originally entrapped. In the Nisei 3rd Battalion, Company K was down to seventeen riflemen and Company I to eight riflemen. Sergeants were running both companies because there were no officers left.

The men of the Lost Battalion later presented a plaque to the 100th/442nd, thanking it "for the gallant fight to effect our rescue after we had been isolated seven days."

Major Claude D. Roscoe, a much-decorated member of the 1st Battalion, 141st Regiment, gave me this description of the rescue when I met him in Italy after the end of the war.

Just before dark on the seventh day we heard firing in the area to our rear and could tell that the fighting was coming closer to our closed-in position. Just at dark we could see troops moving up the hills to our positions. . . . it was difficult to distinguish the Americans and Germans. But orders had been given not to fire until it was definitely determined if it was enemy or friendly troops. And to our great pleasure it was members of the 442nd Combat Team. We were overjoyed to see these people for we knew them as the best fighting men in the ETO [European Theater of Operations].

Later we found out from information by people who were fighting into us how tough it was to fight continuously to rescue us and the tremendous number of casualties it had sustained in the rescuing effort. In all our association with this Combat Team we have always found them one of the best outfits that we worked with in the ETO. Many combat instances may be forgotten but in the memories of those members of the 141st Infantry, 1st Battalion, who were in this operation the 442nd will never be forgotten.

When the 442nd broke through to us we were very tired, hungry and cold and, in all probability, would not have been able to hold more than 36 hours longer. . . .

The first man I met of the 442nd was T/Sgt Takeo Senzaki of Los Angeles. We all had tears in our eyes and were glad to see them and our emotions were so pent up that we could not speak for ten or fifteen minutes. We were so happy to see the men of the 442nd, to be rescued by the men of the 442nd, that it would be difficult to describe our feelings at that time.

When fighting men get together, especially from the 1st Battalion of the 141st Regiment, they will always speak with pride and the deepest feeling of appreciation toward those men of the 442nd.[23]

The 100th and 3rd Battalions were awarded Distinguished Unit Citations for effecting the relief of the Lost Battalion. The 232nd Engineer Company won the Distinguished Unit Citation for "heroic achievement" in keeping supply lines to the 36th Division open. And, in a subsequent ceremony, the 2nd Battalion was awarded a Distinguished Unit Citation for taking Hill 617 and for distinguished service in a later battle in Italy.

Despite the censorship that allegedly had been in effect ten days before to prevent crediting the 100th/442nd with helping free Bruyeres, when word spread on October 30 about the relief of the Lost Battalion, GIs throughout the European Theater of Operations were quick and lavish with their praise of the Nisei. Letters to *Stars and Stripes* expressed what GIs felt about the 100th/442nd Regimental Combat Team:

"We, as infantrymen, realize what a tough squeeze the 'lost battalion' had, but it was the Japanese Americans who fought their way through to them," wrote one sergeant.

"We should like to read a substantial article on the Japanese-American soldiers. They have had more than a year of actual combat and it was they who recently displayed their ability by taking the pressure off the 'lost battalion,'" another sergeant wrote.[24]

There was to be no rest for the Nisei after they rescued the Lost Battalion. Despite the decimation of their ranks, they were now ordered to continue along the ridge of hills to the highway that led to Saint-Dié. Tattered, wet and cold, suffering from respiratory diseases and trench foot, mourning their dead and wounded comrades (many of them relatives, some brothers), the remnants of the 100th/442nd Regimental Combat Team plodded the mountain trails, losing more men to sickness. They were not taken off the line until November 9. The next day, what remained of the 100th Battalion was detached from the Seventh Army and sent to the Maritime Alps.

On November 12, General Dahlquist ordered a dress review to thank the 100th/442nd for what they had done. When the small group of Nisei—those left from the carnage—showed up, he rebuked their officers for not having all the men present. At full strength the Combat Team had numbered slightly more than 4,000 men and officers. All that remained of the 100th Battalion was in the Maritime Alps; a few men from the 2nd and 3rd Battalions were on guard duty; the 442nd's casualty list resulting from fighting with the 36th Division numbered almost 2,000 (140 men killed, 1,800 in hospitals). Those who attended Dahlquist's farewell ceremony were angry. Some blinked back tears. None would ever forgive his harsh treatment of the 100th/442nd.

On November 13, the day after the dress review, General Dahlquist called out the ravaged 442nd's 2nd and 3rd Battalions for patrolling and reconnaissance duty, in case the enemy mounted a counterattack. So the tired, tattered Nisei soldiers, still mourning their dead and wounded, trudged back onto the line.

The Germans, however, were busy elsewhere. On November 11 they had evacuated women, children, and the aged from Saint-Dié. (All able-bodied men between the ages of eighteen and forty-five had previously been sent to Strasbourg, presumably to be used as slave labor.) For the next two days, German soldiers looted the evacuated area; at noon on November 13, they began burning the city, whose history dated back more than twelve centuries. The first building to be torched was the home of the local pharmacist, Monsieur Duminel. On a wall of his office there was a plaque commemorating the fact that Saint-Dié had sent the first shipload of men and supplies from France to America during the Revolutionary War, when America fought for its freedom from the British Empire. The burning of Saint-Dié was a signal that the Germans were finally withdrawing.[25]

On November 17, when the Nisei reached Saint-Dié, they were at last relieved from duty with the 36th Division. Officers and men watched with tears in their eyes (and some men sobbed) as the thin lines, all that was left of the Nisei Combat Team, made their way to rest areas. In his farewell message of November 18 to the Combat Team, Dahlquist wrote: "The courage, steadfastness and willingness of your officers and men were equal to any ever displayed by United States troops." They had taken every objective assigned them. Japanese names were on crosses throughout nearby Épinal National Cemetery.

After the war, when bodies were being transported back to the United States for reburial at home, the people of Bruyeres wanted to keep one grave at Épinal in memory of the Japanese Americans who died in the battle to free their town. They asked the family of SSgt. Tomosu Hirata of the 100th Battalion to leave him buried at Épinal. He had been killed the first day of the Battle for Bruyeres, October 15, 1944.

Tomosu was the youngest child of a close-knit Hawaii family. They were torn by the request: some felt that leaving Tomosu's body at Épinal would look as though they didn't care about him. But one brother, who had been a medic in the 100th Battalion, felt that Tomosu would have wanted to remain buried in the cemetery that had sheltered many of his friends. So the family decided to let its son stay in Épinal, where his grave is carefully tended by the people of Bruyeres.

After the brutal battles in the Vosges Mountains, the 100th/442nd was to be transferred to another command. Even though the unit never received official credit, it had helped deliver to General Dahlquist the prize he wanted: the highway that would ultimately lead him and his 36th Division from Saint-Dié to Sélestat and into Germany. The Department of Defense notes in its biographical sketch of General Dahlquist: "This was the first time in military history that this portion of the Vosges Mountains had ever been successfully attacked."

German troops, fleeing toward their own border to escape the Allied onslaught, left behind them the debris of their long occupation of this part of Alsace-Lorraine. Cities and villages around Saint-Dié were, at last, free. One of these was Schirmeck, a small city about twenty miles northeast of Saint-Dié where the Nazis had built one of their notorious concentration camps. Here they had incarcerated Jewish men, women, and children not only from Saint-Dié but also from other areas of France.

News of the torching of Saint-Dié, the flight of the Germans, and the approach of Allied forces had filtered through to the prisoners who had waited—and prayed—so long for their freedom. Somehow—whether through the FFI or other French underground communication we do not know—they had also learned about the Nisei troops who had been fighting in the Vosges Mountains. For many years the Nisei veterans were unaware that their occupation of Saint-Dié had led to freedom for the prisoners in Schirmeck's concentration camp. It was discovered through a note left at a memorial to the 100th Battalion in Biffontaine.

This memorial, placed at the edge of a wooded area, was built by Gerard Henry, later the mayor of Biffontaine. As a boy he had listened to the terrible battle the 100th Battalion fought to free his town of Biffontaine and had vowed that someday he would erect a memorial in their honor. The first monument he built was made of branches and rocks he had gathered; this was where the note was found.

"Thank you for liberating us from the concentration camp Schirmeck," the note said. The message was signed: "M. and Mme. Raymond Gruber of St. Die."[26]

Bruyeres was another town that would never forget the Nisei. In the years to come, its people would annually commemorate their liberation from German occupation on October 30, the day the 100th/442nd broke through German lines to rescue the Lost Battalion on Hill 345573. This hill represented the last threat to Bruyeres.

Quietly, Bruyeres began building a memorial honoring the Japanese Americans who had helped liberate their city. At first only a well-kept path led to the monument. Now a road wide enough for tour buses leads there. It is called "The Avenue of the 442 Infantry Regiment."

The monument is simple—granite on a concrete slab, resting in the forest where the Nisei fought their way through German lines to reach the little city. A bronze plaque tells the story in French and in English:

To the men of the 442nd Regimental Combat Team, U.S. Army, who re-affirmed an historic truth here—that loyalty to one's country is not modified by racial origin.

These Americans, whose ancestors were Japanese, on October 30, 1944, during the battle of Bruyeres broke the backbone of the German defenses and rescued the 141st Infantry Battalion which had been surrounded by the enemy for four days.

In Biffontaine the monument first built by Monsieur Henry to honor the 100th Infantry Battalion was a simple one, but he dreamed of a granite monument to commemorate those men. In time, Pierre Moulin of Bruyeres heard about the mayor's dream. (Pierre is the son of Max-Henri Moulin, who had led FFI forces in Bruyeres and received the OSS Certificate of Merit from Maj. Gen. "Wild Bill" Donovan.) Moulin told John Tsukano—writer, historian, and veteran of the 100th Battalion—about Monsieur Henry's dream, and Tsukano in turn told the story to Jean Bianchetti, owner of a French monuments company, when he visited Hawaii. At last, through this serendipitous chain of events, the dream was realized. Bianchetti helped build, transport, and erect the granite monument that now stands in Biffontaine.

Then, to further honor the 100th Infantry Battalion, Bianchetti constructed a monument at San Angelo, on the slopes of Monte Cassino, where the 100th earned the name "Purple Heart Battalion."

In spite of such accolades, much resentment was harbored by the surviving Nisei about their treatment during the brutal battles in the Vosges Mountains. In a speech nearly forty years later, Col. Young O. Kim told an audience of Japanese-American veterans:

> My memories of France still show the bitterness burnt deeply into my soul. Later, Colonel Gordon Singles [commander of the 100th Battalion], while filling a Brigadier General's position at Fort Bragg, refused to publicly shake General Dahlquist's hand at a full dress review. . . . Years later after he retired, General Pence [commander of the 100th/442nd RCT] could not mention Dahlquist's name without his voice shaking with anger.[27]

When the Nisei of the 2nd and 3rd Battalions were finally separated from the 36th Division, they joined the 100th Battalion in the snow-covered Maritime Alps, bordering France and Italy, where Germans still held territory from the foothills of the Apennines to the Swiss border. When the Nisei were on leave they sampled the nearby Riviera, playground of the rich and famous, now to be enjoyed by soldiers who knew little of such luxury. With typical GI humor they dubbed this "The Champagne Campaign."

CHAPTER 13

THE PHILIPPINES RECAPTURED

etween their fight to free Bruyeres and their struggle to rescue the Lost Battalion, the 100th/442nd learned that Gen. Douglas MacArthur had landed in the Philippines on October 20. Reading the announcement, many 100th/442nd men knew it was inevitable that their relatives, who were linguists with the Military Intelligence Service, would be with MacArthur. MISers had been through every bloody island battle in the Pacific leading to this goal: recapture of the Philippines. The 100th/442nd men could say nothing about their MISer relatives; it was secret. But *Beachhead News* reported the Combat Team's reaction to the news:

The invasion was marked by a big cheering section from the Four Hundred and Forty Second. . . .

"I hope they get worse than they gave us at Pearl Harbor," offered Sgt. Jitsui Yoshida who saw the attack in Hawaii and won't forget it.

But it was left for Sgt. George Y. Morikawa, who resided for 12 years in Japan, to express the fondest hope for all members of the Combat Team. Said he: "Soon they'll be able to bomb Japan like Germany—that'll be the end of Japan as such."

"What we want to do is win the war and get home as quickly as possible—just like everyone else," explained Corp. Fred T. Matsuo. "It would be the same thing if we were fighting the Japs— we'd kill 'em just the same."[1]

As noted earlier, the captured Z Plan, translated at ATIS, had provided crucial information that led to the Japanese fleet's decisive defeat in the Battle of Leyte Gulf. During this action one of the last survivors of the Japanese fleet in the Pearl Harbor attack, the aircraft carrier *Zuikaku*, was sunk.[2]

Nobody knows how many Japanese-American MIS men were with troops fighting to retake the Philippines. Hundreds is the best number anyone can give. MISers were with all units landing at Leyte Gulf during the initial assault—four divisions on a ten-mile-wide front. More Nisei waited in the stifling holds of ships to go ashore in the next two days with other units. Before General MacArthur himself waded ashore, Nisei linguists were already on the beach at Dulag with the headquarters troops. Among them was Warren Tsuneishi, who, years later, would head the Asian Division of the Library of Congress. That day he was busy searching for information in documents the Japanese had abandoned in their retreat from American preinvasion shelling.

During the initial assault, LST 552, offshore at Tacloban, was attacked by a kamikaze; Tsuneo "Cappy" Harada and Spady Koyama were wounded. Harada arrived at an evacuation facility without a shred of clothing except what corpsmen had wrapped around him. Koyama was placed on the beach in the rows of dead awaiting burial. Only when he was picked up did the burial crew realize he was alive; he couldn't be operated on, however, until he reached Spokane, Washington.[3] (Earlier, when Koyama was serving in New Guinea, he had read a letter in his hometown newspaper, which complained about seeing "Japs" on the streets of Spokane. His reply: he offered the Spokane citizen his New Guinea foxhole.[4])

After the first assault, teams of MISers continued to land on Leyte, and later some would parachute into remote regions to help negotiate enemy surrenders. MISers worked day and night translating captured documents and diaries seized during the invasion, and identifying, from tags found on dead enemy soldiers, which Japanese outfits were pitted against American troops. In rare instances when enemy soldiers could be taken alive, Nisei were up front to question them.

The Nisei moved with the GIs through the mountainous, jungle terrain, hoping they would not be shot because of their Japanese faces. Filipinos, whose hatred of Japanese had become lethal during Japan's harsh occupation of their islands, would shoot a Japanese on sight, or at the very least pelt him with rocks. So the Nisei were often withdrawn from front lines to command posts to ensure their safety.

One of the MISers on Leyte was Frank Hachiya, a native of Hood River, Oregon, and a veteran of nearly three years of Pacific invasions. He had flown from a rest area in Hawaii to replace a MISer who had to be evacuated because of dysentery. Hachiya was soon offered the chance to return to Hawaii to resume his furlough, but he refused because he wanted to stay on Leyte until the end of the campaign. In a letter dated December 3, he wrote his friend Yasuo Baron Goto: "I'll not be back in time for Christmas, as I had hoped. Instead, celebrate it in some muddy foxhole with can of GI rations."[5]

Hachiya was working with the 32nd Infantry Regiment headquarters as it moved along a ridge that paralleled another ridge where the enemy had infiltrated. When the regiment called for help to confer with Japanese prisoners, Frank volunteered to climb into the valley. As his commanding officer, Lt. Howard M. Moss, explained:

> It was essential to get the information from the POW immediately as some of our units were in a bad spot. . . . When they reached the bottom of the valley a Japanese sniper let them have it at close range, when he (Hachiya) tried to talk to the Japanese in the valley in Japanese. Frank emptied his gun into the sniper. Then he walked back up the hill where he was given plasma. . . . At the hospital he was given every possible care but the bullet had gone through his liver.[6]

Although critically wounded, Hachiya staggered up the hill to his commanding officer and delivered the information about enemy positions and troops. He died four days later—on January 3, 1945—and his Silver Star award was granted posthumously.

Five weeks earlier, on November 29, 1944, the American Legion post in Hachiya's native Hood River, Oregon, had painted out the names of all sixteen Japanese-American servicemen who enlisted in Hood River on the municipal memorial roll inscribed on the wall of the courthouse, and announced that the post would support efforts to prevent former residents of Japanese ancestry from returning to the area. Although Hachiya's name had never been placed on the city's memorial roll—he had not enlisted from Hood River—a thunderous outcry arose, protesting the Hood River action. It happened while Hachiya's Silver Star award was being processed, and many people recognized that it was a vicious slap in the face to valorous Japanese Americans.

The Hood River American Legion post's anti-Japanese resolution stated: "This community has long been disturbed by an alien minority whose children are citizens of an enemy country." The resolution also stated that the post would cooperate with any group working to drive out the Japanese; it wanted Japanese land titles "carefully investigated," anti-Japanese codicils included in land deeds, and creation of a corporation to buy Japanese-owned property. It called for formation of a corporation to appraise and buy "all real property remaining in title to persons of Japanese origin" and to prevent their buying or leasing land in the future.

The Hood River incident created a nationwide protest by officials of the American Legion, outraged citizens, government officials including Secretary of War Henry Stimson, and publications including *Colliers* and *Stars and Stripes,* which cited the fighting record of Japanese-American troops in Europe. Newspaper editorials, such as this one in the *Pittsburgh Post-Gazette,* were scathing:

> From now on Frank Hachiya won't have to give a damn about what the American Legion post of Hood River, Oregon, thinks, says, or does about him. On Leyte, the Japanese American volunteered to cross a valley under enemy fire to scout their position. As he was doing so, a Japanese bullet stopped the American.
>
> Out in Hood River, Oregon, some of the old-timers who fought for America a quarter of a century ago never did learn, apparently, what they were fighting for. Over the strenuous protests of national Legion officials, they voted to strike the names of 16 Japanese Americans from the county memorial roll. It didn't make any difference to them what General Eisenhower or General MacArthur or General Mark Clark might think of such fellows fighting under their command. Under their definition of Americanism, any man with Japanese blood in his veins was out.
>
> What is an American? We are no race, no color, no creed. The melting pot of all the world was welded together out of a common faith in the equality of man, as best expressed in the Declaration of Independence, the Constitution with its Bill of Rights,

the Gettysburg Address, and, for that matter, the Sermon on the Mount. When any man risks his life for this country on an especially hazardous mission, it is only fair and reasonable to assume that as an American he knew what he was fighting, what he was dying for.

In April 1945 when the names of Japanese-American servicemen were restored to the Hood River municipal roll of honor, Hachiya's name was included. Three years later, when his body was returned to the United States for burial, his funeral became headline news and his honorary pallbearers included bankers, educators, and a former state governor. His longtime Hood River friend Min Asai gave the eulogy, and Hachiya was buried in the Japanese section of Idlewilde Cemetery, just outside of Hood River, where vandals had overturned gravestones during the war. This somber ceremony helped turn the tide of anti-Japanese sentiment.

During the funeral service, Hachiya's former teacher, Mrs. Martha Ferguson McKeown, quoted from a paper he had written in college, reflecting on a trip to Japan:

I really now think that living in Japan four years has done me one great good [teaching me] the appreciation of America or the love of one's country. Now I don't mean I don't like Japan, but I will never get so that I like her as well as America. As I was born and reared here, I am an American though I was born of Japanese parents. I read where some people stated that they did not fully appreciate their country until they had travelled abroad. And I, too, after living across the sea, realize it now.

I am not very handy with words. Maybe if it were Byron or other writers, they would be able to express their thoughts and feelings, but with my humble vocabulary it is impossible. The love of one's country, America! It is queer and mystifying is all I can say.

My cultural background of two widely separated institutions has afforded me many headaching conflicts. Our position in this nation is not too agreeable, but I hope that it is nearly at its worst. The source of all this ill treatment being forced upon us is the inconsistency between the theory and the practice of democracy.

Mrs. McKeown commented on this last idea in her eulogy: "Frank did not question democracy. He had become a student of democracy. The Frank Hachiya I knew was a thinker. He was a boy who wanted to make his life count for democracy."[7]

Thirty-two years after Frank Hachiya was finally laid to rest, an article by Alan K. Ota in *The Portland Oregonian* carried an announcement of the dedication of a building in Hachiya's memory at the Defense Language Institute at the Presidio of Monterey, California. The courageous Nisei had at last been given his due. The *Oregonian* concluded:

> Hachiya—who became a national sensation after his death when it was mistakenly believed that his name had been erased from an American Legion honor roll because of his ancestry—will finally have a resting place in the memory of future generations of American soldiers.

Frank Hachiya died at a time of desperate fighting on Leyte. By late December 1944 American troops had encircled and divided Japanese forces there, and the 1st Cavalry Division finally broke through enemy lines to try to capture the Ormoc Valley. Final capture of Leyte was in sight; but before troops could be sent to Luzon, MacArthur's next objective, it was essential to learn what enemy reinforcements were being sent to Leyte. Rumors persisted that massive Japanese reinforcements, including tanks, were entering through the port of Ormoc. One of the MIS men assigned to the 1st Cavalry Division was Stanley S. Shimabukuro. He had previously been on a language team that went into Guam with the 3rd Marine Division.

Shimabukuro was the only Nisei linguist allowed at the 1st Cavalry's frontline headquarters, because it was so difficult to protect the Nisei from the Filipinos. He and William Dozier, head of the 1st Cavalry Division's language section, were in charge of questioning prisoners. Dozier credited Shimabukuro with obtaining crucial information General MacArthur needed: "Captured letters and notebooks the hakujin [whites] and Nisei could make no sense of, he could read, even though parts of words were obscured by rain, sweat or blood."[8]

For fifty-one hours, without rest or breaks, by daylight, flashlight, and lantern light, Shimabukuro studied captured diaries, letters, messages, and reports. He determined how many Japanese reinforcements had gotten ashore, how many were lost at sea, how many enemy troops were at particular locations. Shimabukuro's information and that from other intelligence sources made it clear that plans could go forward for MacArthur's invasion of Luzon, site of the Philippine capital, Manila.[9] Meanwhile, smaller outlying islands would be gradually reclaimed by American troops, and mopping-up operations would continue on Leyte. On December 27 MacArthur's communique stated that the Leyte campaign was closed: "General Yamashita has sustained the greatest defeat in the annals of the Japanese Army."[10]

On the morning of January 9, the U.S. Sixth Army began landing on the shores of Luzon's Lingayen Gulf to form a continuous beachhead four miles deep. More divisions, including paratroop units, followed, and the drive for Manila, one hundred miles away, began. Nisei were with them all, everywhere.

Mamoru Noji was among the Nisei linguists who arrived on Luzon with the 43rd Division. He remained there until mid-1945, when Luzon was declared secure. Another Japanese-American linguist who landed at Lingayen Gulf was Harry Fukuhara. He had been turned down three times (by the army draft, navy, and marines) before finally volunteering from the Gila River internment camp as a linguist for the Military Intelligence Service, which accepted him.[11] By the time he reached Luzon he had worked all over New Guinea and on New Britain Island, where the Japanese had initially established their Southeast Area Fleet and Eighth Area Army headquarters. On Luzon he headed one of the MIS teams that went into the northern section of the island to help search for Gen. Tomoyuki Yamashita, commanding general of the Japanese Imperial Army in the Philippines.

On January 29 another contingent of Nisei landed near Subic Bay with the 38th Division. Among these was Arthur Ushiro Castle, who had led a detachment of linguists to Australia in 1942. Since then, he had been in battles throughout the long, tortuous length of New Guinea—from the Buna-Gona-Sananandra area to Salamaua and Lae. After Castle's unit landed near Subic Bay, it circumvented Japanese troops to reach Bataan.

Among veteran Nisei intelligence men in the Luzon invasion was Minoru Hara, who joined the Military Intelligence Service from the internment camp in Poston, Arizona, and saw two years of service in the Pacific before landing on Luzon. Within an hour after the 6th Infantry

Division established a command post on the island, Hara, attached to its headquarters company, questioned his first prisoner, who was dressed in a civilian white shirt and khaki pants. Hara's interrogation revealed that the man was a spy. He told Hara that his commanding officer had ordered him to remain behind when other Japanese units retreated so that he could get information. The man had stolen a white shirt from a Filipino clothesline but kept the trousers of his Japanese army uniform. Following a trial, the man was hanged.

Hara, who was later attached to 6th Division's 1st Infantry Regiment, went on to fight a Japanese detachment, and in February he participated in a bayonet charge at Munoz, where he tried unsuccessfully to talk a Japanese colonel into surrendering.

With Shiz Kunihiro, who had volunteered for MIS from the Gila River camp, Hara was then assigned to the 1st Infantry Regiment in Zambales Province. He stopped at Bataan Peninsula, where he saw the trenches that Lieutenant General Wainwright's troops had used in that last effort to save the Philippines.

Hara's diary includes a further description:

> We walked into the hills and saw a portion of our trenches and found ammo and hand grenades in front of their positions just as they left it when they were told to surrender by Lieutenant General Jonathan Wainwright in 1942. Later on, I asked a Japanese infantryman who initially landed on Bataan why they [the Japanese] fought so fanatically. He said, "You might say that now, but you should have seen your forces. They too fought bravely and fanatically when we cut off Bataan in 1941."

When Hara asked the Japanese soldier why American survivors of Bataan had been made to walk through a hundred miles of harsh terrain under the hot tropical sun, the reply was: the Japanese "didn't have enough trucks."

Nisei linguists were with American troops sent into the jungles of northern Luzon to capture survivors of Japan's giant battleship *Musashi,* who were hiding there. Hara recorded one nearly fatal encounter:

> A prisoner came in one day stating that he saw about fifty Navy personnel all laid up with dysentery in the jungle . . . so our Regi-

mental C.O. gave me the okay to accompany our patrol. . . . After going inland about five or six miles, we ran into a Japanese patrol, 15–20 of them, armed to their teeth. . . . We immediately opened up with a few rounds . . . and I then pursued the scattering enemy patrol. As I was firing ahead at the scattering patrol, I sensed someone behind me, so I hit the ground, rolled over and saw a Japanese soldier about twenty yards away with his rifle aimed right at my back. . . . I emptied three or four rounds into him before he could drive his bolt forward.

The Nisei were being sent into every corner of the Philippines as Americans fought to dislodge Japanese forces from remote areas. When the 503rd Parachute Infantry Regiment launched an airborne assault on Corregidor in mid-February 1945, it needed a Japanese linguist. Harry Akune had volunteered for service with the MIS from an internment camp; now he volunteered again. After one practice jump on Mindoro Island he jumped into enemy fire on Corregidor. His job was to obtain information from Japanese prisoners and translate captured documents throughout a day and a night at the command post. Forty-six years later (on July 4, 1990) Akune was honored at the fiftieth anniversary of the founding of the U.S. Army Parachute Troops. Also honored that day was George Kojima, who served with a parachute infantry regiment in the Southwest Pacific.

Technical Sergeant John Tanikawa headed a team that was shipped to the Philippines from New Guinea with the 41st Division and landed at Zamboanga on Mindanao. Among those on his team was Hisao Matsumoto, who years later would head the Japanese Section of the Library of Congress. Tanikawa had been one of the first Nisei to work in the Pacific, heading a team of linguists on Guadalcanal. At age forty-one, he volunteered for the MIS from the Tule Lake camp. Tanikawa had also been a volunteer in World War I, though underage, and was awarded a Purple Heart and croix de guerre for valorous action in that war. He won another award for valorous action on Mindanao, this time a Bronze Star.

It was in the Cagayan Valley of northern Luzon that another MISer was killed—Sgt. George Ichiro Nakamura, who was serving with the 63rd Infantry Regiment. Nakamura had been in the Tule Lake internment camp when he volunteered to serve as a linguist.

According to fellow MISer Kiyoshi Fujimura:

> We always called him "GI" Nakamura. He was like the rest
> of us Nisei GIs, doing our best in the war effort—translating, in-
> terpreting, and interrogating the enemy. "GI" and I were mem-
> bers of the same language team that graduated Fort Snelling [Military
> Intelligence Service Language School] and was sent to the South
> Pacific to do our work . . . He met his demise while working in
> the front line. . . .
>
> I was away on an assignment and didn't even have a chance
> to shake his hand. But by the time I returned to this outfit, "Our
> Team," the word was around that a Nisei interpreter was killed
> while trying to talk a unit of Japanese soldiers to surrender. That
> guy was "GI"—always trying his best to help out. He could have
> killed, or could have ordered the American forces to kill them.
> But not "GI"—he wanted to save the Japanese soldiers so they,
> too, could have a chance to go back home to see their families
> and loved ones. He wanted them to surrender and save their lives.
> He sacrificed his life that others might live. He was killed by the
> enemy as he tried to talk to them. That was the spirit of "GI,"
> and when I heard of the incident it made me feel real "low" and
> I really felt bad because he and I were known as the babies of
> the outfit. He was 19, I think, and I was only 18 years old at that
> time.[12]

When American air raids began battering Manila in December 1944,
prior to the invasion of Luzon, General Yamashita had moved his
headquarters to Baguio City, which he thought he could protect by blocking
Luzon's mountain passes. Yamashita's headquarters remained at Baguio
four months. Then, as Americans began advancing through the mountains,
the headquarters was forced to move farther north. General Yamashita
was holding out in northern Luzon with a hundred thousand troops
when American forces moved to encircle them. Harry Okubo, one of
the early graduates of the MIS Language School, acting on behalf of
the 32nd Division, would be the one who finally accepted Yamashita's
surrender. Accompanying the Japanese general on the plane to Manila was Kei Sakamoto, one of the MISers who served with Dr. Burden on Guadalcanal. From that point on, Nisei linguists would be

Yamashita's means of communication with American officialdom throughout his incarceration and trial.

While General Yamashita had occupied northern Luzon, his head-quarters group held a valuable prisoner—Richard Sakakida, the American CIC agent captured after the American surrender at Bataan, tortured by the Kempei Tai, then released to the judge advocate general's of-fice where he gathered information to forward to MacArthur's head-quarters. His story is one of the most amazing of the war. Because Sakakida was a Nisei, the Japanese treated him disdainfully, but he was useful because he knew the English language. They never sus-pected that he was using his knowledge of the Japanese language to purloin secret information.

One of Sakakida's most significant reports concerned Japan's *TAKE* convoy, destined for the Netherlands East Indies and western New Guinea in an effort to stop MacArthur's approach to the Philippine Islands. It was one of the largest troop convoys Japan mounted: nine trans-ports and seven escorts, carrying 12,784 troops from Japan's 32nd Division plus troops from its 35th Division. Sakakida reported to his Filipino guerrilla contacts that the *TAKE* convoy departed Manila at 0400 on May 1, 1944. It was then tracked by Intelligence. The subsequent American attack on the convoy resulted in such huge losses of Japanese troops and materiel that Japan's military leaders suspected either that their codes had been broken or that there were spies on the Manila water-front. Sakakida remained undetected.[13]

I asked Sakadida how he obtained information about the *TAKE* convoy. His answer:

A lieutenant legal officer from the Judge Advocate's Office where I was working was selected as a member of the TAKE expedition from the JAG office. While assisting him in pack-ing and preparing for his departure he was able to "accommo-date" me with the answers to some of the questions I posed very innocently. Furthermore, I was able to lay my hands on "Orga-nizational Orders" classified Secret, outlining in detail the or-ganizational structure, assembly point and destination.[14]

More than a year before the American invasion of the Philippines, MacArthur's headquarters had ordered a guerrilla unit to try to rescue Sakakida, but the effort failed. Now, with the Japanese in retreat, Sakakida could no longer be of help to the United States, so he decided to make a break for freedom and rejoin American forces. He describes what happened next:

> Since I had developed beri-beri and was troubled with malaria attacks on a daily basis, I took advantage of this and gave the Japanese the impression that I was too weak to be of any further service to them. They were so occupied with their own problems that I was left back, with instructions to catch up to them when my health permitted.

This was about early June 1945, and Sakakida escaped into the mountains. He was taken in by a local tribe but decided to make his way alone.

> I found myself caught in the cross-artillery fire between the American and Japanese forces. Suddenly a Japanese artillery barrage landed close by and I remember 3 shell explosions. Thereafter I was unconscious. I do not know how long I was lying there but when I regained consciousness I felt my stomach area was wet. I realized I was bleeding and also realized that I was unable to walk. I crawled and slid down the hill for a few hundred yards to a little stream. Here I was able to at least wash and cleanse my stomach wound. Having no medication I merely kept on washing it out. Three days later the infection and stench became unbearable. After washing off the infected area I found a piece of shrapnel imbedded. Knowing that as long as I had that piece of shrapnel the wound would never heal, I got my razor blade out and performed personal surgery. In lieu of medication I gathered whatever weeds were growing around me and, by mashing them, made a poultice with which I covered the wound.
>
> When I finally became mobile, I decided the best way to return to civilization was to follow the river downstream. I was unable to make any distance, suffering from malaria, beriberi, dysentery and my stomach wound.

Sakakida wandered alone and ill for nearly three months (until September), teetering between consciousness and unconsciousness, eating grass and wild fruits, not knowing what was happening in the warring world outside the jungle. He did not know that the Philippines had finally been liberated, that atomic bombs had been dropped on Hiroshima and Nagasaki, or that Japan had surrendered. He was still trying to locate American forces by following a river to the coast. One day he saw a group of white soldiers and crept as close to them as he could. The uniforms or helmets were not familiar to him, and he thought perhaps they were Germans because their helmets were rounded instead of the pie-plate shape Americans used at the beginning of the war. Then he heard them talking and caught their American slang. Scared that they would mistake him for the enemy, he came out of the jungle yelling: "Don't shoot! I'm an American!" Sakakida remembers the scene:

> I was in rags and tatters. My hair was bushy. I was unshaven. Naturally it was difficult for them to believe I was an American. It confused them that I spoke English, but typically good-natured Americans, they gave me cigarettes and chewing gum and gave me directions on how to reach their headquarters. It took me another day and a half to finally reach there.[15]

At the battalion headquarters Sakakida identified himself as an American intelligence agent and gave his serial number and other pertinent data. A commander, although suspicious of this strange-looking creature, finally put a call through to the CIC field office. A couple of hours later a jeep appeared and two lieutenants from the Counterintelligence Corps identified Sakakida as the agent MacArthur's headquarters had ordered them to find. From there Sakakida was taken to the CIC field office, where he was welcomed with a festive banquet. Unused to such rich food after his months of starvation, he took a week to recover from the meal.

He was then sent to Manila to be debriefed; finally he was returned to Hawaii, where, on December 26, 1945, he was reunited with his mother. Officially he was on a two-week leave, but, still recuperating from malaria, he spent one week in a hospital. After that he was returned to Manila to assist the War Crimes Commission investigating crimes committed by Japanese units. He also testified during the trial of General Yamashita. (In 1953 Sakakida was a major witness in the trial of a white U.S. Army staff sergeant, John Provoo, who had given major assistance to the Japanese during their occupation of the

Philippines. Sakakida had witnessed Provoo offering aid to the Japanese. In this war where white Americans had questioned the loyalty of Japanese Americans, it is ironic that a white man had been the disloyal one, with a Japanese American offering testimony against him.)

For his work in the Philippines, Richard Sakakida was awarded a Bronze Star, and his name is in the U.S. Army Intelligence Hall of Fame. When he retired from the military in 1975 as a lieutenant colonel, he had been on active military duty for thirty-four years and was commander of the Air Force Office of Special Investigations (AFOSI) in Japan. Today Sakakida still suffers the aftermath of Japanese torture during his imprisonment. The Philippine government has awarded him four medals in recognition of his services during World War II: the Resistance Medal for helping guerrilla warfare; the Philippine Defense Medal for participating in World War II; the Liberation Medal, marking Filipino freedom from Japan; and, by order of the president of the Philippines, the Legion of Honor Medal "for exceptionally meritorious conduct in the performance of outstanding service to the Filipino-American Freedom Fighters as the United States undercover Counterintelligence Agent from 22 April 1941 to 20 September 1945."

During the spring of 1945, ATIS had moved its headquarters from Australia to the Philippines to help with the occupation and to prepare for a propaganda campaign that would be aimed at Japan itself. A site with maximum security was needed, and the Santa Ana racetrack in Manila, with a high wall entirely surrounding the racecourse, was chosen. Here the Translation Section and the Reproduction and Information Sections could be housed. The advanced echelon moved in before reconstruction work was finished. When three ships bearing the main ATIS unit reached Manila, special arrangements were made to guard them from the Filipinos. Thinking these men were Japanese prisoners of war, Filipinos crowded gates and scaled walls to stare at them. It took lengthy explanations by American officers to convince them that the ATIS men were actually Americans.

Tad Ichinokuchi, one of the Nisei arriving in the Philippines with the ATIS group, gives this description of Filipino hatred of Japanese: "Even with a U.S. uniform a Japanese countenance causes many of the younger kids to shout, 'Baka, Baka' [meaning stupid, dunce, blockhead]. A reminder of their days under the Japanese enemy occupation."[16]

Landing with the ATIS group was Arthur Komori of the Counter-intelligence Corps. He had accompanied Richard Sakakida to Manila before the Pearl Harbor bombing as a Nisei undercover agent and had assisted Colonel Mashbir in formulating ATIS rules for handling Japanese POWs. Komori joined American officials who were still searching for Sakakida, hoping he was alive.

Preparation for General Yamashita's trial was getting under way. Filipino hatred of the general was a constant threat. Tad Ichinokuchi, who served as Yamashita's interpreter, later wrote: "We had to smuggle General Yamashita in a Red Cross van daily to a private residence . . . in Manila to prepare the defense arguments. If the Filipinos knew the general was there they would have bombed the place."[17]

A U.S. Army tribunal found Yamashita guilty of brutality against Americans and Filipinos; he was hanged on February 23, 1946. A week later General Masaharu Homma, found guilty of allowing brutalities during the Bataan Death March, was shot by a firing squad. At the conclusion of the war, Tad Ichinokuchi was among the MIS interpreters sent to Japan to gather evidence for the war crimes trial of Adm. Hideki Tojo, Japan's wartime prime minister.[18]

In addition to interrogation of Japanese captured in the Philippines, Nisei worked with the Psychological Warfare unit of ATIS, broadcasting to Japanese troops who had not surrendered. As a result "a number of prisoners were taken and several well-prepared and well-supplied positions fell into our hands," according to the official postwar report of ATIS intelligence operations, which also states:

> The excellent results of these broadcasts served as additional proof that Psychological Warfare, when considered a weapon to be used in direct support of infantry troops, and when used with as much care and organization as the other supporting weapons, can do much in saving the lives of our own men.

Nisei of ATIS also began publishing a newspaper, *Rakkasan* [Para-chute] *News*. During the last stages of the war in the Pacific, millions of these leaflets, designed to conform with the makeup of regular Japanese newspapers, were dropped by B-29s on Japanese troops and the Japanese homeland to weaken morale by informing them of the true picture of the war.

Japanese Americans serving in the Pacific had become recognized as an important factor in every facet of the war. With peace in sight, their contributions were increasingly needed. When Japanese envoys arrived at Nicholas Field in the Philippines in August 1945 to negotiate the surrender, General MacArthur's official party included two officers of Japanese ancestry: Lt. Thomas T. Imada, from Hawaii, and Lt. George K. Kayano, of San Francisco. Although Kayano and Imada, along with the other Nisei present, were considered indispensable, the men all were asked to turn in their weapons that day.

Back in the United States, old prejudices still flourished. On November 20, 1944, one month after Nisei of the MIS landed on Leyte with MacArthur's troops, President Roosevelt held a press conference during which he was asked:

> Mr. President, there is a great deal of renewed controversy on the Pacific Coast about the matter of allowing the return of those Japanese who were evacuated in 1942. Do you think that the danger of espionage or sabotage has sufficiently diminished so that there can be a relaxation of the restrictions that have been in effect for the last two years?

The president's answer:

> In most of the cases. That doesn't mean all of them. . . . A good deal of progress has been made in scattering them through the country, and that is going on almost every day. . . . And, of course we are actuated . . . in part by the very wonderful record that the Japanese in that battalion in Italy [sic] have been making in the war. It is one of the outstanding battalions we have.[19]

Still unwilling to confront the hate and misunderstanding, Washington was endeavoring to "scatter" Japanese Americans.

While such contention continued at home, Japanese Americans still fought to advance the line in Europe. And three months after President Roosevelt's press conference, Nisei of the Military Intelligence Service would be involved in the bitter battle for Iwo Jima.

CHAPTER 14

CAVES OF HELL

Iwo Jima was an ugly little island trashed by the debris of evolution. One war correspondent described it as "hell with the fire gone out."[1] But this stark volcanic island was vital to the final conquest of Japan. American B-29s needed it as a base for long-range bomber flights over Japanese cities and as a landing place for crippled American planes.

The fight for Iwo Jima began on February 19, 1945, with the heaviest preinvasion bombardment of the war. One-quarter million U.S. marines, sailors, soldiers, and airmen were poised to take the island from its twenty thousand defenders. It ranks as one of the greatest battles in U.S. Marine Corps history and the most costly for the marines in human life and wounds—the Pacific counterpart of D day on the Normandy beachhead. The largest conglomeration of press, radio, and newsreel personnel since the Allied landing in France was on hand to witness it. Secretary of the Navy James Forrestal was there. So were Ernie Pyle, Pulitzer Prize–novelist John Marquand, and Robert Trumbull of the *New York Times,* who radioed his paper:

> The mortar bursts marched methodically back and forth along the shoreline. Our advance is a matter of running 10 yards on the slithery footing of dry volcanic cinder, dropping into a hole, and then up and 10 yards to another hole.

Robert Sherrod of *Time-Life* compared the tanks struggling to climb through the volcanic ash to "so many black beetles struggling to move on tar paper."

Unnoticed among the marines, correspondents, and celebrities were more than fifty Japanese-American linguists of the Military Intelligence Service. Unnoticed also was the fact that three years before on that date President Roosevelt had signed Executive Order 9066, which consigned to internment camps the families of many of these MISers now waiting to go ashore.

Victory on Iwo Jima would be of enormous psychological value because the island was part of the Tokyo prefecture and would be the first conquest of Japanese home territory. Equally important was its menacing position seven hundred miles south of Tokyo: it had served as a base for Japanese attack planes during battles for the Mariana Islands and MacArthur's invasion of the Philippines, and its radar gave Tokyo advanced warning of American bombers en route to bomb Japanese cities.

One of the Volcano Islands, Iwo Jima had been heaved out of the sea by volcanic eruptions. The terrain consisted of boulders, cliffs, ridges, scrubby hills, and twin cones. Rain turned the volcanic dust into slippery, clinging mud. The scraggly, sharp-edged *kunai* grass that grew out of the volcanic dust was infested with typhus-carrying mites. There was no wildlife—no birds, butterflies, or mammals. The island totaled eight square miles, measuring about five miles long and two and a half miles at its maximum width. It had two airstrips, and the Japanese were constructing a third. From Iwo Jima they could ravage American ships almost at will.

At the southeast end of the island a mass of gray, black, and brown rock rose precipitously 546 feet. This was Mount Suribachi, a dormant volcano that served as an observation point for the entire island. A few footpaths led to its hollowed-out top. At the peak and along the slopes was a labyrinth of caves and tunnels that were being utilized by the Japanese troops. Around the base of this volcanic cone was a narrow neck of land composed of pulverized sand.

From the neck of Suribachi the island widened to its maximum at the center. The middle of the island had occasional ridges, the highest being nearly three hundred feet. Sulphur, spewing noxious fumes, still bubbled to the surface around a volcano near the center. At the north end a rocky plateau rose straight up from the sea, and steep hundred-foot cliffs dropped to shallow beaches along its sides.

During the preinvasion bombardment, there was little responding enemy fire. The Japanese, dug into the hillsides, just waited. Their commanding officer was reputed to have been personally selected by Emperor Hirohito. He was Lt. Gen. Tadamichi Kuribayashi, a descendant of five generations of samurai warriors who had served Japan's emperors.[2] Under his command, Japanese soldiers and Korean laborers had worked feverishly, day and night, to convert the island's vast skein of lava tubes into a terrifying mosaic of tunnels leading to some fifteen hundred caves, which hid cannons and machine guns and living quarters for soldiers who would man them.

One of those reinforced positions was described by *Time-Life* correspondent Robert Sherrod in his book *On to Westward:*

> The outer walls were 40 inches of steel-reinforced concrete. The vent opened . . . slantwise toward the upper beaches. Thus the 120-mm. gun inside the blockhouse opening could fire on the beaches and on some of our ships, but could not be hit except from a sharp angle. Our naval gunfire simply could not reach inside. . . .
>
> A demolition charge tossed into the vent would have no effect on occupants of rooms to the rear. . . . A pillbox . . . sat atop it and contained a heavy machine gun. Next to this . . . was an excellent artillery range-finder. The whole affair was covered by eight to ten feet of sand . . . to make it look like just another sand dune. There was a trap-door exit in the rear.[3]

Preinvasion air strikes failed to damage the island defenses significantly. In fact, the defenses were so well hidden that air observers failed to detect most of them. Japan's command was: Iwo Jima must be defended at all costs. As American ships and planes pounded the island, General Kuribayashi ordered: "Every man will resist until the end, making his position his tomb. Every man will do his best to kill ten enemy soldiers."[4]

The result: the United States would suffer almost twenty-nine thousand casualties before the battle was finished.

Teams of Nisei linguists converged on Iwo Jima from all sections of the Pacific: from ATIS headquarters in Australia, from other islands where their work was completed, and from the Joint Intelligence Center,

Pacific Ocean Area (JICPOA), based in Hawaii. The Nisei sent from JICPOA and attached to the 4th and 5th Marine Divisions, sailing from Pearl Harbor, almost didn't make it. When they tried to get to their ships, a sentry told them: "No Japs allowed to enter Pearl Harbor." They were infuriated at being called Japs. It took a while for one of their sergeants to calm them down and accept an officer escort to their ships.[5]

Each of the Marine Corps divisions had a team of Nisei linguists assigned to it. The names of most Nisei who served on Iwo Jima are lost to history, however, because neither the navy nor the Marine Corps accepted Japanese Americans in their ranks and, therefore, did not record the services of Nisei attached to their units. We do know, through the diligent work of author Joseph D. Harrington, about a few of them. But there were many more anonymous soldiers. They were the ones who risked their lives going into caves to convince Japanese soldiers to surrender instead of killing themselves. Others worked day and night in the holds of ships to translate diaries and battle orders taken from dead Japanese soldiers. The documents yielded many enemy secrets—locations of guns, strategy, and living conditions. Other Nisei interviewed prisoners, extracting every bit of information possible.

Nobuo Furuiye, a veteran of the Aleutians campaign, landed on D-plus-1 and spent the first three days and nights on the beach "just staying alive." Later, interrogating Japanese prisoners, he found one of the most important men the United States had ever captured in the Pacific: a cipher specialist, who was immediately put on a plane for Honolulu to be interviewed by intelligence personnel there.[6] From Iwo Jima, Furuiye was sent to Saipan to help with Japanese civilians, then to Yap to interpret during its surrender, then to Guam to work on a cannibalism trial, and finally to Japan to interpret during war crimes trials.[7] His experience is a prime example of the way Nisei linguists were shifted from one place to another and pitched into diverse situations.

American strategists had figured that the battle for Iwo Jima could be won in five days. After eight days, however, General Kuribayashi's plans and battlements were still working. The Japanese held about three-fifths of the island, including the best observation posts and areas for cover and concealment. The rock-encrusted top of one of the heaviest armed volcanic hills, for example, held six antiaircraft guns with barrels readied for point-blank fire. Each gun was connected to an elaborate tunnel system, one of which had been cut through a thousand feet of rock and had seven entrances on three sides of the hill to supply ammunition and troops for the emplacements.[8]

The most dangerous work the Nisei did on Iwo Jima was to enter these many tunnels, trying to flush the enemy out of the caves. One of the MIS men, T5g. Terry Takeshi Doi, acknowledged by Japanese Americans as one of their World War II heroes, risked his life repeatedly in the caves. Doi's family had sent him to Japan for schooling and his command of Japanese was better than his English. Because he was a dual citizen, he had been forced to serve in the Japanese army, which meant he lost his American citizenship. As a result, after graduating from the Military Intelligence Service Language School, he was kept at the school pending clearance for service in a combat zone. He had to petition and appear before Judge Robert Bell in U.S. District Court in order to get his American citizenship restored.

Doi was among several Nisei linguists who landed with the first waves of marines, and he volunteered to search the caves. Armed with only a flashlight and a knife, and stripped to the waist to show he had no gun, he crawled through cave after cave, tunnel after tunnel, urging Japanese soldiers to surrender. He brought them out, one, two, three at a time, sometimes up to a dozen.

Most Japanese soldiers were prepared to follow the ancient Japanese Bushido custom and kill themselves rather than be taken prisoner. But a dead Japanese soldier was of no use to U.S. intelligence personnel. They needed to know where enemy weapons were located, how many men were in what places, and what commands they had been given. Speaking to Japanese soldiers in their own language was the only way to make them understand that they wouldn't be killed if they agreed to come out of their caves. Some did. Others blew themselves up. They shot at Doi repeatedly. Once a bullet knocked off his helmet. But Terry Doi got out as many Japanese as he could, then sent them to the rear to be questioned by Nisei linguists.

Doi's commanding officer, Lt. Wesley H. Fishel, later wrote Judge Bell:

> You will be happy to know that Terry did one of the finest pieces of work possible. Doi was one of the first GIs to land on Iwo Jima. The limits of censorship prohibit details, but I can say Terry is one of the bravest and most capable men I have seen out here.[9]

Another Caucasian officer, a graduate of the MISLS, wrote to Brig. Gen. John Weckerling, who had helped start the first school for interpreters and later was deputy assistant chief of the War Department Intelligence Section:

> There was nothing but praise for the Nisei, particularly a boy by the name of Doi. . . . There is a story about him people tell which goes something like this. He was continually going into caves with a knife and flashlight and hollering to the enemy to "get the hell out or else." Mr. Doi's middle name is now "Guts."[10]

Though Doi's exploits may have been the most spectacular, other Nisei were also crawling through these caves and tunnels. Yutaka Masuda was nearly captured when another American patrol bumped into his patrol; explanations were necessary to save him from being mistaken for an enemy. He also worked with two prisoners, Yamada and Hoshino, at caveflushing. Using names given him by the captives, Masuda called out to soldiers still hidden in a cave. Many came out, most of them wounded. Two officers, however, were holdouts and lobbed a grenade at Masuda. It blasted him off the hill but didn't severely injure him. Another blast sounded as the officers killed themselves.

Exploring another cave, Masuda instructed the captive Hoshino to look in the corners. They found a sergeant and were leading him out when another soldier tried to follow and two officers tossed grenades at him. Masuda commandered a team of medics and the man's life was saved. The officers killed themselves.[11] From an estimated garrison of more than twenty thousand Japanese soldiers on Iwo Jima, only 216 were taken alive.[12]

The danger of being mistaken for the enemy was ever present. After three nights of enemy mortar barrages, Ben Yamamoto went looking for sandbags to put around his hole. A Seabee officer knocked him down, stuck a .45 against his head, and demanded: "Who the hell are you?" After Yamamoto produced ID cards showing he was assigned to the U.S. Marine Corps, the officer let him go but warned him to stay in his own area so another Seabee wouldn't shoot him.[13] Ben was one of those Hawaii Nisei who had been in the war since its first day.

One of the diaries found on Iwo Jima told the story of the determined American advance on the island. On D day a Japanese soldier wrote: "Today we annihilate those who have landed." Four days later, on the morning of February 23, his diary asked: "There are no reinforcements for us. Are we not losing the battle?"[14]

On February 24, at sunrise, a forty-man patrol began an assault up the steep slopes of Mount Suribachi, the hill that overlooked all of Iwo Jima. It had become an evil symbol for the marines struggling in its shadow, and the men were determined to reach its peak. They were carrying an American flag measuring fifty-four inches by twenty-eight inches. At about 1030 they reached the top after fighting up the slopes with bayonets and grenades. Somewhere along the way they had found a piece of pipe and they pushed it into the top of the hill and tied their small flag to it. Marines who had been watching from below stopped fighting long enough to cheer. It was the first symbol of victory in this dirty battle.

The flag was so small that some marines decided to replace it with a larger one that could be seen more clearly throughout the island. An LST anchored offshore contributed a flag measuring ninety-six inches by fifty-six inches, and the men started toward Mount Suribachi with it. Joining them was Associated Press photographer Joe Rosenthal. When they reached the top of the mountain they raised this flag, and Rosenthal snapped the picture that was to become the most famous of the war.

Photographer Rosenthal had been close to the action on this and other islands, and he was one of the relatively few who appreciated the value of the Nisei linguists:

> They work so close to the enemy that along with the danger of being killed by Japs they run the risk of being shot unintentionally by our own marines. Many have paid with their lives. They have done an outstanding job, and their heroism should be recognized. It has been recognized by the Marine commanders where I saw them in action at Guam, Peleliu and Iwo.[15]

The questioning of prisoners by MIS linguists yielded much interesting information. Mineo Yamagata and other Nisei linguists were able to get from their captives maps and charts of Iwo Jima, Tokyo, the Inland Sea, and other areas, which were of help in the present battle and in future ones. They also learned more personal things—the thoughts and fears of the POWs. One prisoner told Yamagata that he had heard that the marines severed body parts of dead Japanese soldiers to send home as souvenirs. Another POW commented that they had been impressed when they saw the road up Mount Suribachi, which Seabees had built in two days. The Japanese, they told him, had had forces on Iwo for nearly two decades and weren't able to build a road up those steep slopes.[16]

James Yoshinobu was a veteran of World War I whose work interrogating prisoners on Iwo Jima won him a Silver Star. Also interrogating prisoners and translating documents was George Inagaki, a veteran of Saipan and Tinian. A few months later, on Okinawa, Inagaki would play a significant role in the interrogation of a Japanese colonel sent to help plan that island's defenses.[17]

Much of the success the Nisei had in dealing with Japanese prisoners was due to knowledge of Japanese mores, gleaned from their parents. They knew that kind treatment of Japanese prisoners would extract more information than the harsh treatment being used in Europe. And they knew, from their own strict home training, that if a Japanese POW were caught telling lies, he would be greatly ashamed; he would then be likely to break down and give the intelligence personnel the information that was wanted.

While these Nisei were flushing Japanese soldiers from caves and interrogating those they captured, dozens of other MISers were diligently working at less glamorous jobs—interpreting maps and translating diaries and orders taken from prisoners or found on dead bodies. They worked fast and accurately, and coordinated closely with the troops in the field. Within minutes of discovering the location of an enemy gun emplacement, Marine Corps guns could be set and firing. This was particularly valuable, since air observation had been hampered by bad weather and by placement of so many main weapons inside cave or tunnel entrances where they couldn't be detected. In one area the Nisei pinpointed thirteen targets where air observation had reported only five.

At 1800 on March 16, Iwo Jima was officially declared secure after twenty-six days and nine hours of fighting. But it wasn't until eleven days later that General Kuribayashi admitted defeat. On March 27 he stabbed himself in the stomach; an aide then slashed his neck with a sword and buried him.[18]

Iwo Jima was the most costly battle in the 168-year history of the

Marine Corps. At the end of Admiral Nimitz's special press release marking the conclusion of the Iwo Jima campaign, he stated: "Among the Americans who served on Iwo island, uncommon valor was a common virtue."[19]

While mopping-up details were still in progress on Iwo Jima, teams of Nisei were being briefed for the invasion of the Ryukyu Islands. There some of the Nisei from Hawaii would rescue Okinawan relatives who had remained in their native land rather than emigrate.

And in Europe the 100th/442nd was still in the Maritime Alps. Plans were under way to ship the Combat Team back to Italy. Its 522nd Field Artillery Battalion, however, was earmarked for Germany, where the Nisei would see firsthand the infamous Nazi concentration camps.

CHAPTER 15

THE CHAMPAGNE CAMPAIGN

With their ubiquitous sense of humor, the Nisei dubbed their new assignment in France "The Champagne Campaign." They could spend their leaves on the Riviera beaches. After the horrors of fighting to rescue the Lost Battalion in the Vosges Mountains, this assignment seemed easy: guarding a twelve-mile stretch of the Franco-Italian border to keep the enemy from crossing into France and heading for the strategic port of Marseilles. The 100th Battalion reached there shortly after mid-November 1944, followed by the rest of the Combat Team a few days later.

In the snow-covered Maritime Alps the men wore white parkas when on patrol. Although it was comparatively quiet, Germans and Italian Fascist units were watching from the mountain mass, and men were still killed or wounded by sniper fire and sporadic shelling. The cold was hard to take, especially for those from Hawaii, but the dugouts were comfortable compared to the cold ground of the Vosges Mountains forests. Kitchen crews sent up hot meals and, sometimes, candy bars.

The candy was optional and cost a few cents. Mike Tokunaga remembers the time he was sharing a dugout with a kotonk new to the 100th Battalion and had to give him a lesson in Island ethics.

"He said to me, 'Mike, lend me a dime to buy some candy.' And I told him: 'Hey! How do I know you won't be killed before you can repay me? No! I won't *lend* you a dime. I'll *give* you one. And when I need, then you *give* to me.'"

What's mine is yours was the credo of the easygoing Islanders. What's mine I have to guard carefully was the lesson many of the mainlanders had learned from their suspicious neighbors at home.

Supplies in the Alps were delivered on the backs of mules. The mule skinners had a hellish time dragging, pushing, and cajoling their animals up the steep, slippery mountainsides. For Capt. George Grandstaff, in charge of supply operations, this was one of his worst experiences. He had coddled and sworn at both mules and mule skinners all through Italy, but the Maritime Alps were a nightmare for him and his GI crew. Grandstaff had high praise for the Nisei under his command. When the war was over, he would go up and down the West Coast of the United States telling audiences about the Nisei with whom he had worked. Grandstaff and his hardy mule skinner crew managed to get supplies to the troops wherever they were, forcing mule teams up narrow, snow-covered trails so slippery and steep that the animals sometimes fell off the cliffs. The mule skinners were tired and cold from repeated climbs, and they were constantly angry with the obstreperous mules. Summing up his never-ending bouts with the beasts, Pfc. Masao Suenaka told me: "You can kiss them, cuddle them and still they won't go."

To lighten this chore, the men gave nicknames to their mules: Hammerhead, named for a shark found in Hawaiian waters; Manini (another Hawaiian fish), for a small mule who was inclined to kick; and Big Herman, who was a brute. Then there was Big Red, a mule who could stand in one spot "long enough to grow roots," according to Pfc. Anse Arakaki. On one long hike up snow-covered mountains, Arakaki tried all the tricks he could think of to make Big Red move. "I stroke him. No good. I swear at him. Nothing happen. I push him. He don't move."

The feud between Big Red and Arakaki became personal and, after choice swear words in a mixture of Japanese, Hawaiian, and pidgin, Arakaki let go with a swift right uppercut to Big Red's jaw. The medics were sympathetic. What happened to Arakaki was listed officially as "simple fracture of the right wrist due to slipping on a mountain trail." Big Red moved only a few inches; no one knew if he had a sore jaw.

"So I land in the hospital," Arakaki confessed. "Good rest. No mules!"

Tragedy could strike quickly and unexpectedly along the Italian border. In the mountain hamlet of Sospel is a plaque memorializing two of K Company's men: SSgt. Kenji Sugawara and T5g. Larry Miura, both of whom had been through the bitter onslaughts in the Vosges Mountains. On a quiet, sunny day shortly after Thanksgiving 1943, an enemy tank appeared suddenly and shelled the town, killing the two men before it raced back across the border. It was in this attack that Pfc. Takaji Goto lost both his legs.

There was another brief skirmish around Sospel at the beginning of 1945 when a Nisei patrol discovered enemy troops hiding in a hunting shack. Fourteen prisoners were taken, but two prisoners and one Nisei, Sgt. Masa Sakamoto, died of wounds. The chaplain later said:

> I was told to go up and get his body and bring it down. We had a little service in the cave there and it was my duty as the chaplain to search his pockets in order to get everything that could be sent home. I found a letter. . . . All of his brothers were in the army in Japan. . . . Some vandals in California had burned down his father's home and barn in the name of patriotism. And yet this young man had volunteered for every patrol that he could go on. You know, you can't give a medal high enough for a man like that.[1]

Perhaps the saddest of all duties fell to the three chaplains of the 100th/442nd: Capt. Masao Yamada, Capt. Hiro Higuchi, and Capt. Israel Yost. They had to comfort the injured and dying. They had to go through the belongings of the dead, searching for personal items to be shipped home—a last note, a picture, a cherished letter—and then compose words of condolence to a bereaved family. It was often heart wrenching. Once, a dying Nisei handed his wallet to a chaplain, saying: "Give to someone who needs it. I won't anymore."

The chaplains were not just rear-echelon figures. They were the ones who went between the lines, under the Red Cross flag, to evacuate the Nisei dead, as Masao Yamada had done during the campaign to cross the Arno River. It was Israel Yost who led a party into no-man's-land at Anzio to confer with Germans about dead Americans lying there. Each of the chaplains was awarded the Legion of Merit, and two of them, Yamada and Yost, received Purple Hearts with Oak Leaf Clusters.

All three chaplains of the 100th/442nd represented Protestant denominations. Although a large percentage of the Nisei were Buddhists, no Buddhist priests were included in the Chaplain Corps. But all faiths filled the ranks at every service these chaplains held. Differences in religion didn't seem to matter to men at the front.

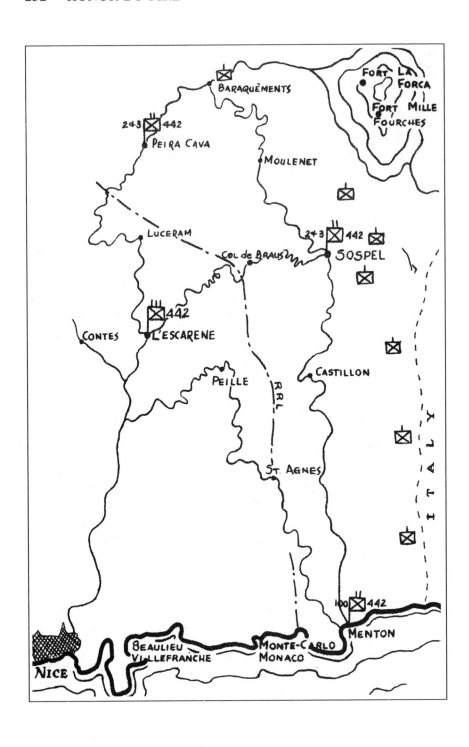

During the Battle of the Bulge in France, when Germans broke through Allied defenses in the Ardennes (December 1944), the French-Italian border was tense. Both sides were sending spies across the border, and patrols were put on alert for German paratroopers dressed in American uniforms, who might infiltrate behind the lines. Nisei observers didn't miss even the most devious tricks. During one artillery skirmish, observers directing artillery fire spotted women working in a field between the lines. As shells began to explode among them, the figures pulled up their skirts and ran. When the skirts went up, the Nisei spotted uniforms and boots under them. They were Italian Fascists, and they didn't get past the Japanese Americans.

Brigadier General Ralph C. Tobin, whose command in the French Maritime Alps included the 100th/442nd, became a dedicated admirer of the Japanese-American troops after this experience with them. He told me when I met him later:

> I was faced with the job of catching two German prisoners of war. After using all "normal" agencies to prevent the Germans from rejoining enemy troops with valuable information, I called in the 100th/442nd to do the job. By 5 P.M. the same day the regiment reported it had caught them.

Tobin used the regiment to catch another batch of the enemy—a company of about seventy-five, which the Germans, desperate for information, had flown across the Franco-Italian line.

"I sent out a platoon of 30 men from the 100th/442nd and they took care of the Germans fine," he said. "The tougher the situation, the better they are."

The most notable prize of the Combat Team during this campaign was the minisub its Antitank Company captured on December 19, 1944—along with its one-man crew, a German corporal—as it headed into the harbor at Menton. The German thought he had reached Ventimiglia—five miles away on the Italian side of the border. After a brief skirmish, the German surrendered, the 232nd Engineer Company pulled the sub ashore, and the Nisei packed crew and submarine off to a fleet base. It was the only time during the war that the U.S. Navy is known to have received a captured sub from the U.S. Army.

What added the "champagne" to this campaign, however, was the five-day leaves the men spent on Riviera beaches. In Menton they could stay at a luxurious hotel, complete with a well-trained staff to wait on them. And plenty of French families opened their homes to these fun-loving but exceedingly courteous Japanese Americans. The Nisei also dated the daughters of the French, trying to find the smallest girl for the shortest man in the outfit. That was, of course, "Shorty"—Larry Kazumura.

Shorty had been spoiled during his long hospitalization in Naples after he was wounded in the battle for Hill 140 in Italy. The nurses were captivated by this brave, cheerful man. They treated him "just like a baby," as he put it. After three months, he rejoined the 100th/442nd, just after it was transferred to France. He had no proper-sized boots, however, so he was given a two-week leave, and the Quartermaster Corps sent him back to Italy to get two pairs custom made by a cobbler who specialized in GI footgear. He got the boots, but they were still a half size too big—size three.

When Shorty returned to France, the fight to rescue the Texas Division's Lost Battalion was just beginning. Captain Joe Byrne, who had always taken special care of Shorty, delegated him to the supply depot because he didn't think the man was well enough to go back on the line. That was where Shorty was when he learned that Captain Byrne had been killed.

The Nisei loved Joe Byrne, who towered above them all at six feet three inches tall. He had known Japanese Americans ever since his army service in Hawaii before the war. He was one army Caucasian who knew how to pronounce their sometimes complicated names. The Nisei knew they could count on Byrne to be with them in any situation. When I Company faced Banzai Hill during the fight to rescue the Lost Battalion, Byrne grabbed a BAR from a fallen soldier and charged with them up the hill, his tall figure a sure target during that all-out frontal assault. For his valor that day he won a Silver Star. Soon afterward Byrne was killed by a Bouncing Betty mine. But I Company men would never forget him. They chipped in and bought a loving cup, had it inscribed in his memory, and presented it, along with his Silver Star, to his older brother, a West Pointer.[2]

The Champagne Campaign was, of course, too good to last. In early March, rumors began floating around that the 100th/442nd would be moving out. The destination was top secret. The guessing began: Would they go to the States? The Pacific? Maybe, at long last, get to Paris? Adding to the confusion was the fact that the 522nd Field Artillery Battalion had been separated from the rest of the Combat Team to work with General Patch's Seventh Army. It was the first time the 522nd would not be part of the Combat Team.

As the 100th/442nd boarded trucks and headed along the coastal road toward Marseilles, the destination was still a mystery. Now came the strangest of all commands—first oral, then on notices hung in latrines where nobody could miss them:

> All organizational markings of any sort, including shoulder patches, insignia on helmets, vehicle designations, etc. will be obliterated or taken off all items of equipment of individuals and units within the Combat Team.

They did as they were told, wondering how anybody could mistake their Japanese faces for anything other than 100th/442nd soldiers. Axis Sally was saying in her radio broadcasts that "America's Secret Weapon" (meaning the Nisei) was being transferred to Italy. Nobody wanted to believe her. Italy, with its mud and mountains, summer scorching heat and winter freezing cold, was the last place any of the old-timers wanted to see again.

The men didn't have to wait long to learn of their destination. Their mission was urgent, apparently; they were piled on ships as fast as the army could get them there. After that, news about the 100th/442nd was absolutely nonexistent. They might as well have dropped off the face of the earth.

It was at this time that I reached Paris. Nobody at SHAEF headquarters would tell me where the 100th/442nd was or what they were doing, so I roamed around and covered some stories for my former employer, the Associated Press, which was shorthanded. Eventually press headquarters gave me a jeep and driver and headed me into Germany. The roads were clogged with people trying to escape the fighting—women and old men with their few remaining possessions piled on pushcarts or on their backs, children playing with dolls, oblivious of the war all around them.

I was still trying to locate our soldiers from Hawaii when I saw, for the first time, a Nazi concentration camp. It was in the First French Army area, located outside a small village near Karlsruhe. Max Borden, of NBC, and I were the first Americans to enter it. When the prisoners heard that Americans were there, they crowded around us until French guards had to push them back. The French were busy that day, burying the last of approximately eighteen thousand Jews who had died during the war years in this abominable place.

After we left the camp, my GI driver made his way to a Seventh Army bivouac, secluded in a forested area. I hoped someone there could tell me about my friends from Hawaii. It was sheer luck, of course, but I landed where two U.S. Army generals had their headquarters: Lt. Gen. Alexander M. Patch and Brig. Gen. Ralph C. Tobin. Word must have spread fast that a stray reporter was around, because within a few minutes the two generals materialized. When I told them that I represented a Hawaiian newspaper and was searching for the Japanese-American soldiers, the ice broke. A trailer was put at my disposal, a GI was ordered to get me anything I needed, and I was invited to dinner. I shouldn't have been surprised: both officers had had the Nisei in their commands and admired them tremendously.

At dinner, conversation revolved around the generals' contacts with the Nisei Combat Team—one story after another. Said Tobin:

> There is something about those kids that gets under my skin. I go into a hospital where they are and as soon as I get into the room they say: "Hey, General, I'll be back on the line in ten days." They never kick. They are the most alert soldiers, and they are well behaved. I have never heard of a case of AWOL among them.

Both men went into great detail about the difficulty in finding clothes to fit the Japanese-American soldiers. They said they had been at their "wit's end" during the winter, trying to find warm clothes for the regiment. "We finally had to turn the problem over to the experts in army salvage and the Quartermaster Corps to find shoes and parkas small enough," General Patch admitted.

Then they got on the subject of rice. Tobin was proud that he had secured a 10 percent increase in the Combat Team's rice rations. One of Tobin's favorite stories, however, was about the boy from Hawaii whom he was decorating with the Distinguished Service Cross. Despite his fearlessness on the front lines, the boy "shook like a leaf" during the presentation. The general told him to be thankful the French weren't awarding the decoration because they would insist on kissing him.

I didn't realize then that General Patch had known Nisei of the Military Intelligence Service in the Pacific. Their work was secret at that time, but he left no doubt concerning his feelings about the 100th/442nd Regimental Combat Team. "I really feel I would give that unit a desperate mission and truly and sincerely trust them to fulfill it," he said.

Where was the 100th/442nd at this point? It had returned to Italy, but there was an artillery battalion of Nisei under his command, Patch told me, and he would see that I got to them the next morning. So I was caught between two fronts. I decided to take a look at the 522nd Field Artillery Battalion here in Germany and then—somehow—get to Italy.

The infighting among U.S. Army generals for command of the 100th/442nd Regimental Combat Team may have been the reason that the 522nd Field Artillery Battalion was separated from the rest of the Combat Team—as a compromise. General Patch had commanded the first U.S. Army force sent into the Pacific, to which some of the first Nisei graduates of the army language school were assigned. And, in late 1942, Patch had gone to Guadalcanal as commander of the combined army and marine forces there and met more Nisei linguists. Shifted to the European Theater as commander of the Seventh Army, Patch knew all about the record of the 100th/442nd in the Vosges Mountains. Confronted with the challenge of defeating German forces in their own country, he had fought for the best troops he could get. Though he lost the Nisei infantry to Gen. Mark Clark, he was successful in adding the Nisei 522nd Field Artillery Battalion to his force.

CHAPTER 16

GERMANY AND THE DEATH CAMPS

The 522nd Field Artillery Battalion moved out of the French Maritime Alps on March 9, 1945, for a three-day, 619-mile ride to the Saarland village of Ipplingen. It was the beginning of the 522nd's life as a roving battalion, shifting to whatever command most needed the unit at any particular time. Before the war was over, the men would supply supporting fires for almost two dozen army units. They would travel eleven hundred miles across Germany, from the Saar and Rhine Rivers in the west to the Austrian border in the east, fire 15,219 rounds, and take every objective of their fifty-two assignments.

On reaching Ipplingen, the 522nd reinforced the 63rd (Blood and Fire) Infantry Division. The Nisei crossed the Saar River into Germany near midnight on March 12 with the Blood and Fire boys and fired their first round on German soil the next morning. They were still with the 63rd in the breakthrough of the Siegfried line, which was dotted with German corpses frozen in snow. Soon after that, at the village of Neumchlerhot, they captured a big prize: a German 150mm howitzer. They then fired the gun on its previous owners, with better results than they had had with their own 105mm howitzers.

A commendation sent to their battalion commander, Lt. Col. Baya M. Harrison, Jr., by the commanding general of the 63rd Infantry Division stated: "The manner in which all missions were accomplished indicated a well organized, well directed and well disciplined battalion. It reflects great credit upon the personnel of your command."

The Nisei supported the 45th "Thunderbird" Infantry Division's crossing of the Rhine River near Worms and captured twenty-one Germans near Ripperterhof. Then the battalion was shifted again, this time to the 44th Division, with which it finally crossed the Rhine River via a treadway bridge in the early morning on March 27. It was too dark and the men were too tired to enjoy the thrill of breaking through another barrier.

Two days later they were back with the Blood and Fire boys, shifting from one unit to another as they moved northeast through a series of villages and towns whose names were like a cartographer's nightmare. In early April they were with the 4th Reconnaissance Troop. They placed fire so effectively on enemy troops near Aub that the Germans there surrendered en masse. The 522nd was moving so fast through the German countryside that it sometimes displaced three times a day. Each displacement meant uncoupling the heavy howitzers from trucks, digging new gun pits, anchoring the pieces with sandbags and logs, stretching camouflage nets on poles to hide them from enemy aircraft, then waiting for a call from the fire direction center, which would relay a point of aim from forward artillery observers. Each piece had a name and its own pit and crew. One, manned by Nisei from Hawaii, was called Kuu Ipo, which means "sweetheart" in Hawaiian. When the shooting began, some men stuffed cotton in their ears to keep from injuring their eardrums.

Sometimes new orders were slow in coming; then crap games, gossip, and paperbacks so old they were falling apart relieved the boredom. Gun crews slept in the fields in blanket rolls or in pup tents alongside the gun emplacements. The remainder of the battalion slept in village farmhouses or barns (when available), where they set out blanket rolls and found places to keep the many pets they seemed to accumulate. When new orders arrived, they would start all over again: taking down everything they had set up, packing up their pets, hooking up the howitzers, loading other paraphernalia onto trucks, and moving forward to repeat the whole process in a new location.

After leaving the headquarters of General Patch and General Tobin, we drove a couple of hours by jeep, riding behind the front lines, before I found the 522nd. I had arrived at an inopportune time: some of the men from Hawaii had discovered a water hole and were relishing a skinny-dip. When they saw a woman approaching, they yelled a warning and scrambled for cover. The "coconut wireless" took over then, and within minutes everybody in the battalion knew I had arrived. After that I felt at home, luxuriating in their pidgin-speak and outrageous good humor and sharing their noon meal of captured German macaroni and beets. Dessert was canned pineapple, which the men from Hawaii loathed. They hadn't had a grain of rice for three weeks. Then I toured their gun emplacements, where I met up with Kuu Ipo and the stray pets—from a pheasant to enough dogs to bench a good-sized dog show—which they pampered outrageously.

Mail arrived that day. It was never enough, but they were happy to see it, even when they received newspapers five months old. They read every inch of print, including "help wanted" and "for sale" ads. Gun crews were firing, but those men not working were writing letters, reading, or playing games. A hundred feet down the road lay a dead German, but nobody paid any attention to him.

In late afternoon we packed up to move forward. One gun crew was so hot on the heels of retreating Germans that it captured a chicken still roasting on a spit and promptly ate it. The battalion cleared the barns and houses in their new location and established a mess and sleeping quarters while worried Germans looked on. Some villagers tried to help, but the nonfraternization rule prevented this. A GI with a different outfit had recently been choked to death with piano wire somewhere around Regensburg.

In this new town the Nisei found a French soldier who had been a prisoner of war for almost five years, since being captured at Dunkirk. He warned them that the Germans had mined the roads ahead. The Nisei fed him, gave him a map, pointed the way toward France, and wished him good luck. It wasn't long before the men had strung communication lines, uncoupled their howitzers, put up pup tents, taken care of their menagerie of pets, found a supply of potatoes to make their favorite midnight snack—something that tasted like french fries—and settled in for the night.

They had found the best feather bed in the village for me and established a corner in the operations office where I could write. I set up a typewriter on the only surface available—a sewing machine table. On the other side of the room, officers were busy getting directions from forward observers, then relaying them to the gun crews who would set a point of aim.

Lieutenant Colonel Harrison, a quiet, distinguished lawyer from Tampa, Florida, had commanded the 522nd Field Artillery Battalion since its training days at Camp Shelby, Mississippi. The battalion had a roster of headquarters officers that included some of the most astute forward observers of any artillery unit. Most were Caucasians who had had no experience with Japanese Americans before the war, but the officers quickly learned to appreciate them. They also learned to understand the pidgin spoken by the men from Hawaii—which Colonel Harrison concluded was "guaranteed to defeat any Germans listening in on radio commands."

That night the artillery was shooting at some targets in the direction of Munich, and the big guns were busy until morning. The men who weren't on duty spent the evening gathering fresh eggs in the village. (They were meticulous about paying for what they took, either in occupation money or staples.) The next morning they fried the eggs for breakfast on a long sheet of metal over an open fire. The few leftovers went to their pampered pets.

When it was time for me to leave—to head for Italy and find the rest of the Combat Team—two men from Hawaii, Richard Sugiyama and Ernest Miwa, were assigned to drive me to a press camp where I could file the stories I had gathered from the 522nd. Before we set off, I watched the two men scrutinizing a map for a long time. A wrong turn could lead to enemy territory and capture. It had almost happened to me en route to the battalion. But I had great confidence in my Nisei friends: they took pride in doing a job thoroughly.

A few scanty news reports had reached us, telling of fierce fighting in the Apennine Mountains. With fighting still going on in Germany and in northern Italy, I would have to make an end run, by plane back through Paris and Rome, then work my way north in Italy to catch up with the infantry and engineers of the 100th/442nd Regimental Combat Team.

When I left the 522nd, it was moving southeast, still shifting its support among army units and heading for a crossing of the Danube River—if it could find a bridge the enemy hadn't smashed as they retreated farther into Germany.

The battalion finally did find a narrow bridge just north of the small town of Dillingen. The outfit crossed the river on April 26 to set up their guns in the village of Weisengen, a few yards from the front lines.

But front lines everywhere were disappearing fast as Germans fled before the final Allied onslaughts.

On April 1, Hitler moved from his chancellery to a bunker dug deep below the chancellery grounds. In midmonth, the Soviet Union opened its offensive against Berlin.[1] In the town of Dachau, ten miles northwest of Munich, Hitler's crack SS troops were preparing for an inevitable Allied push and were moving Hitler's most prominent prisoners from subcamps to the main camp at Dachau.

Between 1933 and 1945 the Dachau administration controlled and supplied prisoners for a total of 240 auxiliary camps, each created to provide labor for a particular construction project or factory.[2] Among Hitler's elite prisoners taken to the main Dachau camp as Allied forces approached were some of the most prominent statesmen (and their families) of Europe, including Leon Blum, former chancellor of France, and Kurt von Schuschnigg, former chancellor of Austria.

Approximately 150 of Hitler's most important prisoners were finally gathered at Dachau, and, after dark on April 24, they were herded into open trucks to be transported under SS guard away from approaching Allied troops. A few days later approximately eight thousand other prisoners were marched out of the extermination camp, presumably toward a Dachau subcamp in the Tyrol. The mild spring weather had suddenly changed to bitter cold and it started to snow. Prisoners, whose sneakers and striped cotton prison garb offered little protection, began dying from the cold.

Meanwhile, the 522nd Field Artillery Battalion, pursuing the vanishing Germans, had moved into the area where the Nazis had scattered Dachau subcamps. When the Nisei came upon a camp, they would knock down the gates and free the prisoners. (We heard, but couldn't confirm, that at one subcamp they smashed a gate by backing a truck into it.) No one kept track of which subcamps they entered, but it is known that on April 27 they occupied a position at Horgau, the location of one Dachau subcamp, and next to the city of Augsburg where another subcamp was located.

The battalion continued to move south, firing all the while on Munich. Their original orders were to head toward Berchtesgaden, Hitler's Alpine retreat near the Austrian border, where he might seek refuge from Russians then converging on Berlin. On April 25, however, more than three hundred

British bombers had smashed Hitler's mountain refuge. German forces were disintegrating so fast that there were no longer enemy "lines," and 522nd scouts ranged out from their bivouac areas toward Dachau, seeking information about German pockets left in the wake of retreat.

Once Dachau had been a quaint market town, a mecca for German artists. But in the late nineteenth century industry began to supplant the rural life. Whatever beauty remained was extinguished during World War I, when extensive stands of old pine and fir trees were cut down to provide space for a huge factory built to produce ammunition for German battlefields. Rows of small, red-roofed houses were constructed for the thousands of workers needed to manufacture ammunition, and the factory complex was surrounded by a long concrete wall.

It was this abandoned factory that had prompted Heinrich Himmler, head of Hitler's SS, to place the first Nazi concentration camp in the old town. Dachau became the model and training center for SS-organized camps. By 1936 the camp, planned for five thousand persons, was too small, and prisoners were forced to build a larger compound, surrounded by miles of electrified barbed wire and guarded by watchtowers.

A report issued by the Counterintelligence Corps of the Seventh Army estimated that about 229,000 prisoners had been processed at Dachau since its inception in 1933. Some were kept at the main camp; others were dispersed to the subcamps spread throughout southern Germany and into Austria.

Few GIs fighting in Europe knew much about Nazi concentration camps. News of the death camps and the labor camps was obscured in the rush of Allied troops toward the heart of Germany itself—Berlin. On April 29, however, American forces broke into a ghastly scene that would, at last, focus world attention on the Nazi death camps. Many GIs cried as they tried to understand what had happened here. A graphic description was given in an Associated Press dispatch dated April 30, 1945:

> Dachau, Germany's most dreaded extermination camp, has been captured and its surviving 32,000 tortured inmates have been freed by outraged American troops who killed or captured its brutal garrison in a furious battle.

Dashing to the camp atop tanks, bulldozers, self-propelled guns—anything with wheels—the Forty-second and Forty-fifth Divisions hit the notorious prison northwest of Munich soon after the lunch hour yesterday. . . .

Controversy has continued about whether the 42nd or 45th Division reached Dachau first. Questions also exist concerning these notes from the diary of T4g. Ichiro Imamura of the 522nd Field Artillery Battalion, which were not revealed until TSgt. Chester Tanaka discovered the diary during research for his book *Go For Broke,* published in 1982, nearly forty years after the end of the war:

Two liaison scouts from the 522nd Field Artillery Bn, 100/442 RCT, were among the first Allied troops to release prisoners in the Dachau concentration camp. I watched as one of the scouts used his carbine to shoot off the chain that held the prison gates shut. He said he just had to open the gates when he saw a couple of the 50 or so prisoners, sprawled on the snow-covered ground, moving weakly. They weren't dead as he had first thought.

When the gates swung open, we got our first good look at the prisoners. Many of them were Jews. They were wearing black and white striped prison suits and round caps. A few had shredded blanket rags draped over their shoulders. It was cold and the snow was two feet deep in some places. There were no German guards. They had taken off before we reached the camp.

The prisoners struggled to their feet after the gates were opened. They shuffled weakly out of the compound. They were like skeletons—all skin and bones. . . .

We had been ordered not to give out rations to the Dachau prisoners because the war was still on and such supplies were needed to keep our own fighting strength up, but we gave them food, clothing and medical supplies anyway. The officers looked the other way. These prisoners really needed help and they needed it right away. They were sick, starving and dying. . . .

We stayed near Dachau for several days and then got orders to move on. During this time, I found some large chalk-like bars, sort of oval-shaped, with numbers stamped on them. I was about to "liberate" a couple of them as souvenirs when an MP told me they were the remains of prisoners. The numbers were for identification. I put the bars back.[3]

None of the Nisei mentioned in Imamura's diary would talk to Tanaka about their experience. Three years later, John Tsukano published *Bridge of Love,* his book about the 100th/442nd Regimental Combat Team; he had met the same silence when he tried to get more information from the men named in Imamura's diary. In 1987, Ben Tamashiro, a 100th Battalion veteran and historian, wrote a series of articles for *The Hawaii Herald* about the meeting of Dachau prisoners and 522nd men. Information about the Dachau-522nd experiences began spreading through the American Jewish community and then through the European Jewish community. When a group of 522nd veterans visited the Dachau camp shortly afterward, the Jews of Munich turned out to welcome the Japanese-American veterans. An official of B'nai B'rith told the group: "Call me, call us, any time you are in Munich and you will always be welcomed. . . . We shall never forget what you did at Dachau in 1945."[4]

One former Dachau inmate wrote the Nisei: "We thank you for freeing us from the Dachau camp in 1945. . . . We want you to know what a lot your arrival in front of the Dachau camp gates in 1945 meant to us."

Since then other former prisoners have verified that they were helped by the Nisei. One of them, now a bookstore owner in the New York area, said he was liberated by soldiers who were like no others he had ever seen: "short, dark, straight black hair and their patch had a field of blue with a white flame." They made a distinct impression on him because it was the first time he had seen anyone of Asian ancestry.[5]

According to an article in the November 11, 1991, issue of *The New Yorker* magazine, one former Dachau inmate testified:

I was standing with a blindfold waiting to be shot, but the shot didn't come. So I asked the woman next to me: "Do you think they're trying to make us crazy, so we'll run and they won't have to feel guilty about shooting us?" She said, "Well, we're not going to run. We'll just stand here." So we stood and stood and suddenly someone was tugging at my blindfold. He tugged this way and that way, and then he jumped up because he was short and he pulled it off. I saw him and I thought, Oh, now the *Japanese* are going to kill us. And I didn't care anymore. I said, "Just kill us, get it over with." He tried to convince me that he was an American and wouldn't kill me. I said, "Oh, no, you're a Japanese and you're going to kill us." We went back and forth, and finally he landed on his knees, crying, with his hands over his face, and he said, "You are free now. We are *American* Japanese. You are free."

The day after Dachau was liberated, the 522nd captured the town of Moerlbach, south of Munich, opened the gates to a Dachau subcamp there, and liberated its French prisoners. Even this, however, was not the last meeting of Japanese Americans and of the prisoners of the Nazis.

On May 2, 1945, three days after American troops entered Dachau, the Nisei had another encounter with Dachau survivors. Colonel Harrison, commander of the 522nd Field Artillery Battalion, gave me the following account:

> Entering the town of Waakirchen, south of Munich, the battalion was met and cheered by 5,000 Dachau prisoners. . . .
>
> There was snow on the ground and the weather was so cold that a few towns back the men volunteered to mark the route so they could stand by the burning buildings to keep warm. Yet, the Dachau men were clad in cotton uniforms with cotton bathrobes as their only outer wrap.
>
> They had been taken from Dachau a week before when the Nazis knew the Americans were coming and had been forced to march through the Bavarian mountain roads.
>
> Of the 8,000 who started the march, 5,000 survived. The rest were either shot by the Germans when they got too weak to keep up or died by the wayside.
>
> The Nazi guards fled to the woods, leaving the prisoners free for two hours before the advent of the American troops [the 522nd Field Artillery Battalion].
>
> The battalion had seen some dead Dachau men as it approached town but the sights when the battalion entered the town were unforgettable. Some of the Dachau men were tearing strips of meat

from dead animals, while Germans stood and watched. The prisoners hadn't eaten for three days and the 522nd battalion, although short on rations, shared food with them.

All of the Dachau prisoners were suffering from malnutrition and many from typhus and trench foot.

There were some doctors among the prisoners and within 24 hours after liberation they had established a hospital and were treating the sick.

Six prisoners died the first night. Meanwhile the Germans were ordered to feed them and many were outfitted from local stocks.

Japanese Americans of the 522nd Field Artillery Battalion would never forget the suffering and deaths of these prisoners from the notorious death camp at Dachau. They took hundreds of pictures of the skeletal creatures they met at Waakirchen. After V-E Day they visited Dachau to see again the prison and the ovens in its extermination chambers where so many men, women, and children had died.

At war's end Hideo Nakamine returned to Hawaii, married, and raised a family. But his memories of the Dachau prisoners remained—vivid and painful. Nakamine began attending Jewish meetings on the mainland, and he was a guiding factor in forming the 522nd's Dachau Research Committee in Hawaii to learn more about this devastating chapter of world history.

While the 522nd Field Artillery Battalion was fighting Germans in their own country, the rest of the 100th/442nd Regimental Combat Team was pushing German forces through the Apennine Mountains and back to the Alps to bring freedom once again to Italy.

CHAPTER 17

VICTORY IN EUROPE

A xis Sally had been right—again! The 100th/442nd Regimental Combat Team landed back in Italy. On March 25, 1945, the 100th/442nd reached Leghorn after a one-and-a-half-day trip from Marseilles and was immediately trucked to a staging area in Pisa. There were a lot of newcomers in the ranks because so many of the old-timers had been left behind in hospitals or graves in France. The new men were interested in the sights. The famous Leaning Tower, however, puzzled some of them. One Nisei from Hawaii alarmed the Italians when he assured them: "We are going to fix that tower so that it won't lean so much and be a hazard to our troops."[1]

At the staging ground, the Combat Team drew new equipment. The men were not permitted to leave the area because their presence was still classified "secret." General Clark had fought all the way up the line to General Eisenhower to get the Nisei back to Italy. He hadn't wanted to let them go to France in the first place, but General Devers, commander of the Sixth Army Group, had needed fresh troops and had demanded the 100th/442nd. Everybody wanted them, it seemed. This time Clark won: he needed them for the drive to end the war on the Italian front. His Fifth Army was pitted against the last great German defense south of the Alps.

The fight among generals for the Japanese-American Combat Team had gotten quite intense. In a letter to the Nisei outfit at the close of the war, Maj. Gen. Alfred M. Gruenther detailed the controversy:

> To show you how your reputation as a fighting unit had grown
> I must tell you of the behind the scenes battle which took place

over the assignment of the 442nd. Every division in the Fifth Army insisted that the 442nd be assigned to it. General Ryder insisted that there was only one logical place for it and that was with the 34th Division and that was General Clark's decision.

Two months later the assignment of the 442nd was again to be the cause of considerable pleading and counter-pleading. General Devers commanding the Sixth Army Group which invaded Southern France appealed to the Joint Chiefs of Staff for the 442nd. General Clark resisted vigorously and many messages passed between the Joint Chiefs of Staff and the two commands on that subject. In a letter which I received from the officer in the Operations Division of the War Department while the argument was at its height he said: "One would think that the 442nd RCT was the only unit in Italy the way you fellows are squawking about giving it up!"

The decision was made in favor of the Southern France assignment and you left Italy September 1944.

Although you were out of sight you were not out of mind and General Clark never gave up the idea that he would get you back. . . . General Devers protested vigorously but General Clark won out.[2]

Still operating in secrecy, the Combat Team moved on the night of March 28 to an area north of the walled city of Lucca, the central marketing town of Tuscany. Captain Grandstaff bartered there for mules, which he would need for the coming mountain battle.

On April 3, General Clark reviewed a formation that the 100th Battalion held in his honor and greeted the troops:

I welcome the 100th Infantry Battalion back to Italy. I hated to see you leave the 5th Army, but it was considered necessary that you go to the support of the invading troops in southern France. I have followed closely your splendid record. . . . I remember the time when the 100th Battalion received the Distinguished Unit Badge and more than 100 other medals that I have presented at various times. I have seen you in action and know your ability.[3]

Spring was late in coming to the Apennine Mountains, but trees were beginning to leaf out as the Combat Team trained and practiced maneuvers. The coming battle was going to be tough. The engineers explained to newcomers the type of mines the Germans were using: nonmetallic Shu mines, which couldn't be spotted by mine detectors. The Todt Organization, which had constructed the fortifications at Monte Cassino, had spent nine months building the Gothic line, using an estimated fifteen thousand Italian slave laborers. They drilled through rock to make gun pits and trenches, which were reinforced with concrete. Bombs dropped from planes did little damage to these fortifications. From their mountaintop positions the Germans had unobstructed views of any approaching armies, and they controlled all approaches. And they had interlocking firepower, just as they had had at Cassino.

After crossing the Arno River, Allied forces broke through the center of the Gothic line, which stretched from the Ligurian seacoast in the west across the Apennine Mountains to the Adriatic Sea on the east coast. But the advance had been stopped near Pietrasanta, on the west coast, by enemy fortifications in the mountains that commanded the Ligurian coastal road northward. The Combat Team's orders were to conquer this last sector of the Gothic line and drive the Germans out of the mountains onto the western coastal plain, then up the coast toward the great naval base at La Spezia. Continuation of the Allied advance northward depended on the Combat Team's success in conquering the hitherto impenetrable mountain bastion. And General Clark hadn't forgotten that the Germans increased their troop strength wherever the Nisei were on the line. He was counting on it this time. If the Germans did shift troops to face the Nisei regiment on the west coast, it would help the Allied line to push the Nazi troops through Bologna, then into the Alpine passes and out of Italy. For this operation, the Combat Team would be attached to the 92nd Division, a black unit.

The mountains facing the Combat Team rose to heights of three thousand feet, one after the other, looking like a series of ocean waves in an angry storm. Even the old-timers who had climbed Italy's mountains from Salerno to the Arno River thought these were the most daunting they had ever faced.

The command question was whether to make a frontal attack or try to encircle the Germans' formidable mountain defenses. Either way, the enemy could look down from its heights and see what was coming. The answer was to conceal the Nisei approach by moving at night, then make a surprise pincers attack at dawn. In this operation they would have help from the Partisans, those Italian civilians who had denounced fascism and Mussolini and thrown in their lot with the Allied armies. As the war progressed in Italy, Partisan forces had grown stronger. The Allied forces could use these natives to guide them through the difficult mountain passes.

At dark on April 3, the 100th and 3rd Battalions began moving toward their assembly areas. The 100th moved into a location near Vallecchia, at the foot of the western edge of the mountain mass; the men would climb toward the German defense line during the next night and be ready for a dawn attack on April 5.

While the 100th was moving toward Vallecchia, the 3rd Battalion hiked eastward all night, via goat paths and mountain trails, to the village of Azzano near twenty-eight-hundred-foot Mount Folgorito. Adjoining it is three-thousand-foot-high Mount Altissimo, which looks down on the whole area. The 3rd Battalion would remain hidden around Azzano throughout the day on April 4, climb to the saddle between Mount Cerretta and Mount Folgorito that night, then attack across the mountaintops at dawn on April 5, moving westward toward the eastward-moving 100th Battalion—squeezing the German defenses between them. The two battalions would meet somewhere along the mountain saddle and, together, push the Germans north. There the 2nd Battalion, which would be climbing Mount Folgorito during the night of April 5, would tackle the retreating German forces; its goal was to push off Mount Belvedere the crack Machine-Gun Battalion Kesselring, named in honor of Field Marshal Albert Kesselring, who, until recently, had been the formidable commander of all German forces in Italy.

When the 3rd Battalion reached Azzano after its all-night hike, a tired and weary patrol was dispatched to the rock-strewn valley in front of Mount Folgorito. They hid in a rock hut throughout the day to check for enemy patrols in the valley. Radio silence had to be maintained, so one man, TSgt. Chet Tanaka, was sent, with a Partisan guide, to get information from the patrol hidden in the valley and report back to Colonel Pursall at battalion headquarters. Halfway there, however, the guide disappeared, leaving Tanaka to find his way alone in unfamiliar territory.

Throughout the day on April 4, 3rd Battalion men hid in the olive groves and small houses of Azzano and prepared for the mountain climb, rubbing dirt or soot on their faces to obscure them from enemy observation, cleaning weapons, resting when they could. They were ordered to go up the mountain in absolute silence—no talking, no smoking, no radios, dog tags tied so they wouldn't clank together. Even if a man fell off the mountain he wasn't to cry out.

It was 2200 on April 4 when the 3rd Battalion hiked through the valley floor to begin tackling the 60 percent incline between Mount Folgorito and Mount Cerretta. On the steep, slippery, shale-encrusted slopes it seemed that for each step forward they fell two steps backward. Laden with full packs, rifles, and ammunition, they crawled and pulled themselves up by grabbing onto scrawny bushes, the leg of the man ahead, or his rifle butt, digging into the mountain with hands bloodied by sharp stones. One man dislodged a rock and it fell on him. A few men fell down the mountain—without uttering a sound. It was freezing cold in the mountain air, but the men sweated under their heavy packs. They gasped for breath as they climbed, then slipped and fell and crawled again. At 0500 on April 5 they reached the summit to begin their all-out attack against the strong enemy defenses.

On the west end of the mountain mass, the 100th Battalion had also climbed undetected during the predawn hours. At daybreak it was positioned to begin the attack after a rolling artillery barrage. The 100th's first objective was a knob of solid rock, which had more than a dozen gun emplacements. The Nisei advanced 150 feet unopposed. Then the battalion ran into a minefield, which killed and wounded many of them, and the Germans opened up from their well-concealed nests and foxholes with machine guns, rifles, and grenades. The advance was scattered and nearly stopped until Pvt. (later SSgt.) Henry Y. Arao reorganized his squad and took over. He crawled alone to a machine-gun emplacement, threw a grenade, then charged, killing the gunner and forcing his assistant to surrender. By then another machine gun was shooting at him, so he tossed a grenade and killed that crew as it came out from a shelter.[4] As one Nisei dropped, another replaced him, killing the enemy in their positions until the Germans fled to a shelter dug into the mountainside.

In thirty-two minutes the Nisei had driven the Germans from the crucial rockbound entrenchments that had repelled unending, persistent attacks for more than five months.

In a nearby shell crater lay the torn body of Pfc. Sadao Munemori, one of the heroes of this crucial battle in the Apennines. Munemori had taken charge of his squad when its leader was injured. Fighting beside him were two Nisei privates. When a machine gun opened up, they all ducked into the shell crater. But the machine gun had to be silenced, so Munemori crawled from the hole and knocked out two machine-gun nests with hand grenades. By then heavy enemy fire was concentrating on him, and he ran back to the crater. He stopped at its edge and was preparing to throw another grenade when an enemy grenade bounced off his helmet and rolled down into the crater. There wasn't time to throw it out and, in a split-second decision, Munemori threw himself on top of the grenade, bending his head over his chest and hunching his shoulders to smother the blast. He was killed instantly. The other two men suffered only minor wounds, but they were haunted the rest of their lives by the memory of Munemori's sacrifice to save them.

At the Manzanar, California, internment camp, Munemori's family was handed the War Department notification of Sadao's death. Munemori was awarded the Medal of Honor—the only such medal granted the 100th/442nd during World War II despite other recommendations. It was awarded at the conclusion of the war in Europe, but only after Mike Masaoka, a member of the Combat Team's Public Relations Office and a wartime leader of the Japanese American Citizens League, contacted his longtime friend Senator Elbert Thomas of Utah. Why, they asked, had no previously recommended Medals of Honor been granted to Japanese Americans but had been awarded in other units for actions that were no more heroic? The question remains: Was this yet evidence of wartime racial prejudice?

Three years later the ten-thousand-ton troopship *Wilson Victory* would be renamed *Pvt. Sadao S. Munemori,* the first ship to honor a Japanese American.

Sadao Munemori was nineteen years old when he volunteered for the army a month before Pearl Harbor. He was eventually sent to the MIS Language School and had attained the rank of sergeant, but he decided he wanted to be with the 442nd Regimental Combat Team. He had to take a loss of rank—to private—to get there. By that time his family had been sent to the Manzanar camp. Munemori was among the first replacements sent by the 442nd to the 100th Infantry Battalion, following the Battle of Cassino. He had fought in the breakout from the Anzio beachhead, the battle to take Lanuvio on the road to

Rome, up the Italian coast, across the Arno River, and in the battles of Bruyeres, Biffontaine, and the rescue of the Lost Battalion in France.

Sadao was a fun-loving boy who got along well with the old-time 100th men from Hawaii. He even learned to speak their crazy pidgin dialect and hoped to go to Hawaii after the war. His only peculiarity was that he preferred to eat potatoes instead of rice, but his new friends tolerated this aberration and called him "Spud." He liked the nickname.

Although Munemori's action was the most outstanding that day, there would be other heroes as the Combat Team fought along the mountain saddle. The battle raged as the Germans were driven north.

The next morning, at dawn, Lt. Col. Jack Conley, current commander of the 100th, was on the radio: "We are running into Shu mines. It is just like a fortified line. They won't come out. You have to dig them out. Can you get us some flamethrowers so we can burn them out?" They eventually got five flamethrowers but no operators for them.

Two hours later a call went out to bomb the slit trenches on the reverse slopes where Germans were hidden. Finally, four planes were up and circling. They were directed over the target by a round of smoke, then circled and dived and hit a target. More planes came up. More targets were hit. "My whole damn reserve and some front line are standing on the hill watching the air show," Conley radioed.

German fire was coming in from Mount Altissimo. Men were being killed by artillery fire, and sometimes nobody knew which side had killed them. And "Anzio Annie" had moved north. The big railroad gun, now at Punta Bianca, near La Spezia, was throwing in round after round. Company L of the 3rd Battalion moved through the fire to fight Germans hand to hand. All along the ridge Germans and Nisei were fighting, with bayonets, rifles, from behind rocks, on slopes.

On April 6 the last enemy stronghold on the mountain saddle fell. The 100th and 3rd Battalions linked up, and the 2nd Battalion began an attack that would lead it onto Mount Belvedere. There, as it faced Machine-Gun Battalion Kesselring, TSgt. Yukio Okutsu knocked out three machine-gun nests. He crawled toward the first, then threw two grenades and killed the crew. He hit the second with a grenade, wounding two Germans and capturing two. Then he charged the third with his tommy gun and captured the whole crew—four men. Another DSC.[5]

After the Germans were knocked off Mount Belvedere, the 2nd Battalion began fighting its way through adjoining mountain strongholds to join the other two infantry battalions in their push north on the coastal highway to Massa. Then they were on to Carrara, where they crawled through hillsides that Michelangelo had once walked to select the marble for his masterpieces.

April 13 was an unlucky day for the troops. The infantry had moved so fast that their artillery couldn't keep up with them. Germans had them directly under observation from a mountain peak, and the 3rd Battalion, now in Carrara, was being pounded by rounds from the big railroad gun up north. Word began to filter through to the troops that President Roosevelt had died the preceding day. For many men, Franklin Delano Roosevelt was the only president they had known since childhood. Like American troops throughout the world, they mourned his loss. Not understanding the complexity of American government, most didn't realize that the incarceration of their families in internment camps was based on a presidential order. They wondered what the new man, Harry Truman, was like. "Will he be good?" they asked anyone they thought might have an answer.

In ten days the Combat Team had knocked the Germans from their Apennine Mountain strongholds overlooking Italy's west coast and swarmed northward, obliterating enemy troops in their path. German troops were rushed from their Bologna position to stop the Nisei advance, just as General Clark had hoped. The big push could begin at last. On April 15, the Allied armies facing Bologna launched their drive to push the Germans into the Po Valley and the Alpine passes.

The 100th/442nd infantry moved so fast up Italy's west coast that supplies couldn't keep pace. At one point they moved seventy-six miles in five days. Crews worked night and day keeping wires intact. Retreating German forces wrecked everything as they moved north, which kept the 232nd Engineer Company working around the clock. The Nisei engineers rebuilt roadways where Germans had buried shells and paved them over so they would blow up men and vehicles passing along them. A bridge over the Frigido River was blown, so the engineers worked in rubble and mud, using huge searchlights at night, to build a bypass. The men were so grubby and encrusted with mud that you couldn't tell the Nisei from the Italian laborers working with them.

The engineers' job was one of the worst in the Combat Team. To the infantry went the glory of fighting the enemy. Engineers didn't earn DSCs for knocking out enemy machine-gun crews, although, too often, they had to use their weapons to remain alive under enemy fire. In this action, their commander, Capt. Pershing Nakada, and several of his men were wounded. The infantry couldn't have won battles, however, without the support of the engineers. When the engineers finished their work, troops could ride on trucks instead of walking mile after weary mile. Food and ammunition could get to them so that they could push the retreating enemy faster and harder. And, in this fight for the west coast of Italy, the 232nd Engineer Company shared with the 100th/442nd Infantry a Distinguished Unit Citation for ten days of bitter action, April 5 to 14.

In this campaign, as they had throughout the war, the Nisei used audacity as well as weapons. I was told this story about a ten-man patrol that encountered fifty Germans somewhere near La Spezia. A reconnaissance patrol from Baker Company of the 100th Battalion was sent to observe the German self-propelled guns. To communicate with their command post, they laid a wire as they proceeded. They set up their observation post in a building they thought was two hundred yards from the enemy, based on information the Italians had given them. They soon discovered they were only fifty yards from a house occupied by Germans.

An enemy patrol found the communications wire the Nisei had strung and traced it to their position. A young German corporal entered the house and ordered them to surrender. Instead, the Nisei demanded that the Germans surrender. When the corporal refused, the Nisei took him prisoner. Thus began a seven-hour battle with the Germans, who threw machine-gun, bazooka, and mortar fire at them. Their prisoner sat in a corner throughout the fight. When he was wounded by shrapnel from his own guns, the Nisei gave him cigarettes, lighting them for him when his hands shook so that he couldn't hold a match.

"We figured we were not going to get back," one of the Nisei told me, "so we gave our cigarettes to him."

Their conversation with the German was in Italian, but they managed to understand that the Germans thought the Japanese Americans were "sort of crazy" because of the way they fought.

When the men failed to return to headquarters, 1st Lt. Bert Tanaka led a patrol from Charlie Company to find them and discovered that the wire leading to the surrounded men had been cut. Tanaka's patrol

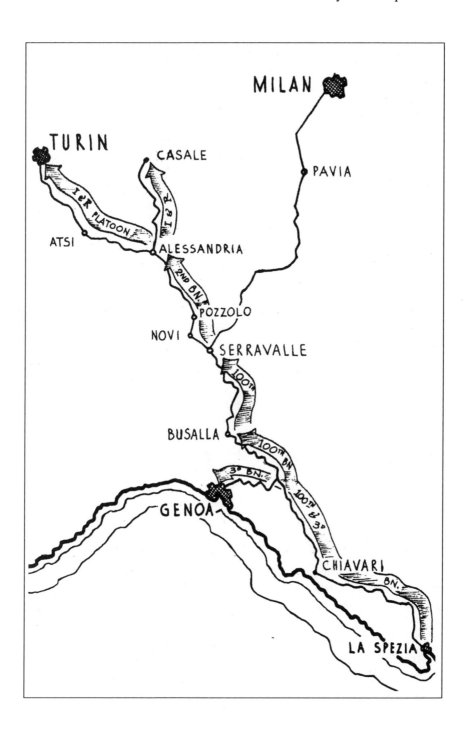

fought it out with the Germans, and that night they evacuated the wounded and dead, using every able-bodied man to carry litters. The task took all night. But the Nisei had obtained the information needed about the enemy self-propelled guns.

By the time the Combat Team entered Genoa, Italian Partisans had taken over the city. Everybody in Genoa seemed to be wearing something red, the Partisan symbol, including the 100th Battalion's Colonel Conley, who had worked closely with Partisans during the west coast drive. He sported a red scarf.

There remained one major problem confronting the Japanese Americans. They had to prevent Germans retreating from the west coast from joining German units along the rest of the front line. To do this, the Nisei had to stop them at Mount Nebbione, the last strategic area leading to the vital road center at Aulla. If Germans retreating from the coastal areas got through Aulla, they could link up with their troops along the center of the line to stiffen resistance and bar Allied entrance to the Po Valley.

By April 20 the Germans had blown up their big naval guns near La Spezia and were retreating east. At Mount Nebbione the three Japanese-American infantry battalions regrouped to stop them. The next day 2nd Lt. Daniel K. Inouye led a 2nd Battalion platoon to Colle Musatello, a strategic ridge overlooking the town of San Terenzo and a vital road the Germans were using to resupply their troops. Here the Nisei faced an enemy even tougher than the Germans, the Bersagliere—a crack Italian mountain unit made up of diehard Fascists who had refused to acknowledge Italy's surrender in 1943 and joined the Nazis.

Inouye's platoon encircled and destroyed an enemy patrol and mortar observation post, then advanced to within forty yards of the main enemy force, which was shielded in a hilltop rock formation with three machine guns hidden in a bunker. There was no cover on the hillside leading to it. Inouye crawled up the hill alone to locate the weapon emplacements; as he was taking out a grenade, he was hit in the stomach by machine-gun fire. The blow knocked him down, but he managed to get up, pull the pin from the grenade, run to within five yards of the nearest machine gun, and throw the grenade inside the position. As the gunners struggled to their feet, he raked them with his tommy gun.

His men ran to help him but were pinned down by enemy fire. Inouye, bleeding from the stomach, staggered farther up the hill and threw two more grenades into the second position before he fell again. He dragged himself toward the last machine-gun nest, stood up, and pulled the pin from another grenade. He had just drawn back his right arm to throw it when his right elbow was smashed by a rifle grenade, which almost tore off the arm. By reflex action, his right hand was still clenching the grenade and its safe handle. His men ran to help him but Inouye yelled at them: "Go back!" Reaching down with his good left hand, he took the grenade out of the clenched fist of his shattered right arm and threw it at the remaining machine-gun nest, destroying it. Then, with his left hand controlling his tommy gun and his right arm flapping against his side, he started finishing off the surviving gunners. Before he was through he was hit again by gunfire, this time in his right leg, and he fell down the hill. When his men ran to help him he yelled: "Get back up that hill! Nobody called off the war!" Inouye refused to be evacuated until his men were deployed in defensive positions against a possible counterattack.

In this attack, twenty-five enemy troops were killed and eight others captured. Inouye's right arm had to be amputated. His dream of becoming a doctor was ended, but he had earned the Distinguished Service Cross—and the United States would hear more about Daniel Inouye in the years ahead.

Only the capture of Aulla remained to seal off the retreating German troops. On April 25 a task force led by Maj. Mitsuyoshi Fukuda poured into the city, forcing the Germans to withdraw. The place was a shambles, littered with dead donkeys, broken carts, and the debris of shattered houses, but the Italians greeted the Fukuda task force with flowers and wine and kisses.

On April 28 Benito Mussolini and his mistress, Clara Petacci, were executed by Partisans in a village on Lake Como. The next day their bodies were taken to Partisan-held Milan, where they and a male Fascist were hanged, upside down, in front of a gas station. When I saw them, dried blood was still caked on Mussolini's face. Italians were pelting the bodies with stones, but some solicitous soul had tied the woman's dress to her legs so that the skirt would not fall away and bare her body.

I was headed for General Clark's headquarters and, finally, found him. We talked in a briefing room where a very large map was hung, and he traced the route the Combat Team had taken in this last push through Italy. As we talked, an aide handed him a slip of paper and the general told me: "Scouts from the 100th/442nd are in Turin now. They're wonderful fighters. Their record is one of the most magnificent jobs of this war."

General Clark's press release that day announced:

> Twenty-five German divisions, some of the best in the German army, have been torn to pieces and can no longer effectively resist our armies. Thousands of vehicles, tremendous quantities of arms and equipment and over 120,000 prisoners have been captured, and many more are being corralled.

For Hitler's army in Italy, the war was almost over. The U.S. Fifth Army and the British Eighth Army had smashed the Germans in the Bologna area. American forces were racing through the Po Valley. The New Zealand Corps was driving into Venice and, in its fight toward Trieste, would link up with Marshal Tito's forces at Monfalcone. From the west to the east coast of Italy, Germans were surrendering as fast as they could. I watched hundreds of them, guarded by only a few GIs, as they made their way along the dusty roads. They were tired, dirty, hungry, and thirsty. But, at long last, they wouldn't have to fight anymore. Some even looked happy as they were herded to camps where they would now be prisoners of war. At least they were alive. And they were not prisoners of the Russians!

The Nisei received another Presidential Unit Citation—this one signed by the man who had refused to accept the 100th among his troops— General Eisenhower. The citation, awarded to the 100th/442nd Infantry and the 232nd Combat Engineer Company, stated (in part):

> When the 92d Infantry Division with the 442d Regimental Combat Team attached was ordered to open the Fifth Army offensive by executing a diversionary attack on the Ligurian Coast of Italy, the Combat Team was ordered to make the main effort of the attack. It was done by executing a daring and skillful flanking attack on the positions which formed the western anchor of the formidable Gothic Line. In 4 days, the attack destroyed positions which had withstood the efforts of friendly troops for 5 months. This was accomplished in the face of skilled enemy forces

nearly equal in strength to the attacking forces and who had at least 5 months in which to improve their position. The 442d Regimental Combat Team drove forward, despite heavy casualties. Allowing the enemy no time for rest or reorganization, the Combat Team liberated the city of Carrara, seized the heights beyond and opened the way for further advances on the way to the key road center and port of La Spezia and to Genoa. It accomplished the mission of creating a diversion along the Ligurian Coast, which served as a feint for the subsequent breakthrough of the Fifth Army forces into Bologna and the Po Valley. The successful accomplishment of this mission turned a diversionary action into a full scale and victorious offensive, which played an important part in the final destruction of the German armies in Italy. The gallantry and esprit de corps displayed by the officers and men of the 442nd Regimental Combat Team in bitter action against a formidable enemy exemplify the finest traditions of the armed forces of the United States.

With still another Presidential Unit Citation pending—its seventh, to be awarded in Washington by President Truman—and 18,143 individual decorations, the 100th/442nd Regimental Combat Team had become the most decorated unit for its size and length of service in American history.

During the final weeks of the war, hundreds of Japanese-American recruits had continued to flood into Italy to join the 100th/442nd. Among them was a quiet man from the 100th Battalion, Corp. Hershey Miyamura, from Gallup, New Mexico. He would go on to fight in the next war— Korea—to carry on the Nisei tradition of courage and win the ultimate distinction: the Medal of Honor.

An eerie quiet hung over the Italian front as the German army crumbled and Allied troops waited for orders. There were none. On May 2 the Germans surrendered in Italy, though the war went on in Germany itself. Men who had saved whiskey or cognac, even grappa, to mark this moment in history were silent. There may have been celebrations in the cities but there were none on our front.

In the small town of Alessandria, not far from Turin, I sat with a few of the Combat Team's officers in front of the potbellied stove in the parlor of a small stone house. They seemed too stunned by the suddenness of the German collapse in Italy to talk much, so I left to wander alone up a winding, narrow road until I found some of my GI friends. They were crowding into the world-renowned Borsalino factory to select hat felts, which they paid for with cigarettes, the universally accepted exchange for anything in a war zone. When they got home they would have them made into stylish hats, they told me. I wondered just how comfortable the men from Hawaii would feel with felt headgear in their tropical climate.

For such a long time the Nisei had planned and fought for this moment. Now that it was here, they wondered what would come next. Would it be combat on the other side of the world or occupation jobs in Europe? Or would they go home to the internment camps to collect their families and try to find places for them to live? Whatever happened, it would be a major change. Soon the old friends with whom they had lived and worked, and the battles they had fought together, would become just memories.

Five days after the end of the war in Italy, all German forces in Europe surrendered. The surrender documents were signed at 0141 on May 7, 1945, central European time, at Reims, Germany, to become effective May 8.

Victory in Europe, however, didn't mean the war was over. On the other side of the world, the battle against Japan still raged. And in Europe, work went on. The 100th/442nd celebrated V-E Day with a five-mile march in the hot sun. For the 232nd Engineer Company it also meant stripping to the waist to pour the final concrete slab in reconstructing a bridge that American bombers had damaged.

Ceremonies honoring comrades who had fallen in the Apennine Mountains and along Italy's west coast in the last campaign of the war were held throughout the Combat Team—in grassy fields, in rough parking lots, in newly plowed farmland. Their commander, Col. Virgil R. Miller, told them:

> In combat you have been an outstanding organization. A high ranking general in the European theater stated that you are probably the best assault troops in the army.
>
> By your fighting you have made for yourselves stronger friends than ever—friends who will go to bat for you to the last ditch.

The award ceremony for valorous actions during the final push in Italy was held on the big, dusty airfield at Novi Ligure under a scorching sun. I stood beside a visiting colonel during a regimental parade, the first time I had seen the 100th/442nd banners flying and the entire Combat Team marching. After that, the ceremonies began and the colonel mopped sweat from his face repeatedly as medals, ribbons, and commendations were handed out and the names rolled on and on. Finally, I heard him mutter: "The only thing wrong with this outfit is it has too damned many heroes."

When the fighting ended, the 522nd Field Artillery Battalion remained in Germany, carrying out orders diligently. A number of SS men were being sought who, by subterfuge, had escaped detection in other Allied areas. The Nisei were told to watch for them. By May 18, the 522nd Field Artillery Battalion had been transferred to the small town of Donauworth, located near a Danube River bridge. The SS men who had managed to get through guard points in other areas hit a snag at Donauworth. The Nisei detected them by a simple method others had overlooked: they ordered any German man trying to cross the river to strip, then looked for the SS tattooed on their arms.

General Tobin's faith in the Nisei was, once more, repaid. A German named Frederick Kops, a member of the Nazi Party's art collection group, had left Hitler's home at Berchtesgaden with a number of boxes and trunks in the back of an Opel. Outposts at strategic points were notified, but the man managed to drive through 150 miles of carefully policed U.S. Third Army area to Donauworth without being apprehended. There the 522nd caught him, despite the fact that he had changed his name, switched cars, and no longer had the trunks and boxes. The alert Nisei noticed that his physical description corresponded with information from army headquarters.

When General Tobin was informed about Kop's capture, he asked who had caught him. Told that it was the 522nd Field Artillery Battalion, his response was: "I might have known."

For the Nisei in Italy it was a long, hot summer. They were trucked 125 miles north to the dusty, barren Ghedi Airfield (near Brescia) where they processed more than eighty thousand German prisoners, most of whom were ragged, unkempt, and ridden with lice, but docile. Day after day the prisoners lined up on the baking airfield with all their possessions spread beside them on the ground. They were allowed to keep personal items, but everything else was confiscated: knives more than three inches long, firearms, cameras, maps, and binoculars.

Many prisoners had smashed their cameras, watches, and binoculars to prevent Americans from getting them. Nevertheless, every one of the huge hangars lining the field was packed, from ground to rafters, with loot from all of Europe: vodka from Russia, silverware, silk stockings and underwear, antiques, cameras, binoculars—whatever scrounging soldiers could find amid the ruins of war. Wagon loads of German contraband came in, pulled by horses or oxen. The Germans had run out of fuel, due to the Allied air forces' efficient bombing of the Alpine passes.

Private 1st Class Charlie Arakaki went through the lines, day after day, examining the prisoners: "It's a filthy job. But killing them is filthy, too," he concluded. "It is either them or us."

Sergeant Andy Okamura, however, was undoubtedly the most unhappy of the American supervising crew. "The krauts are everywhere," he griped, "and there's not one to build a latrine."

One day, as I walked a line of prisoners with Capt. Bert Nishimura, an arrogant English-speaking German staff officer challenged him: "America hasn't yet won the war," the German said.

When Nishimura asked what the United States must do to win, the German replied: "America must first fight your people and then the Russians." Indignant, Nishimura informed him that the 100th/442nd was an American unit.

The POWs at Ghedi were only lightly guarded, but there were no known escape attempts: after all, they had three square meals a day and clean latrines, and were told that if they tried to escape and were caught they would be sent "north"—meaning to the Russians.

This POW camp, however, was different from any other: Hawaiian music blared via loudspeakers all day long. If the Germans didn't know "Hilo Hattie" and "Manuela Boy" by the time they were released, it was no fault of the Islanders.

One bright spot in this dreary picture was the plentiful supply of rice available from the Po Valley, the great food basket of Italy. Throughout the war a favorite quip of both officers and men had been: "Feed them rice and mark them duty." Now big trucks, overloaded with rice, appeared daily on roads leading into the Combat Team's bivouac areas.

The white officers weren't happy about it, but they could eat elsewhere: the camp was near Lake Garda and the officers could now enjoy meals at a lakeside restaurant, complete with waitresses and music. As they took off for nearby towns, they would tell my friend Chet Tanaka: "You're the 'Provost Marshal' and you are in charge of Ghedi Airport."

With only a limited knowledge of German, Tanaka found an Austrian POW who could speak English. "He did a great job translating orders," Tanaka says. "The most urgent job was to keep the prisoners busy. I had them clearing up the area, putting on shows at our improvised theaters. . . . Many of the prisoners were Austrian and they hated the Germans. Their story was: 'If we don't fight, the Germans will kill our families.'"

Then it was time for me to fly south to attend the Fifth Army Memorial Day service at the recently finished cemetery—the largest in Italy— where twenty-seven hundred enemy dead lay alongside six thousand Americans. The cemetery sits on a hilltop at Nettuno, just above the Anzio beachhead where so many men died. The white crosses stretch back to the hills from which Germans had pounded the Americans clinging to their narrow holding on the beachhead below. Each cross is marked simply and unforgettably with a soldier's dog tags.

Following the speeches and the benediction, a salute of three volleys was fired and taps was sounded. And then, preceding the national anthem, there was a moment of absolute and stunning silence—no sounds except those of birds, contrasting with the booming of enemy guns just a year ago.

One of the 100th Battalion's representatives at the memorial service was Lt. Allan Ohata, the man who, with one companion—Mikio Hasemoto—had repelled an enemy onslaught and protected his company's flank during a two-day attack on the approach to Cassino. Ohata was a quiet, dedicated, modest man who never wore the Distinguished Service Cross he had won.

When the service was finished we walked the rows of crosses looking for the names of friends. There were so many of them. And then we left.

From there, I went to Naples to visit the big hospitals where wounded Nisei had been sent from the Apennines campaign, awaiting shipment back to the United States. I found a group of them at one hospital, playing cards, shooting craps—so cheerful that it was hard to remember they had been hurt until you looked more closely. You wouldn't have believed that Dan Inouye had been wounded until you saw that one arm was missing. (The next time I saw him, many years later, Hawaii had become a state and he was the first Japanese-American member of the U.S. Congress.)

In another hospital I was looking for men from Hawaii when I noticed a boy, obviously in great pain. Sagie Nishioka was lying flat on his back in a narrow hospital cot. Casts started near his hips and ran to the bottom of both legs, holding him rigid. His face was so pinched with pain, his brown eyes so clouded, that I couldn't talk with him that day. "I'll come back later," I told him.

In a couple of days I returned and found him in a wheelchair on the sunporch with other Japanese-American soldiers who had been wounded in that last push up the Italian coast.

"You look so much better!" I exclaimed. "What did they do to you?"

"They gave me another transfusion," he said.

"How many have you had?"

He hesitated. "Maybe fourteen or fifteen. I don't remember."

"Where are you from?" I asked.

"Hood River, Oregon," he replied. Then he told me about his family and the letter from his mother, telling him that the American Legion post in Hood River had taken the names of all Japanese Americans off the list of men in service.

"It didn't seem real," Nishioka said. "I couldn't believe it."

He had been too busy fighting just then to worry about Hood River. And soon afterward his legs were smashed and his back and stomach riddled by German gunfire.

When he remembered the letter, it was between operations—five of them—and between transfusions. The medics managed to save his legs, holding them together with pins through the knees.

And now? He'd heard that the names of Japanese-American servicemen had been put back on the Hood River roll after a nationwide outcry.

"But if we return to Hood River, will the white people there make trouble for us?" he asked me. "And if we do go back to the farm, will I be able to work it again with my legs so busted up?"

I had no answers.

By the time I left Naples the 100th/442nd had finished its prisoner-of-war duties at Ghedi Airport and had traveled north to Lecco, in the mountain foothills of northern Italy—a welcome change. But the Nisei faced another problem: War Department officials back in Washington had hatched a new scheme, an idea that could only result in more racial tension. They wanted to train GIs for fighting in the Pacific war by having Nisei veterans use Japanese weapons and dress in Japanese uniforms in maneuvers. Insensitive Pentagon bureaucrats still had not learned that the 100th/442nd men were Americans and valued that identity above all. The resulting cries of indignation from both the Nisei and their Caucasian officers were loud and exceedingly clear. First of all, the Nisei didn't know anything about Japanese methods of warfare. Many of them couldn't even speak Japanese. They warned that the result of such identification with the enemy would be escalation of racial antagonism toward Japanese Americans, especially for those leaving the internment camps to return to their West Coast homes.

After talking over the situation with Mike Masaoka, the Japanese American Citizens League (JACL) leader and mentor, I wrote a letter to Secretary of the Interior Harold Ickes. If anyone could get something done in Washington, we figured, it would be that crusty old gentleman. He had shown great concern regarding the Japanese problem in the United States, and I thought he might be interested in hearing about some of the problems facing men in the Japanese-American regiment. The pertinent sections of the letter follow:

> One of the most pressing problems which Mainland men here face is that of finding homes for their displaced families. The regiment, according to present War Department plans, is due to remain here for a number of months—with the exception, of course, of high point men. At the same time it is their and my understanding that War Relocation Camps are due to be closed by the first of next year. According to these two schedules the men here are prevented from assisting their families in getting relocated at a time when such assistance is vital. For your information, the regiment has just been relieved of its prisoner of war guard duties and is now merely slated for recreational and educational routine in northern Italy, with no other duties assigned it.

> In speaking with many of them regarding recent cases of west coast violence, they have told me they believe the situation might possibly be alleviated if some of them were allowed to return to

the west coast in uniform. They said the men now going back from relocation centers have not, of course, served in the armed forces of the United States and that the presence of Nisei in American uniforms might make a big difference in the treatment of returning Nisei families.

Regarding the recently reported War Department program of using Nisei troops dressed in Japanese uniforms for training GIs for Pacific combat, nothing I can say could convey to you the feeling of consternation it has aroused in 442nd men. Again, I have talked with numerous men of that unit (including some of their Caucasian officers). Their reactions are, briefly, these:

Many told me they would rather go back into combat—anywhere—than have to dress up in Japanese uniforms and use Japanese weapons in this training program. They said they could not understand why Caucasian soldiers could not do the same training inasmuch as Nisei don't know anything about Japanese warfare in the first place and, therefore, have to be trained by the War Department in such methods. They believe the use of Nisei for such work—particularly when they are required to copy Japanese enemy troops to the exact detail of even dress—will only serve to increase racial antagonism. They think a feeling of doubt and hatred toward Japanese Americans cannot help but be engendered among unthinking GIs who train under such a program. To substantiate that argument they point out that even in maneuvers between purely Caucasian troops one unit learns to hate the unit pitted against it.

Then I told Secretary Ickes about Sagie Nishioka, the boy from Hood River whom I had talked with in the Naples hospital.

My letter was referred to Dillon S. Myer, chief of the War Relocation Authority. Here are excerpts from his reply, dated July 17, 1945:

I should like you to know that we will make every effort to get in touch with T/4 Sagie Nishioka when he gets to this country . . .

I was interested in your account of the feelings of the 442nd members toward the War Department's program for using Nisei soldiers to train other troops in Japanese tactics. When I first heard of this program, my reaction was similar to that of the men with whom you spoke, and for about the same reasons. Later, when I was able to talk with some of the Japanese Americans actually assigned to this training, and found them quite unconcerned about it, I let the matter drop. However, in view of the reaction you report, I am taking the matter up with the War Department.

No action was taken by the War Department regarding training methods, and no special consideration was given Sagie Nishioka when he returned to the United States.

Back in Europe, veterans of the 100th/442nd were volunteering for the war in the Pacific. Rather than being used as guinea pigs in any War Department training programs, they wanted to fight in the ranks alongside other GIs. Many had hoped for duty in the Pacific when the 100th Battalion and the 442nd Regimental Combat Team were first formed. Now that the war in Europe was finished they wanted to help settle the score with Japan, whose attack on Pearl Harbor had brought to Japanese-American families anguished years in internment camps. Four officers and 194 enlisted men with knowledge of the Japanese language were finally sent to the Military Intelligence Service Language School for further training as linguists in the Pacific.[6] When they graduated they were sent to Japan, Korea, and other Pacific areas to help in the peace to come.

CHAPTER 18

OKINAWA: GATEWAY TO JAPAN

In the spring of 1945, while the 100th/442nd Regimental Combat Team was preparing to battle its way through Italy's Apennine Mountains and the 522nd Field Artillery Battalion was racing through Germany, Japanese Americans of the Military Intelligence Service were heading into the greatest land battle of the Pacific war: Okinawa, the threshold of Japan, 360 miles to the northeast.

Code-named Operation Iceberg, the invasion was set for April 1, and fifteen hundred ships—the mightiest fleet the world had ever seen[1]— and 548,000 Americans of all services had been assembled for it. The campaign would last eighty-two days, with 180,000 American combat troops involved in the fighting, and another 368,000 American troops supporting them. Before it was finished, more than a quarter-million lives would be lost.[2] This was the final battle before the planned invasion of Japan itself, and Nisei linguists would unveil two pieces of information that would prove vital for an American victory.

In 1853, nearly a century before most Americans ever heard of Okinawa, largest of the Ryukyu Islands, Commodore Matthew Perry raised the American flag there and forced the king of the Ryukyus to sign a treaty guaranteeing friendly treatment to American ships. The United States government failed to follow through on Perry's arrangements, and twenty-six years later Japan seized the islands.

A docile people with no history of warfare, Okinawans were primarily farmers who worked small plots of scabby land, raising mostly sugarcane, rice, and sweet potatoes. Because Okinawa was so distant from Japan's main islands, its people were often treated as second-class citizens.

In hopes of finding a better life, Okinawans began migrating to the Hawaiian Islands near the end of the nineteenth century. Descendants of those Okinawan immigrants were among the Nisei linguists in the invading force. They would use knowledge of their ancestral home and dialect to help win an American victory on this strategic gateway to Japan.

The Ryukyu Islands, with their harbors and ample land area for air bases and troop concentrations, were vital to both sides in this conflict: the United States would need them to support an invasion of Japan; Japan needed them to protect its home territory. Faced with a critical threat to their home islands, the Japanese army had forcefully drafted twenty thousand men between twenty and forty years of age from the Okinawan population to augment its own forces and to form a Home Guard, the Boeitai.[3]

Although Okinawa was the main objective of the invasion, command of a chain of islands, Kerama-retto, lying off its west coast, was necessary to provide harbor and repair facilities for American ships. Another objective off Okinawa's northwest coast was the small island of Ie Shima and its large airfield, which would be used as a base for bombing Japanese cities and to protect American forces in an invasion of Japan.

When it appeared that capture of Okinawa would be necessary, Tom Ige, whose Okinawan parents had settled in Hawaii, suggested to the MIS Language School that a special contingent of Nisei of Okinawan-descent be sent in with the invasion force. He pointed out that knowledge of the Okinawan dialect (a form of ancient Japanese) would be essential to converse with inhabitants of the Ryukyus and to differentiate between local residents and Japanese soldiers masquerading as Okinawans. The War Department approved Ige's suggestion, and a team of ten Nisei of Okinawan-descent, led by Lt. Wallace Amioka, was formed for the invasion in addition to the regular Nisei language teams.[4]

Ige, a graduate of the University of Hawaii with postgraduate study at the Universities of Chicago and Wisconsin, had been turned down by the U.S. Navy and the Army Air Forces, neither of which accepted Japanese Americans, before he became involved with the MIS. He had settled into a job as an economist for the War Labor Relations Board and was working in Detroit when a visit from a boyhood friend changed his life and led him to volunteer. In his book *Boy from Kahaluu,* Ige, a former administrative assistant to Hawaii's Senator Daniel K. Inouye, describes the feelings he and other young Japanese Americans had as they faced the war with Japan:

> Within the broad spectrum of the values we developed during our formative years in school and in our exposure to American society, specific factors inextricably guided us to make specific decisions. Peer pressure was certainly a major factor. We all registered for the draft—one by one we were being called to the colors. To have refused to participate in this ultimate test of citizenship would not have been tolerated, not only by the law but, even more importantly, by our circle of friends and relatives. In no instance did the Issei parent encourage an American son not to register for the draft or refuse induction after being called. . . . Peer and family pressure to do your part was overwhelming.
>
> In my own case, my former [school] housemates, Joe Takata and Tadao Beppu, were already in uniform. When I visited Camp McCoy as a student and civilian, and saw so many of my classmates preparing to go overseas with the 100th Infantry Battalion, I felt very uncomfortable. Finally, when Technical Sergeant Beppu came all the way from Camp Shelby in Mississippi to Detroit to inform me that Sergeant Joe Takata had been killed in Italy, I could no longer remain aloof.[5]

In addition to Ige, the Okinawan language team led by Lieutenant Amioka included Jiro Arakaki, Shinyei Gima, Leslie Higa, Seiyu Higashi, Hiroshi Kobashigawa, Kenzo Miyashiro, Kazuo Nakamura, Kosei Ohiro, and S. Sakihara. The team was misdirected by the army to Saipan, then to the Philippines, then back to Guam, but it finally reached the Ryukyus in time for the invasion. Eventually members of this special team would be reunited with relatives on Okinawa whom they hadn't seen since childhood, when they left Okinawa with their parents.

Among other Nisei landing with the first American troops on the Kerama-retto islands were Frank Mori and Mac Miyahara, veterans of the Guam campaign. Mori, who had volunteered for the MIS Language School from the Gila River internment camp, had also been with American forces invading the Marshall Islands. All his family except one sister was in Japan.

Nisei who had served in other Pacific campaigns followed in the second and third landings on the Keramas. Among them: Kunio Endo, a veteran of the invasion of Guam; Vic Nishijima, who had volunteered from the Tule Lake camp and was also a veteran of the Guam invasion; and Mitsuo Shibata, veteran of the Aleutians and Guam campaigns, who was later killed by American sniper fire on Ie Shima. With the 77th Division Headquarters were four Nisei of the Kerama-retto linguist team. One of them, Eddie Fukui, died when a kamikaze attacked his ship as he was intercepting enemy radio communications.[6] He had volunteered for the MIS Language School from the Tule Lake camp and was a veteran of the Guam campaign.

Soon after landing on the Keramas, the Nisei helped locate the newest, and potentially devastating, weapon the American troops would face in the area, the *shinyo*. These were mass-produced suicide boats, the sea-borne equivalent of the kamikaze planes. The twenty-foot-long motor-driven craft had two depth charges in the bow and a third in the stern. The plan was for a lone sailor to run a boat alongside an enemy ship, then detonate the three charges, which were strong enough to break apart most warships. Of course, the Japanese sailor would also be killed. It was Vic Nishijima who found these boats hidden in caves, where they were mounted on narrow-gauge rails for easy launching. By March 31, American forces had captured 360 of the suicide boats and completed their five-day conquest of the Keramas.[7]

On April 1, Easter Sunday, more than thirteen hundred ships ringed Okinawa, and five army and marine divisions landed on a five-mile beachhead so quickly and with such little opposition that American officers were astonished. But Lt. Gen. Mitsuru Ushijima, commander of the Japanese troops, had planned it that way. He would allow American forces to occupy the flat beaches and wheat fields of the coastal areas, then stop them as they advanced into the interior, beyond the protection of supporting firepower from their ships, and where his defenses were dug into mountains and caves.

With its mountainous terrain, volcanic boulders, coral crags and ditches, and rainfall that could reach eleven inches a day, Okinawa was one of the most torturous strongholds the American troops had ever tackled. And, as at Saipan, there were huge volcanic caves, fortified by the Japanese army, where enemy soldiers and frightened civilians hid. There were also large family tombs, which the Japanese had converted into heavily armed redoubts.

The Nisei eventually spread all over Okinawa, risking their lives to persuade civilians and Japanese soldiers to leave the caves and tombs. They interrogated POWs and gained the confidence of the Okinawan civilians, who would provide information about Japanese entrenchments.

Ige explains how the Nisei linguists worked:

> The ability of most of our team members to speak the Okinawan dialect proved most helpful in interrogation of Japanese prisoners. . . . This was especially valuable and effective in separating out the Japanese soldiers masquerading as Okinawan civilians. A few basic questions to them in the Okinawan dialect immediately unmasked their disguise. Very few Japanese soldiers could understand, much less speak, the dialect. They would be embarrassed when unmasked and, thereafter, would be in a more cooperative mood.
>
> Interrogating prisoners of war was one of our main activities. . . . There was one particular prisoner . . . who was a graduate of the Tokyo Imperial University. . . . This prisoner had been hastily drafted and was disgusted to have some country bumpkin push him around. He had surrendered without resistance and gladly cooperated with me. He could, and did, easily translate, in an hour or two, documents that would have taken me days. I knew enough Japanese so I could determine if he was translating correctly. In this manner my translation work was not only made easier but far more accurate.[8]

Ige also relates a meeting with a highly educated captured civilian, the manager of a large sugar refinery on Okinawa. He turned out to be an old family friend who had worked with Ige's father at a sugar plantation in Hawaii prior to getting a degree in engineering at the University of Chicago and returning to Okinawa. "He proved to be most useful to our military government during the occupation and was later appointed chief executive of the Ryukyu Government."

Takejiro Higa also had old friends on Okinawa, and he had known about—and dreaded—plans for this invasion for nearly six months. He and his brother, Warren, were serving as linguists on Leyte with the 96th Infantry Division when Takejiro was suddenly ordered to report to the XXIV Corps G-2 photointerpreting section. His brother had informed their officers that although Takejiro was born in Hawaii, he had lived on Okinawa from age two to sixteen, because of family illness and deaths, and might be of help if the island was invaded. Because of his knowledge of the country and its language, Higa was assigned to the advance unit of the 96th Division Headquarters, which landed on the western side of the island. A few days later, he was called to question a refugee suspected of being a Japanese soldier. Higa recognized the man immediately as his seventh- and eighth-grade teacher, who had been caught while looking for potatoes to eat. After Higa identified the man as a teacher, the man was taken to the same civilian refugee camp where his wife and children were.

In May, with U.S. forces pushing through southern Okinawa, Higa was called to interrogate two shabbily uniformed young men. "They were very hungry and fatigued," he says. "I offered them a candy bar, which they refused because they feared the candy bar was poisoned. I yelled '*bakayaro*' [you idiot] and nibbled a portion to show it was safe. They gobbled up two candy bars each and gulped down a lot of water and I started my interrogation."

As the men began to answer standard questions about age, hometown, and so forth, Takejiro sensed they were former classmates. Then he asked: "What happened to your classmate Takejiro Higa from Shimabuku?"

They said they thought he had returned to Hawaii.

"If you saw Takejiro Higa now, would you recognize him?" Higa asked.

"Not sure," they answered.

Higa then yelled at them: "*Bakayaro, dokyusei wo mite wakarani no ka?*" (You idiots, don't you recognize your own old classmate?).[9]

The most dangerous work of the Nisei linguists, as on Saipan, was trying to get civilians and Japanese soldiers to come out of the deep caves and family mausoleums. Teams of MISers were called on to talk these people into surrendering peacefully. Sometimes their efforts were successful. Sometimes they failed, and then the Nisei had to watch as the caves were torched by flamethrowers or destroyed by explosives. Orders were that nobody could be left to threaten the rear of advancing troops. Often, as the Nisei witnessed the destruction, they couldn't help wondering if their relatives were among those dying inside.

"The war became very personal when civilians were involved," Ige says. "There was no greater feeling than to watch frightened civilians meekly walk out of the caves for another lease on life."

On the first day of the invasion Mike Sakamoto entered a cave and rescued two sisters and a little girl whose arm had been blown off. Tatsuo Yamamoto walked into a cave where 350 Japanese soldiers and their colonel were hiding and talked them into surrendering.[10]

Lieutenant Amioka became a hero among the Okinawans and his fellow MISers when he captured and killed an air force colonel whom the civilians hated and feared. The officer had been the leader of Japanese soldiers who were raiding northern Okinawan villages.

Village leaders were caught in a tragic dilemma between American forces and Japanese soldiers. The Americans were highly visible and in charge during daylight hours, but at night Japanese soldiers came out of their hiding places in the mountains and infiltrated the villages to look for food and to punish Okinawans who cooperated with Americans. Villagers were often executed by these night raiders.[11]

One of the most important discoveries on Okinawa was the Japanese defense plan. This vital document correctly predicted the place and date of American landings on Okinawa and how the invading forces would operate. Shortly afterward Dan Nakatsu—a MISer veteran of Saipan, Tinian, and Iwo Jima—helped capture and interrogate the author and supervisor of this defense plan, Colonel Yohara, who had been sent from Japan to assist General Ushijima.

Another crucial discovery was made while American forces still faced the main Japanese defense line on Okinawa. A GI found a map in the pocket of a dead Japanese officer and turned it in. It was a detailed contour map of the island, showing artillery locations and heavy mortar positions. American maps had been based on aerial reconnaissance photos and were inadequate, having many blank areas and only rough terrain sketches. A team of Nisei—Lloyd Shinsato, Thomas Higashiyama, and Saburo Otamura—translated the Japanese army symbols. Hiroshi Ito, a graduate of a Japanese university, translated the handwritten notes on the chart. The resulting overlay, transposed to the U.S. Army map grid, was key to the final conquest of the Japanese defense line.[12] The map was flown to Pearl Harbor, where twelve thousand copies were made, shipped back to Okinawa, and distributed among the troops. There would be no more guesswork about terrain or the location and type of the enemy's great defense bulwark.

As the fighting went on, the Nisei linguists continued their valuable work. Mits Usui, who had worked at Schofield Barracks in Hawaii with a top-secret group planning the invasion of Okinawa, helped bring in civilians and register them at a compound established to shelter native Okinawans.

"The people were brought into hastily made camps, and shelters were made out of old wood covered with palm fronds," he recalled. "They were scared, suspicious, and perhaps a little hateful of their captors. However, they survived and gradually became a little more friendly."[13]

There were many pathetic stories about Okinawan civilians caught between the enemies of this war, and Usui recorded one of the most touching:

> One day as we—a CIC officer and I—were driving . . . we saw a little girl about 10 years old hysterically running down the road, crying and falling as she went along. We stopped her by nearly tackling her, and tried to calm her down. After several minutes we were successful and started to talk to her. Her left arm was shattered and gangrene was starting to set in. She told us a bomb had hit her home and her father and mother were dead. Not knowing what to do, she fled. I said to the CIC officer that I knew the doctor at the field hospital . . . let's take her there. . . . Right away Dr. Red MacDonnell took care of her. Later that evening I went to the hospital tent and found her still under the effects of the sedation. Her arm was severed and all bandaged up, but she tried to talk to me.
>
> Thereafter I started to go to the hospital tent each night to see her and some of the other civilians in the hospital. . . . We became good friends and stayed that way until I was assigned to go to Korea (after the Japanese surrender). When I told her I was leaving, she cried, hugged me and we both started to bawl, holding onto each other.[14]

Warren and Takejiro Higa were credited with saving more than thirty thousand Okinawan civilians from death by coaxing them out of hiding places in caves and family tombs.[15]

One Nisei linguist, Seiyu Higashi, was reunited with his father on Okinawa. Higashi was born in Los Angeles but had been taken to Okinawa for schooling. When he returned to Los Angeles, his father had remained in the family's hometown, Nago, in northern Okinawa. The two met there after an eight-year separation. Another Nisei, Leslie Higa, found a number of relatives. And, before the war ended, Jiro Arakaki located his father and nephews in a refugee camp.[16]

Hoichi Kubo, awarded a DSC for clearing more than 120 civilians out of a cave on Saipan, was among the Nisei doing the same job on Okinawa. He had arrived with his old outfit, the 27th Infantry Division, which had been badly battered on Saipan; on Okinawa, the unit suffered large numbers of casualties as it hit enemy defenses.

On Ie Shima, Vic Nishijima survived an attack by Japanese who had strapped explosives onto their bodies, then rushed out of caves, trying to kill Americans along with themselves. (It was in another attack on Ie Shima that war correspondent Ernie Pyle was killed on April 18 when he was moving up to the front to be with foot soldiers. A Japanese machine gun ambushed the jeep in which he was riding.) And on Okinawa at about that time more than twenty Nisei from ATIS were killed in a plane crash.

And what happened to the man whose idea was helping the United States to conquer this last, vital stepping-stone to Japan? Tom Ige was wounded on Tokashiki Island in the Keramas as he headed for a location where Japanese troops and gun emplacements were located. The battles were over for him, but his contribution to victory was invaluable.

By June 21, marines had blasted their way to the entrance of the cave where General Ushijima had established his command post. It was part of a final defense line—a network of caves, pillboxes, and above-ground tombs converted into machine-gun nests. Cornered now, with no room to retreat, the general prepared to commit suicide. In the early hours of the next morning, after a special feast, he knelt on a clean sheet and, with a sharp sabre, committed seppuku.[17] Ben Honda went with the general's personal cook, whom he had interviewed earlier, to identify Ushijima's body.[18]

In the battle for Okinawa, Honda won an Oak Leaf Cluster to add to the Bronze Star awarded him for operations on Saipan. His award citation provides an example of why the Japanese-American linguists of the MIS were so valuable.

During the Okinawa Island Operation, Technician Honda's skillful screening and interrogation of more than 1000 Japanese prisoners of war was responsible for the securing of information which proved of utmost value in formulating effective plans of attack. Technician Honda's thorough understanding of Japanese psychology and his masterful ability to gain the confidence of the prisoners enabled him to obtain information which could not have otherwise been secured. When the number of prisoners taken per day became exceedingly large, Technician Honda screened them accurately and rapidly, promptly segregating those who possessed tactical information in order that they could be interrogated immediately. His outstanding work decreased the time involved in obtaining vital tactical information and increased the efficiency of the interrogation section. Technician Honda's exceptionally meritorious service throughout this period contributed materially to the success of the Okinawa Campaign and reflected great credit upon himself and the military service.

Okinawa was declared secure on June 22 after nearly three months of some of the cruelest fighting American forces had ever experienced. On July 2 the Ryukyu Islands operation was formally declared ended, although mop-up operations in northern Okinawa did not end until August 4. It had been the bloodiest slaughter of the Pacific war, including the greatest loss of life for the Nisei linguists. Americans lost more than 7,374 dead and 31,807 wounded in the land battle. The U.S. Navy counted 34 ships sunk by kamikaze pilots, 763 carrier planes lost, and 4,907 sailors killed—the worst casualties the navy suffered in any battle of the entire war.[19]

Sporadic fighting continued on Okinawa even after the final surrender of Japan. MISers on Okinawa would continue working in POW camps and in the relief centers that had been established to help the impoverished, homeless population caught in the middle of this war. Helping to adjudicate postwar legalities there was Masaji Marumoto, who had been commissioned a first lieutenant in the Judge Advocate General's Department and attached to military government in Okinawa.[20] He later served in General MacArthur's Supreme Allied Headquarters in Tokyo. Before the Pearl Harbor attack, Marumoto had been practicing law in Hawaii. Despite lameness, he had volunteered for the MIS Language School.[21]

No one knows—or will ever know—how many Japanese Americans worked with U.S. troops in the Okinawa campaign. Language teams were with every unit on the island, but, because they were designated TDY (temporary duty) for the invasion, as they were in all other invasions, most of their records are lost to history.

While MISers were fighting on Okinawa, scores of Nisei linguists were landing on other Pacific islands, trying to persuade enemy holdouts to surrender. Don Okubo, veteran of service with the marines on Peleliu, was working with Tony Sunamoto in the Marshall Islands, sailing inlets to scout possible enemy hiding places, dropping Japanese-language leaflets written by other Nisei linguists. Henry Hikida, Paul Bannai (who would later become the first Nisei member of the California State Legislature), and other veterans of service on New Guinea went into Borneo with Australian troops. Sam Takamura, who had seen bombs drop on Hawaii the day Pearl Harbor was attacked, was among Nisei linguists with the Australian army scouring Philippine islets for enemy holdouts. Nisei linguists were with the British army when it took Rangoon, Burma. The MISers, in short, were everywhere. They had become an indispensable part of every military unit in every part of the Pacific. And they were making contributions in other areas of the world as well.[22]

Since late October 1944, three Nisei (Kazuo Yamane, Pat Nagano, and George Urabe) from the Pacific Military Intelligence Research Section (PACMIRS) had been waiting in Versailles, France, to parachute into Berlin with British commandos and seize from the Japanese embassy documents that might help finish the Pacific war quickly. But the war in Europe ended before this mission could be undertaken.

Japanese Americans on OSS language teams were in North Burma and near Calcutta, India, beaming broadcasts into Japan about that country's defeats and danger.

At Camp Ritchie, Maryland, Nisei of PACMIRS were examining every scrap of information relayed from the Pacific to learn whatever secrets might face Allied troops when they entered Japan.

MISers on Okinawa had also been trying to learn about Japan's plans for fighting an invasion of the homeland. Information they gleaned about potential landing sites on Kyushu and other places, the preparation of civilians to join the fighting, and the state of Japan's armaments was forwarded to intelligence centers preparing for the last great battle of the war.

Stunned by heavy losses of men and ships at Okinawa, the United States wanted to end the war with Japan as quickly as possible and without repeating the disastrous toll suffered in the conquest of the Ryukyu Islands. In August 1943, when Winston Churchill and President Roosevelt met at Hyde Park, the two men had agreed to share the work being done by American and British scientists on the atomic bomb.

The next year, Churchill and Roosevelt discussed the bomb question again. By that time scientific advisers had informed both men that an atomic bomb would "almost certainly" be ready by August 1945. The two leaders initialled an aide-mémoire declaring that "when a 'bomb' is finally available, it might perhaps, after mature consideration, be used against the Japanese, who should be warned that this bombardment will be repeated until they surrendered."[23]

The costly victory on Okinawa clarified the choice: to use this new weapon if it tested successfully or to endure losses potentially far greater than those suffered on Okinawa if Japan itself was invaded. Until a decision was reached, Allied preparations for the invasion of Japan would continue. Japanese Americans of the Military Intelligence Service would face the same double jeopardy there as they had on the Pacific islands: to be killed by the Japanese, along with others in American uniforms, or to be killed by friendly fire if mistaken for the enemy by Caucasians of the Allied invading forces.

Hoichi Kubo had already volunteered to go into Japan with the initial American forces. While he waited, he saw the special planes carrying Japan's delegation to the Philippines to negotiate peace terms. It had been nearly four years since he had seen planes with the Rising Sun emblem—then they were headed through Kole Kole Pass to bomb Pearl Harbor.

CHAPTER 19

PEARL HARBOR AVENGED

B y the time Okinawa was conquered, Kiyoshi Hirano and Yutaka Namba had finished their special assignment in an office hidden above New York City's Fulton Fish Market. Although the two MISers had been working for the Manhattan Project, they knew nothing about the bomb that scientists were trying to build in the New Mexico desert. Their job had been to translate special Japanese technical manuals and papers from files confiscated from the New York branches of two Japanese companies.

Both men had been educated in Japan. Hirano had become a high school teacher, and with his service in the Japanese equivalent of ROTC, he was qualified for a commission in the Japanese army. Instead, in 1939 he returned to California, determined to get an American education. So he got jobs and attended school in his spare time.

His attempts to get an American education were interrupted when Pearl Harbor was attacked and everyone of Japanese descent was ordered off the West Coast. He ended up in the Topaz, Utah, internment camp. Because there was a national shortage of agricultural workers, the camps granted leaves to internees to harvest crops, and Hirano went to Montana to work in the beet fields. "We Nisei were trying so hard to prove our loyalty to our country, the U.S.A.," he recalls.

In December 1942, Hirano volunteered for service as a linguist and was sent to the Military Intelligence Service Language School. On completion of his studies there he went to Camp Shelby, Mississippi, for infantry training with the 442nd Regimental Combat Team, which all MISers received. This was preparatory to going into Pacific combat zones as linguists. But he was suddenly ordered to return to the MIS Language School.

Yutaka Namba, who was born in Hawaii, had attended Meiji University in Japan but didn't finish his education there. Returning home, he joined the Hawaii National Guard and was in the Nisei contingent that sailed from Hawaii for the mainland in June 1942 to become the 100th Infantry Battalion. With other top linguists in the battalion, he was selected by the MIS to attend its language school.

The reason for Hirano's sudden recall from combat training at Camp Shelby was a top-secret message the MIS Language School received from the office of the Manhattan Project requesting two skilled linguists. Hirano and Namba were selected. They were told they were being sent to New York on a highly secret assignment, ostensibly to work for *Yank* magazine, an army publication. Actually, they were assigned to the New York branch of the War Department's Military Intelligence Division and at first were put to work compiling a Japanese military dictionary: English into Japanese and Japanese into English. They also translated two military conversation pamphlets.

When that job was completed they were ordered to report to the RKO Building in Rockefeller Center for an interview with a high-ranking army officer, and they ended up volunteering for an assignment of an "unknown" nature in New York rather than returning to the language school. They were told to go to a room located above a warehouse. This was their introduction to the secret office above the Fulton Fish Market. There they were instructed to translate special Japanese technical manuals. Hirano was given the confiscated files of the New York branches of Mitsui Company and the Ogura Petroleum Company, and asked to identify any metals that might be mentioned in the reports. In translating these documents on metallurgy and polymerization, Hirano deduced that the reason for his assignment was to ascertain Japan's progress in researching powerful explosives. He did discover one very interesting piece of information: the fact that the Germans had not shared with their Axis partner, Japan, the polymerization refining process of petroleum (the Fischer process). Without this, Japan was forced to use obsolete methods throughout the war to obtain the high-octane gasoline needed for its aircraft.

Whatever Namba discovered in his research remains unknown, because the two men never discussed their work, and Namba has since died.

This was not to be the end of Hirano's special assignments, however; at the Japanese surrender, he would be called on to perform a task for which few Americans were qualified. Meanwhile, he was reassigned to the MIS Language School as an instructor, to cope with the ever-increasing enrollment of Japanese Americans volunteering to serve as linguists.

Now that war secrets have been revealed, it is obvious that the attempt to identify metals mentioned in the Mitsui and Ogura files was to ascertain if any were fissionable materials—that is, uranium or plutonium—whose nuclei could be split to produce the energy necessary for an atomic bomb. Since the end of World War II, books and articles in scientific journals, written by both American and Japanese scientists, make it clear that Japan was trying to produce an atom bomb, and, if successful, intended to use it against American forces in the Pacific.[1]

How much the United States learned during World War II about Japan's progress in producing an atomic bomb remains undisclosed. But, by the time Okinawa was declared secure in the summer of 1945, scientists of the Manhattan Project were preparing to test their first atomic device. Also under way at that time were plans for a conference of Allied leaders to be held in Potsdam, Germany.

The Potsdam Conference of the "Big Three" (Britain, the Soviet Union, and the United States) began on July 17. President Truman had been in office only a little more than three months, since President Roosevelt's death on April 12. Roosevelt had never informed Truman of the work being done on an atomic bomb, and the new president had to accumulate knowledge about it from military and scientific advisers. When Truman left the United States for the Potsdam Conference, an atomic bomb had not yet been tested. Because of the enormous losses on Okinawa, however, the decision had already been made to use the bomb if it tested successfully, and if Japan would not otherwise surrender.

The first atomic weapon was tested successfully in late afternoon on July 16. Eight days later, the Big Three agreed to send a message (the Potsdam Declaration) to Japan, calling for the unconditional surrender of all Japanese armed forces. On July 26, Japan rejected the Potsdam Declaration, and when Truman returned to Washington the military process was already under way for using an atomic bomb against Japan.

The USS *Indianapolis* had reached the island of Tinian on July 26 with its special load, a bomb that crew members accompanying it had named "Little Boy." Shortly after 0200 on August 6, Col. Paul W. Tibbets started the engines on his B-29 Superfortress, named *Enola Gay* in honor of his mother. At 8:15:17 over Hiroshima, the bomb bay was opened and "Little Boy" headed for earth.

Three days later, a B-29 took off from Tinian to drop the second atomic bomb, this time over Nagasaki. The next day, August 10, the Japanese government accepted the terms of the Potsdam Declaration, provided that the position of the emperor would be protected. Pending a resolution of the emperor's status, the fighting continued. On August 15, after this issue had been settled, Emperor Hirohito announced that Japan would accept the Joint Declaration issued at Potsdam.

That August day when news flashed around the world that a new kind of bomb had been dropped on Hiroshima, I was with the 100th Battalion. I watched the men as a few who understood what such a bomb meant described it. Then I heard a Nisei officer from Hawaii, who had seen the bombing of Pearl Harbor and had suffered hell on the rock-strewn slopes of Monte Cassino, exclaim: "Good for those goddam Japs!" And another Nisei from Hawaii said: "Those goddam bastards! They cost us plenty at Pearl Harbor. It's time they paid for it."

Some men remained silent, still trying to comprehend what an atomic bomb could do. It was inevitable that some of these Japanese-American soldiers had relatives, even family members, in Hiroshima. However, I didn't hear anyone object to using the new weapon. Japan's attack on Pearl Harbor had changed their lives: it had brought death, suffering, and the hatred and suspicion of other Americans. For these soldiers this new weapon meant that they might no longer have to face the possibility of more war, more deaths, more wounds.

There were more discussions after the atomic bombing of Nagasaki, as men still tried to understand the significance of this new weapon. But the formal surrender of Japan meant that "high-point" men could soon return to the United States, where they would get their families out of internment camps and take them home—if they still had homes—or find new places to live.

For the Japanese Americans who had fought in Europe, the war was over. For Nisei linguists of the Military Intelligence Service, however, there were new and mounting demands as they were called on increasingly for help in a rapidly changing world. To meet escalating needs for linguists in the Philippines, Kiyoshi Hirano had led a team of MISers to Manila. There they helped in the interrogation of thousands of Japanese prisoners. On the night of August 15, Col. Sidney Mashbir (the chief of ATIS) ordered Hirano to check the Japanese language used in the surrender terms. Reluctant to undertake such a daunting task, Hirano refused at first, but Mashbir insisted.

"Sergeant Hirano," he said, "you were a school teacher in Japan according to your service record. You have the best background in Japanese education among the group [of linguists] here. Somebody has to do this very important job to end the war. Please do your duty."

At about 2300 that night, Hirano was escorted to army headquarters in Manila's City Hall to confer with an Australian army officer who had been born and educated in Japan.

"We finished checking the Japanese translation which had been prepared by the ATIS team," Hirano recalls, "but the major and I disagreed about a certain type of Japanese language structure. It took me over a half-hour to convince him that I was right. I then started to rewrite the Japanese, using the Japanese *Compendium of Law* book. It took me three nights to finish."

The task had placed Hirano in an ironic situation. He was a descendant of the ancient Hojo family, rulers of Japan for more than a century (1200–1333), during which Japan had repulsed two great raids led by the Mongol emperor, Kublai Khan. Six centuries later, through twisted paths of migration and war, Hirano was making a final check on the language used in a Japanese surrender.

"When I presented it to Colonel Mashbir on the morning of August 18, he said to me: 'Sergeant! You have done the greatest job! I will give you a commission and a medal.'"

Like many other Nisei, however, Hirano never received either. Instead, he was shipped to the 41st Infantry Division stationed in Zamboanga on Mindanao in the Philippines and eventually landed in Japan, where he was assigned some of the most sensitive jobs facing Allied occupation forces.

As the war ended, Nisei of the MIS were scattered throughout the Far East, helping not only Americans but also the British in the surrender of Japanese troops. The MISers worked at POW compounds and with the OSS teams that parachuted into every known POW camp throughout China and Manchuria, searching for American and British war prisoners. Their most urgent search was for Lt. Gen. Jonathan Wainwright. The day after the first atomic bomb was dropped on Japan, the Soviet Union declared war on Japan and, on August 9, invaded Japanese-occupied Manchuria. Unknown to anybody except top Japanese officials, the highest ranking captive Allied officers, including Wainwright, had been moved to Manchuria from Formosa—their last place of incarceration that the U.S. War Department had been able to identify. With the Russian invasion, the prisoners in Manchuria faced the possibility of being killed by their Japanese captors to keep them out of the hands of invading Allied forces.

Without any previous parachute training, Fumio Kido, a Nisei linguist, jumped into Mukden, Manchuria, with an OSS unit that was searching for Wainwright and other high-ranking American prisoners.[2] The OSS finally traced General Wainwright to Sian. When they reached his place of imprisonment they had trouble recognizing him from prewar pictures. The man they saw was a walking skeleton: emaciated, starved, his clothing in rags.

Japanese-American linguists were needed urgently and in increasing numbers to cope with new situations. Five MIS veterans flew to Atsugi, Japan, to establish protection for General MacArthur's arrival there on August 30: Eddie Yamada, Jiro Yukimura, Mike Miyatake, Akira Abe, and Harry Akune.[3] From Atsugi, MacArthur was driven to Yokohama. It was there that he finally met General Wainwright, whom he had last seen in 1942 when he left him in command of the Philippines. On September 2, at MacArthur's direction, Wainwright was among the dignitaries witnessing Japan's formal surrender on the battleship *Missouri* in Tokyo Bay. Colonel Mashbir, as chief of ATIS, and three Nisei lieutenants of the Military Intelligence Service were also there—including Tom Sakamoto, who made the final review of the surrender document itself, Noboru Yoshimura, and Jiro Yokoyama, all veterans of Pacific warfare. And the man who had first told the world that Pearl Harbor was being bombed was there—Webley Edwards of Honolulu's radio station KGMB.

Immediately after the surrender, Arthur Kaneko, who had been a teacher at the Military Intelligence Service Language School, and other intelligence specialists were flown from Washington to Japan. Their task was to review detailed studies on Manchuria and Siberia that had been made by Japan's Imperial Army and discovered in a mountainside cave.[4]

A month after Japan surrendered, ATIS moved its headquarters to Tokyo. Ultimately more than five thousand Japanese-American linguists worked out of ATIS, covering every aspect of the occupation. They worked in MacArthur's Supreme Allied Headquarters in Tokyo, in prisons, among civil affairs departments, with police, with every segment of Japanese government in the effort to reestablish order. We know who some of these MISers were. Others were lost to history for several reasons: censorship, which kept them anonymous; lack of mention in official records; and the subsequent neglect of historians.

George Koshi, for example, was involved in writing the new Japanese constitution, which pledged that Japan would "forever renounce war as a sovereign right of the nation."

Ray Aka helped prepare Japan's self-defense law. Among General MacArthur's language aides were Shiro Omata and Kan Tagami; Tagami was a veteran of the Pacific fighting and the MARS task force in Burma, who had worked with the British army during the surrender of Kuala Lumpur.

Shigeharu Takahashi, an expert on land reform from the University of Chicago, headed MacArthur's Agricultural Branch, which reviewed Japan's land reform law. Shiro Tobuno worked on agrarian reforms that affected an estimated five million Japanese farmers.

More than seventy linguists, mostly from the MIS, provided all translation services and interpreters for the war crimes trials, which were held not only in Japan but also in China, the Philippines, French Indochina, and the East Indies. Nisei were assigned as defense attorneys and as defense monitors.

Kiyoshi Hirano was again thrust into some of the most demanding jobs. In Yokohama he supervised the large team of interpreters necessary for the spectacular vivisection trials held there, including trials of those accused of the torture and dismemberment of captured B-29 fliers. In Shimane Prefecture Hirano worked with the newly appointed American governor, translating orders to prefecture officials. And it was Hirano who interviewed Dr. Hideki Yukawa, the Japanese scientist who had spearheaded his country's effort to produce an atomic bomb.

When Gen. Hideki Tojo, Japan's wartime prime minister, tried to commit suicide, Harry Urasaki was assigned as his aide at an army field hospital. He bathed, fed, and interpreted for Tojo until the general's transfer to prison to await trial.

Arthur Komori, who had worked in the Philippines before the war as a U.S. undercover agent, was the first Japanese American of the Counterintelligence Corps (CIC) to enter Japan. Following Komori to Japan were approximately a hundred Nisei who had been trained by the CIC at Camp Ritchie, Maryland, and were assigned to every prefecture in Japan to maintain contact with officials of the Japanese government, police, and media.

Nisei of the MIS were spread throughout Japan with the Civil Censorship Detachment (CCD) to oversee censorship and to obtain civil intelligence information that would help the occupation forces to carry out their policies. The Press, Publication and Broadcast (PPB) Division of the CCD worked directly with the mass communication media, maintaining close contact with publications throughout the country.

MISers helped screen six million Japanese soldiers and civilians returning to Japan through four ports of entry, many in such deplorable physical condition that they had to be carried off the ships.

The Nisei also played a major role in screening Japanese repatriated from Russian prisons in Siberia, where approximately 700,000 Japanese soldiers (and some civilians) had been taken as prisoners of war. The object of the screening was to identify potential intelligence agents recruited by the Russians. Only about 350,000 of these Japanese prisoners were released. The rest were believed to have died during 1945–46.

Perhaps the most important contribution of the MISers to both Japan and the United States was the understanding they could impart to a conquered nation. They were able to help two disparate peoples work together toward the common goal of rebuilding a devastated land.

Then, five years after Japanese Americans of the Military Intelligence Service entered Japan, they would be off to Korea, to help MacArthur in another war.[5]

In Europe, the celebration of V-J Day brought another tribute to the distinguished record of the 100th/442nd Regimental Combat Team when it was selected to lead more than fifteen thousand American, British, and Italian troops in a victory parade through Leghorn. Despite the fact that most of the Nisei would soon be going home, they had a tremendous feeling of loss and sorrow as they watched the first of their comrades head for ports of embarkation. GIs who had seen friends killed, and had themselves faced death, wept as they said good-bye to men with whom they had lived in foxholes, shared a last bit of food or water, and endured a shattering cascade of enemy firepower. Ahead of them lay a new way of life still shadowed by the suspicions and hatred of those who refused to accept them as Americans.

On October 19, 1945, Maj. Mitsuyoshi Fukuda became the last member of the original 100th Battalion—the men whose courage at Monte Cassino had won America's first acclaim for Nisei soldiers—to leave Europe. Fukuda had gone from lieutenant to commanding officer of the 100th Battalion and then to executive officer of the 100th/442nd Regimental Combat Team to become the U.S. Army's highest ranking Japanese-American officer in Europe and the first Japanese American to command an infantry battalion.

The 100th/442nd was by then mostly draftees who had seen action only in the last months of war. They would remain in Italy to complete handling prisoners and to guard military installations. But they were to witness the highest honor the United States could bestow on their outfit when they finally brought the 100th/442nd Regimental Combat Team colors home to America.

CHAPTER 20

ECHOES FROM THE PAST

S
o the Nisei came home—the 100th/442nd Regimental Combat
Team from Italy, the 522nd Field Artillery Battalion from Germany, the Military Intelligence Service linguists from China,
Burma, India, Manchuria, London, Paris, the Philippines, little-
known islands in the Pacific, and New York and Washington, D.C.
Japanese Americans, newly graduated from the Military Intelligence
Service Language School, would replace some of the old-timers to
help General MacArthur in Japan.

A few of the 100th/442nd men—the "little iron men" of Europe—
wore their medals. Most, modesty prevailing, kept them in pockets and
backpacks.

The men from the Pacific who had labored over enemy maps and
diaries and battle orders soaked with blood or rain or mud, and the
men who, in far-flung parts of the world, spent thousands of hours
intercepting Japanese communications, returned to face a silence they
were forbidden by law to break until nearly three decades later. By
then, America's interest had passed them by as it focused on other wars.

For men with families still in internment camps, the first task was
to get them resettled—somewhere. It had been left to the War Relocation Authority (WRA) to work out plans to close the camps and try
to alleviate the distress of families, many of whose prewar properties
had been either destroyed by vandals or sold at such low prices that
they had inadequate resources to finance a new start on life.

Unlike others in Washington's ruling enclaves, Secretary Ickes and
Dillon Myer, chief of the War Relocation Authority, had been sympa-

thetic through the years to the plight of those in the camps. Within a week after cessation of hostilities in Europe, Ickes had released a statement to the press condemning "Nazi storm trooper tactics against loyal Japanese Americans and law-abiding Japanese aliens." Dillon Myer talked to people throughout the San Joaquin Valley of California, where many of the terrorist attempts against Japanese families had occurred. He also enlisted the help of decorated Nisei veterans and white officers who had fought with the 100th/442nd to lecture up and down the West Coast about the war record of Japanese Americans. In addition, the WRA had drawn up a plan to try to help those who had been incarcerated in the camps and now had to begin a new life.

Viewed in the light of history, the financial aid seems minuscule and the help piteously inadequate. Government officials had precious little understanding of the devastating hardships—moral and financial—that prisoners in the internment camps had suffered. Also, as yet undiscovered, was the fraudulence of the U.S. War Department in secreting from the Supreme Court of the United States evidence that pointed to racial bias, not military necessity, in putting all Japanese from the West Coast into internment camps. So a nation accustomed to other forms of racial prejudice could only believe that its government had acted correctly in sending one of its minorities into imprisonment. The Supreme Court had said so or, at least, had avoided denying it by clever judicial maneuvers. The fraud remained unknown for forty years—until discovered during research for the book *Justice At War* by Dr. Peter Irons, which states in its foreword:

> This documentary record reveals a legal scandal without precedent in ᴠhe history of American law. Never before has evidence emerged that shows a deliberate campaign to present tainted records to the Supreme Court.[1]

The facts, briefly, are these: By early 1943, three cases challenging the constitutionality of orders issued by Lt. Gen. John L. DeWitt, commander of the Western Defense Command, under Executive Order 9066 were pending before the U.S. Supreme Court. Specifically, the cases questioned DeWitt's military order, which sent everybody of Japanese descent from their West Coast homes into the camps, and a curfew order governing both foreign-born and American-born Japanese. The cases involved Minoru Yasui, a young lawyer from Oregon; Gordon Hirabayashi, a University of Washington student; and Fred Korematsu, a welder who wanted to get married and settle in California. (A fourth case, brought by Mitsuye Endo as a civil suit for habeas corpus, would reach the high court later.)

Yasui was born in Hood River, Oregon, graduated from the University of Oregon law school, and, through the reserve officer training program, had been commissioned a second lieutenant in the U.S. Army Reserve. To support himself while waiting for his bar examination, he worked for the Japanese consulate in Chicago, performing tasks requiring the use of English. His employment ended when Pearl Harbor was bombed. He reported for active duty at Fort Vancouver, Washington, but was ordered to leave the base. Angered, he decided to challenge the military's authority and deliberately violated the curfew order issued under Executive Order 9066 and Public Law 503, which required Japanese, German, and Italian aliens "and all other persons of Japanese ancestry" to be in their homes between 8 P.M. and 6 A.M.

Gordon Hirabayashi, a Quaker and thus a conscientious objector to military service, was arrested for violating the curfew regulation and the mandatory evacuation of persons of Japanese ancestry to a detention center where they were temporarily imprisoned before being transferred to internment camps.

Fred Korematsu's activities had not been intended to test DeWitt's military orders. He had volunteered for service in the U.S. Navy in June 1941 but was turned down when classified 4-F. To conceal his racial features he had undergone plastic surgery before evacuation orders were issued. When he did not report for evacuation, he was arrested.

To argue the government's side in support of Executive Order 9066 and Public Law 503 in these cases, Edward Ennis, a Justice Department lawyer, asked the War Department for any published material it might have regarding the military situation on the West Coast at the time of the 1942 forced evacuation of Japanese-descended residents.

Assistant Secretary of War John McCloy had received copies of General DeWitt's report entitled "Final Report, Japanese Evacuation from the West Coast, 1942." On reading the DeWitt report, McCloy discovered several points that he felt would jeopardize the government's cases:

1. DeWitt stated in the Foreword that he opposed, for the duration of the war, the return of Japanese Americans to the West Coast.

2. DeWitt claimed that it had been impossible to differentiate loyal from disloyal Japanese Americans, saying that "an exact separation of the 'sheep from the goats' was impossible." This, in effect, admitted that the War Department had relegated everyone of Japanese ancestry to the camps without any effort to distinguish loyal from potentially disloyal people.

McCloy decided that the "Final Report," as written, was damaging to the federal government's side in the pending Supreme Court cases of Hirabayashi, Yasui, and Korematsu, and he ordered that all copies of the report be removed from the War Department files and returned to San Francisco. He then instructed DeWitt to submit a revised version of the "Final Report" along with another transmittal letter. He also ordered that the galley proof of DeWitt's original report be destroyed.[2] In this way, McCloy was successful in concealing from the U.S. Justice Department (and, therefore, from the U.S. Supreme Court) evidence of racial prejudice in the military orders and in their execution.

The War Department's tampering with evidence in the Japanese-American cases remained hidden for nearly forty years—until a Japanese-American woman, Aiko Yoshinaga Herzig, discovered a copy of DeWitt's original version of his "Final Report" in a U.S. government file[3] and recognized the significance of the changes that had been made in its revision.

On June 21, 1943, the U.S. Supreme Court upheld a lower court conviction of Yasui for violating the curfew order, arguing that the army had authority to issue orders binding on civilians even in the absence of martial law. (The legality of the evacuation order to internment camps was not an issue in the Yasui case.) In the Hirabayashi case, ruling only on the curfew order, the Supreme Court found that a special danger existed; therefore, the army had the right to impose a curfew on persons of Japanese descent. The Supreme Court returned the Korematsu case to the court of appeals for further adjudication. Therefore, in this judicial round, the Supreme Court had escaped ruling on the legality of the order evacuating all Japanese-descended persons from the West Coast and sending them to internment camps.

On June 29, eight days after the Supreme Court decision was announced, a report from a War Department warrant officer stated:

I certify that this date I witnessed the destruction by burning of the galley proofs, galley pages, drafts and memorandums of the original report of the Japanese Evacuation.[4]

It would be one-and-a-half years before the U.S. Supreme Court decided the Korematsu case and the case of Mitsuye Endo, a civil service employee of the State of California who, along with all other California state employees of Japanese descent, had been dismissed following the Pearl Harbor bombing. After she was sent to an internment camp, a San Francisco attorney, James C. Purcell, filed a civil suit for habeas corpus in federal court in San Francisco, demanding that the government free her or show cause why she should continue to be held in custody. Her contention was that imprisonment had deprived her of her rights as an American citizen.

On December 18, 1944, the Supreme Court handed down its decisions on the Korematsu and Endo cases. In the Korematsu case, by a vote of six to three, the Court upheld the constitutionality of the wartime regulations under which American citizens of Japanese ancestry were evacuated from Pacific Coast areas. In the Endo case, however, the court ruled unanimously that Japanese Americans of unquestioned loyalty to the United States could not be detained in war relocation centers.

The Supreme Court had, in effect, ruled that convictions for violations of the restrictions in the Yasui, Hirabayashi, and Korematsu cases were criminal violations of military orders issued under Executive Order 9066 and Public Law 503, whereas Endo, who had not violated any military orders, was imprisoned in violation of her civil rights. In declaring that the War Relocation Authority could not detain admittedly loyal citizens against their will, the Court's decision opened the way for everyone of Japanese decent to leave the camps governed by the WRA and return to their West Coast homes.

The day before the decision was handed down, the War Department announced the revocation of the West Coast exclusion order against Japanese and their American-born children, to become effective on January 2, 1945.

Raymond Sadamune was serving with a MIS translator team in General MacArthur's battle to retake the Philippines when he heard about the Supreme Court decision overturning the WRA's right to intern loyal citizens. But his joy was short-lived. He also learned that his brother had been wounded in France during the battle to rescue the Lost Battalion.[5]

Some families were able to leave the camps right away. Others waited for family members serving with the MIS or in Europe with the 100th/442nd Regimental Combat Team to return from war and help them. Many would have to search for new homes and new jobs, and try to rebuild their lives as best they could, wherever they could. Their losses in 1942 dollars totaled $400 million, by conservative estimates. A 1948 attempt by Congress to settle their claims became so snarled that they finally settled for an average of ten cents on the dollar. In 1982 the Commission on Wartime Relocation and Internment of Civilians under Executive Order 9066 concluded that "race prejudice, war hysteria and a failure of political leadership" had led to issuance of Executive Order 9066, that no military necessity had justified it, and that $1.5 billion be appropriated for payment to the surviving victims. And on August 10, 1988, President Ronald Reagan signed into law a congressional act acknowledging "the fundamental injustice of the evacuation, relocation and internment" and making restitution of $20,000 to each of those of Japanese ancestry who were alive on the day the congressional act became law.

The executive and legislative branches of the U.S. government had acknowledged a national mistake.

Given the constraints of money, time, personnel, and understanding, the WRA, at war's end, made an effort—though inadequate—to meet the basic needs of an uprooted people.

In his letter to me, dated July 17, 1945, Dillon Myer wrote:

> We have recognized all along that many of the families now residing in relocation centers, including some of these with sons in the Army, would not be able to plan and carry out their relocation unaided. The closing of the [WRA] centers will not mean that these people will be thrust out with no place to go and no one to whom they can turn.
>
> On the contrary, we are doing everything we can to help each individual and each family to draw up its individual plans, on

the basis of adequate knowledge, and to supply the assistance which is needed in each case. . . .

Many evacuees, fearing West Coast reprisals, sought new lives in the East or the Midwest; ironically, this satisfied the desire of President Roosevelt to scatter the Japanese throughout the United States. For many, however, the West Coast had been home and that's where they wanted to go. Some soon learned that they still were not welcome there.

The story of Mitsuo Usui typifies the experience of many returning Nisei veterans:

> Coming home, I was boarding a bus on Olympic Boulevard [in Los Angeles]. A lady sitting in the front row of the bus saw me and said, "Damn Jap." Here I was a proud American soldier, just coming back with my new uniform and new paratrooper boots, with all my campaign medals and awards, proudly displayed on my chest, and this? The bus driver, upon hearing this remark, stopped the bus and said, "Lady, apologize to this American soldier or get off my bus." She got off the bus.
>
> Embarrassed by the situation, I turned around to thank the bus driver. He said: "That's okay, buddy. Everything is going to be okay from now on out." Encouraged by his comment, I thanked him and as I was turning away, I noticed a discharge pin on his lapel.[6]

Captain Daniel Inouye, passing through California on his way home to Hawaii, wanted to get a haircut. He was all spruced up in a new uniform and wearing his recently acquired artificial arm to replace the one he had lost at Colle Musatello. At a barbershop just outside San Francisco he was met on the doorstep by an attendant who told him: "You're a Jap and we don't cut Jap hair."[7]

Soldiers in American uniforms, and wearing decorations for valor in a war to protect the United States, were confronted with signs in streets throughout the West Coast: "No Japs Allowed" and "Whites Only." Working with the War Department and the War Relocation Authority, white officers returning from duty with the 100th/442nd spoke to audiences throughout the West Coast about the Nisei soldiers. One of these was Capt. George Grandstaff, a native Californian who had headed the supply team of the 100th Battalion, working with Nisei to get ammunition and food to soldiers on Italian mountaintops, in the forests of the Vosges Mountains, and in the snow-covered Maritime Alps of France. He told his audiences:

I came home to what I thought would be a land of the free, to a people I thought had learned from this war to respect the rights of fellow citizens, to a people who had, I thought, learned that racial discrimination and democracy don't jibe. And yet one of the first shocks that stabbed me in the stomach like a cold bayonet was to find racial prejudice and discrimination against the fathers, mothers, sisters, and kid brothers of men in my outfit. And I find this same discrimination against even the returned veterans themselves. I asked for and received orders from the War Department to speak on this subject. I don't know of anyone who has a better right to do so.

One night in particular [at Cassino] will always remain in my mind. Some forty enlisted men and I had picked a spot at which to meet at 2000. I was delayed by a persistent mortar barrage and arrived about three-quarters of an hour late. Instead of forty men there was only one. Upon questioning him, I found that the balance were up in that barrage hunting for me because they knew that I was alone. There are many fancy definitions of "loyalty" but when those men straggled in at dawn after an all-night search for me I needed no dictionary for my interpretation of the word.[8]

Loyalty and courage—the two outstanding characteristics of the Nisei soldier—both stemmed from their family values. Loyalty to their country, officers, and fellow fighters; courage, above all. Their families had warned them: come home dead, if you must, but do not bring us shame—*hagi*.

Ample testimony of their courage was the competition among American generals to have the Nisei under their commands and the Germans' fear of them. But, added to this, they were quick, they were smart, they took care of each other. Those who knew them best—the GIs who fought side by side with them—will tell you the Japanese Americans were the best assault troops in the U.S. Army. Some of those GIs could even get belligerent about it.

Technician 4th Grade Fred Yamaguchi of the 522nd Field Artillery Battalion found this out when he lost the Combat Team patch off his shirt while on pass in Brussels after V-E Day. He had walked into a bar, and two half-tipsy GIs from the 36th and 45th Divisions recognized him. They asked for his patch and finally ripped it off his shirt. With Yamaguchi's patch in hand, they went around the room asking others what outfit the insignia belonged to. After getting several vague answers, the two GIs exclaimed: "You know what this is? Goddamn you ignorant bastards. It belongs to the fightingest outfit in Europe, the outfit which rescued the only 'lost battalion' of this war!"[9]

Bill Mauldin, the *Stars and Stripes* cartoonist who created the beloved frontline infantry characters Willie and Joe, said it best, however, in his book *Back Home:*

> No combat unit in the army could exceed [the Japanese Americans] in loyalty, hard work, courage, and sacrifice. Hardly a man of them hadn't been decorated at least twice, and their casualty lists were appalling. And if a skeptic wonders whether these aren't just "Japanese characteristics," he would do well to stifle the thought if he is around an infantry veteran who had experience with the Nisei units. . . . When they were in the line, they worked harder than anybody else. . . . As far as the army was concerned, the Nisei could do no wrong. We were proud to be wearing the same uniform.[10]

So, as their reputation grew, the Nisei were pitched into some of the worst battles. It's not hard to understand why many of them have felt that they were considered expendable. The high esteem in which Generals Clark, Devers, Patch, and Tobin held the Nisei troops and their statements, both public and private, deny this. General Dahlquist, however, used the Nisei more ruthlessly than his own troops, pushing them into death traps, day after day, to reach the Lost Battalion of his 36th Division. Why he did this is a question that still troubles the Japanese-American soldiers who survived that ordeal.

After a half century, General Dahlquist remains a bitter memory among the Nisei. Others have excused Dahlquist, pointing out that he was very short on troops and under intense pressure from his superiors. The Nisei, however, will not easily accept the argument that Dahlquist used them as the best troops he had to rescue his Lost Battalion and thereby save his own military reputation. They remember, all too vividly, the hundreds of Japanese Americans wounded or killed in a battle to rescue 211 Texans who should not have been there in the first place.

Major General Jacob L. Devers, who commanded the Allied invasion of southern France, would never forget the Japanese Americans' contribution to getting Allied fighting forces through the Vosges Mountains and into Germany. After the war, as chief of Army Field Forces, he had this to say about the Japanese Americans:

> There is one supreme, final test of loyalty for one's native land—readiness and willingness to fight for, and if need be, to die for one's country. These Americans pass that test with colors flying. They proved their loyalty and devotion beyond all question. . . .
>
> These men . . . more than earned the right to be called just Americans, not Japanese Americans. Their Americanism may be described only by degree, and that the highest.[11]

Despite the praise of those who had fought with the Nisei soldiers and knew them best, some of America's political leaders were still steeped in racial prejudice. In the summer of 1946, I was standing two feet away from Sam Rayburn, the Texas Democrat who was Speaker of the House of Representatives, as he discussed with two men the possibility of statehood for Hawaii. I heard him tell them: "If we give them statehood they'll send a delegation of Japs here."

The statement stunned me. It had been less than two years since Japanese Americans had rescued the Texas Division's Lost Battalion. Certainly, I thought, even Mr. Speaker had heard about that! By the time Hawaii was eventually admitted to statehood and Daniel Inouye went to Washington as the first Japanese-American member of Congress, Rayburn must have changed his mind, for one reason or another. He personally welcomed the new member from Hawaii and also invited him to sit with the Texas delegation in the House chamber.[12]

The 100th/442nd Regimental Combat Team sailed into New York harbor on July 4, 1946, to be greeted by cheering crowds and by the New York Fire Department streaming arcs of water toward the SS *Wilson Victory*. The Nisei soldiers lined the rails and clustered around the smokestacks. Small craft, decked with streamers, went offshore to welcome them. On shore, crowds shouted and whistled and waved American flags. Some of us watched with tears in our eyes, happy to witness such a welcome, happy to see—once again—those Asian faces that had come to mean so much to us. In command of this last returning group of Nisei was Lt. Col. Alfred Pursall, the officer who had drawn his pearl-handled .45s and led his 3rd Battalion up Banzai Hill, the strategic point from which the final push to rescue that Lost Battalion would be launched.

From New York the Nisei went to Camp Kilmer, New Jersey, to be greeted by officials from Hawaii bearing hundreds of leis to decorate the returning soldiers. They remained there while plans were being made for their reception in Washington, D.C. The plans had not been completed when they reached the capital more than a week later, and they camped on Washington's steaming hot Anacostia Flats while the president's men concentrated on changing his schedule so that he could personally welcome them home. I remember Colonel Pursall striding up and down, waiting for the next message from the White House. We began thinking the president wouldn't make it, and that all our hopes and dreams had been foolish. Finally came the message that everything was "go." The president's schedule had been changed; he would welcome home the 100th/442nd men and their colors.

At last, on July 15—after a two-day wait—everything was in order. Government workers were granted an extended lunch hour so they could watch the parade along Constitution Avenue. They cheered and whistled and clapped hands as the Nisei stepped along, their banners streaming, behind a band playing Sousa marches. Their march ended on the green expanse of the Ellipse, which spreads between the White House and the towering Washington Monument. A driving summer rain had begun by the time they reached there, and their uniforms and regimental colors were drenched. Spectators huddled under umbrellas. Nisei amputees in wheelchairs and other Japanese-American veterans, patients from nearby Walter Reed Army Medical Center, waited along the edges of the parade ground. Colonel Pursall, his khaki uniform splotched black from the rain, nervously looked his troops over as they stood, at ease, waiting for the president of the United States. None of the men had ever seen an American president, except in pictures. Most would never again see a president of the United States in person. This was a moment in their lives to remember, and they snapped to attention as that doughty old veteran of another world war appeared.

With Colonel Pursall at his side, President Truman trooped the colors. Then he faced the men of the 100th/442nd to tell them:

It is a very great pleasure to me today to be able to put the seventh regimental citation on your banners.

You are to be congratulated on what you have done for this great country of ours. I think it was my predecessor who said that Americanism is not a matter of race or creed, it is a matter of the heart.

You fought for the free nations of the world along with the rest of us. I congratulate you on that, and I can't tell you how very much I appreciate the privilege of being able to show you just how much the United States of America thinks of what you have done.

You are now on your way home. You fought not only the enemy, but you fought prejudice—and you have won. Keep up that fight, and we will continue to win—to make this great Republic stand for just what the Constitution says it stands for: the welfare of all the people all the time.

Bring forward the colors.

With rain still beating down, Truman pinned the Presidential Unit Citation on the colors. The twins Conrad and Laverne Kurahara were in the color guard facing the president that day. I would not see them again until years later when we walked among the graves of our friends at Punchbowl—remembering. When the color guard was dismissed and the trooping was finished, the president walked to the side of the field where the wounded had been watching from wheelchairs, on crutches, happy to see an American president honor the colors they loved. He stopped to shake hands with Pfc. Wilson Makabe, veteran of the 100th Battalion, confined to a wheelchair because he had lost a leg fighting in Europe. And then the old warrior went on to shake the hands of the remaining sick and maimed veterans.

The men of the Combat Team were free to go home, having been honored by their country. Thousands of their fellow Nisei, however, the men of the Military Intelligence Service, would return home anonymously, never to receive the illustrious welcome given the 100th/442nd.

A few months later a writer for *The New Republic* journeyed to Hood River, Oregon, and wrote this report:

> If you had never heard of it before, you would have thought that Hood River was just another town, a quiet place sitting in a frame of mountains at the end of the winding loveliness of the Columbia River gorge. . . . Finally, you asked somebody where the courthouse was.
>
> Even in the dimness of twilight, you could see the freshly repainted names of the Nisei. . . . Shortly after November 29, 1944, when the names were wiped off, the Reverend W. Sherman Burgoyne, the Methodist minister, attacked the action as undemocratic and unchristian. . . . Letters poured in from all over and people asked what they could do to help.
>
> To each of them, Burgoyne sent this answer:
>
> "The battle for American decency happened to be here this year. We fought it and won. Next year it may be in your part of America and I'm counting on you to stand true."[13]

The Nisei did come home to Hood River, and Mamoru Noji was, at last, able to be with his family. He wrote to me:

> Unfortunately our war had not ended yet in Hood River. Prejudice was alive and rampant. . . . There was a coalition of sane people who befriended us. They were the true heroes of the period. Eventually sanity began to return to the valley. . . . We can look back and say, nevertheless, it has been a good life here in the valley. We can appreciate it all the more because we have seen the depths to which a war can bring even the most upright citizens.

Sagie Nishioka, the wounded 442nd Combat Team GI from Hood River whom I met in a Naples hospital, was transferred to Fitzsimmons Army Medical Center in Denver, Colorado, the military hospital nearest the Heart Mountain Relocation Center in Wyoming, where his mother, sister, and brother were interned. After sixteen operations he was able to walk again, though with a slight limp. After his discharge from the hospital he enrolled at Lewis and Clark College in Portland, Oregon, where he received a bachelor's degree; soon thereafter he passed the income tax auditor examination. He was placed on the "eligible list," but was turned down as an auditor because the state agency felt that some people who had lost their sons in the Pacific would not approve of dealing with him. This was a violation of the Oregon fair employment practice law, and he was, ultimately, accepted as an auditor.

He wrote me that his mother, brother, and sister had returned to their farm in Hood River, to the family home and the pear and cherry orchard.

The Nisei had come home, but wherever they had been in Europe they had left, among civilians, indelible memories of their kindness, generosity, and thoughtfulness. They were to become a legend in a corner of France: the little town of Bruyeres. Busloads of Japanese-American families come to Bruyeres, including grandchildren who never had a chance to know the Nisei grandfathers who fought or died there. They come to see the monument that the townspeople erected in honor of the Combat Team as evidence of their gratitude and lasting devotion to the men who freed them from the terrors of Nazi occupation. It had been a moment in life when love for fellow humans transcended race and creed.

A German soldier, Karl Schmid, also came to a Bruyeres reunion to thank the Nisei for treating him well when they had taken him prisoner. "I was captured by you near Biffontaine," he told the veterans and their families, "and was treated so humanely that in all the years that followed I never forgot you and always talked about you with my family. We always treasured the hope that some day we would meet you to thank you for our very existence."[14]

The great evergreen forests around Bruyeres have grown back, replacing the shell-shattered trees that fell during the battle to liberate the town. Shrapnel, a reminder of other days, remains buried in the trunks of those trees that survived. And children of Bruyeres still sing the Hawaiian song loved by many of their liberators, "Aloha Oe" (Farewell to Thee), as well as they sing the "Marseillaise."

Before the monument honoring the 100th Battalion in nearby Biffontaine, visiting veterans stand silently with their families, remembering the terrible slaughter when they were surrounded there by enemy troops.

And to Monte Cassino the widows, children, and grandchildren of that Original 100th Infantry Battalion come to read the words of remembrance on the memorial stone and to look up at the monastery window to see the Hawaiian chieftain's helmet and the taro leaf, which are emblazoned on the flag of the Purple Heart Battalion.

The Japanese Americans of World War II are also remembered at the 350-acre Defense Language Institute at the Presidio of Monterey, California, one of the largest and finest foreign-language teaching centers in the world. Its beginning was the Fourth Army Intelligence School class of sixty students who gathered in the decrepit converted hangar at Crissy Field in San Francisco thirty-six days before the Pearl Harbor bombing, to study the Japanese language, which they later used as a weapon in the war with which the United States was then threatened. As World War II progressed and demands for Nisei linguists streamed in from Allied combat zones throughout the world, the language school moved from one place to another—always a larger location—until, at the end of World War II, it was transferred to Monterey. Renamed the Defense Language Institute in 1963, it currently has a faculty of a thousand native-speaking instructors, teaching twenty-five languages and graduating an average of five thousand servicemen and women annually. In 1969 the institute dedicated Nisei Hall in honor of all Japanese-American soldiers of the Military Intelligence Service. And in 1980 it dedicated three of its important buildings in honor of outstanding Nisei linguists of the Military Intelligence Service who died in the Pacific during World War II: Nakamura Hall, in memory of Sgt. George I. Nakamura, killed on Luzon, Philippine Islands; Mizutari Hall, in memory of Sgt. Terry Mizutari, killed in New Guinea; and Hachiya Hall, in memory of Sgt. Frank Hachiya, killed on Leyte, Philippine Islands.

Subsequently, two buildings were named in honor of the men who headed the Military Intelligence Service Language School during that war: Col. Kai Rasmussen, commander, and Col. John Aiso, dean of academic training.

Among those honored in the U.S. Army Intelligence Hall of Fame is Lt. Col. Richard Sakakida, the Nisei who was imprisoned when Japan conquered the Philippines, and was tortured during his captivity, but who still managed to send enemy military information, via Filipino guerrillas, to General MacArthur.

They are old men now, those Japanese Americans who served in World War II. Their numbers dwindle every day as more die of old age or complications from battle wounds. And those who are left, and their children and grandchildren, still know the sting of prejudice. They are caught in a no-man's-land between America and Japan. To many Americans they remain "Japanese." And in Japan some of my friends have been treated as "inferior" Japanese—scorned as Koreans and Okinawans have been over the centuries. Yet they carried into battles of World War II the best inheritance from their immigrant Japanese parents: loyalty to the country of their birth. For the Japanese soldier that was Japan; for the Japanese-American soldier it was the United States.

The Allied victory in World War II was forged from the solidarity of Americans descended from nations around the world. They fought together, they died together, and the trophy they won was freedom from the domination of ethnic-oriented societies of other nations.

A Japanese-American GI captured by Germans answered the question "Why do you fight for the United States instead of Japan?" by saying: "I was born in America." He could still respect the Japanese culture and language of his forebears but he spoke English and wanted to be called "American."

German Americans who, during World War I, had suffered from anti-German feelings in the United States fought during World War II against German relatives to secure the democratic way of life they treasured in America.

Blacks, despite their desperate history of slavery, poverty, and discrimination in the United States, fought in their segregated units beside American whites to defeat a country ridden with ethnic hatred and persecution.

American Indians, though discriminated against throughout American history, stood shoulder to shoulder with other Americans against a foreign enemy, using their unique languages to protect American communications.

I have learned that we are dependent on each other, and that the future will be based on the ability of our diverse races, religions, and cultures to weave an understanding that will rise above inevitable conflicts. My Japanese-American friends have taught me this lesson.

APPENDIX

THE RECORD

100TH INFANTRY BATTALION AND
442ND REGIMENTAL COMBAT TEAM

Eight Major Campaigns In Europe
Naples-Foggia: 9 September 1943 to 21 January 1944, 100th Infantry Battalion
Anzio: 22 January to 5 June 1944, 100th Infantry Battalion
Rome-Arno: 6 June to 9 September 1944, 100th/442nd Regimental Combat Team
Southern France: 15 August to 14 September 1944, 100th/442nd Antitank Company
Northern Apennines: 10 September 1944 to 4 April 1945, 100th/442nd Regimental Combat Team
Rhineland: 15 September 1944 to 21 March 1945, 100th/442nd Regimental Combat Team
Central Europe: 22 March to 8 May 1945, 522nd Field Artillery Battalion
Po Valley: 5 April to 8 May 1945, 100th/442nd Regimental Combat Team

Seven Presidential Unit Citations
1. 100th Battalion, Belvedere, Italy
2. 100th Battalion, Biffontaine, France
3. 3rd Battalion, Biffontaine, France
4. Company F, 2nd Battalion, and Company L, 3rd Battalion, Belmont, France

5. 442nd Infantry Regiment (less 522nd Field Artillery Battalion), Gothic line (Italy)
6. 232nd Combat Engineer Company (attached to 111th Combat Engineer Battalion, 36th Division), Vosges Mountains, France
7. 2nd Battalion, Hill 617 (France) and Pariana, Italy

Decorations[1]

9,486 Purple Hearts
18,143 individual awards and decorations, including:
1 Medal of Honor
52 Distinguished Service Crosses
    100th Battalion, 26
    2nd Battalion, 16
    3rd Battalion, 10
1 Distinguished Service Medal
560 Silver Stars
28 Oak Leaf Clusters in lieu of second Silver Stars
22 Legions of Merit
4,000 Bronze Stars
1,200 Oak Leaf Clusters representing second Bronze Stars
15 Soldier's Medals
12 French croix de guerre
2 palms representing second croix de guerre awards
2 Italian crosses for military merit
2 Italian medals for military valor

MILITARY INTELLIGENCE SERVICE:

Where MIS Language School Graduates Served[2]

Sixth Army Headquarters
    New Guinea, Philippines

Eighth Army Headquarters
    New Guinea, Philippines

Tenth Army Headquarters
    Okinawa

I Corps Headquarters
    Luzon with Sixth Army

IX Corps Headquarters
Hawaii

X Corps Headquarters
Leyte with Sixth Army

XI Corps Headquarters
Philippines with Eighth Army

XIV Corps Headquarters
Solomon Islands, Philippines

1st Cavalry Division
Los Negros, Leyte, Manila

6th Infantry Division
Sansapor in New Guinea, northern Luzon

7th Infantry Division
Attu, Kwaialein, Leyte, Okinawa

11th Airborne Division
Leyte, Manila, Cavite

24th Infantry Division
New Guinea, Leyte, Corregidor, Verde Island, Mindanao

25th Infantry Division
Guadalcanal, New Georgia, Philippines

27th Infantry Division
Makin Island, Saipan, Okinawa

31st Infantry Division
Davao in southern Mindanao

32nd Infantry Division
Buna, Aitape in New Guinea, Leyte

33rd Infantry Division
Baguio in northern Luzon

37th Infantry Division
Munda, Bougainville, Lingayen Gulf, Manila

38th Infantry Division
Recapture of Bataan

40th Infantry Division
   Los Negros, Luzon, Panay Island in Philippines

41st Infantry Division
   Salamaua, Marshalls, Mindanao, Palawan

43rd Infantry Division
   New Georgia, New Guinea, Luzon

77th Infantry Division
   Guam, Leyte, Okinawa

81st Infantry Division
   Anguar, Peleliu, Ulithi

93rd Infantry Division
   Moretai Island, New Guinea, Philippines

96th Infantry Division
   Leyte, Okinawa

American Division
   Guadalcanal, Bougainville, Cebu Island in Philippines

Far East Air Forces Headquarters
   Okinawa, Ryukyu Islands

Fifth Air Force
   Philippines, Southwest Pacific area

Sixth Air Force
   Caribbean area, Calcutta

Seventh Air Force
   Headquarters in Marianas, covered Central Pacific

Tenth Air Force
   Headquarters in India, covered India-Burma area

Eleventh Air Force
   Headquarters in Aleutians, covered Northern Pacific

Thirteenth Air Force
   Headquarters in Southwest Pacific, covered that area

Fourteenth Air Force
Headquarters in Chungking, covered China

Twentieth Air Force
Guam, Mariana Islands

Language Centers
Allied Translator and Interpreter Section
Joint Intelligence Corps, Pacific Ocean Area
Joint Intelligence Collecting Agency, Southeast Asia
Translation and Interrogation Center, Sino Translation
Interrogation Center

Other Units
British, Australian, and New Zealand armies
Chinese Combat Command
Mars Task Force (Burma)
Merrill's Marauders (Burma)
MP detachments
Office of Strategic Services
Office of War Information
Pacific Ocean Area (JICPOA)
Pearl Harbor, Hawaii
Psychological Warfare
U.S. Marine divisions, including 3rd Marines, at Iwo Jima
United States Navy

ENDNOTES

Chapter 1: Pu'uloa Becomes Pearl Harbor
1. On August 10, 1936, President Roosevelt wrote Admiral W. H. Standley: "One obvious thought occurs to me—that every Japanese citizen or non-citizen on the Island of Oahu who meets these Japanese ships or has any connection with their officers or men should be secretly but definitely identified and his or her name placed on a special list of those who would be the first to be placed in a concentration camp in the event of trouble." Peter Irons, *Justice At War* (New York: Oxford University Press, 1983), 20; also Gary Y. Okihiro, *Cane Fires* (Philadelphia: Temple University Press, 1991), 173–74.

Chapter 2: Birth of the Legendary Battalion
1. Ted Tsukiyama, *Honolulu Star-Bulletin,* December 7, 1978.
2. *Puka Puka Parade,* May–June 1982, 58–59.
3. Ibid., 48.
4. Ibid., 56.
5. Ibid., 47.

Chapter 3: Nisei of the MIS
1. Richard Sakakida, personal communication.
2. Ibid.
3. Ibid.
4. Ibid.
5. Ibid.
6. Ibid.
7. Ibid.
8. Joseph D. Harrington, *Yankee Samurai: The Secret Role of Nisei in America's Pacific Victory* (Detroit: Harlo Press, 1979), 133.
9. Charles A. Willoughby and John Chamberlain, *MacArthur, 1941–1951* (New York: McGraw-Hill, 1954), 98.
10. Ibid., 98–99.

Chapter 4: The Killing Fields of New Guinea
1. Unless otherwise noted, all diary excerpts are from File NND745074, Boxes 278 and 279, National Archives Branch Depository, Suitland, Md.

2. Excerpts from Minoru Hara's notes are used with his permission.

Chapter 5: The Proving Ground

1. John Alfred Burden, letter to author.

2. Agawa Hiroyuki, *The Reluctant Admiral: Yamamoto and the Imperial Navy* (Tokyo and New York: Kodansha International, 1979), 328.

3. J. Alfred Burden, letter to author.

4. Edward J. Drea, *MacArthur's Ultra: Codebreaking and the War Against Japan, 1942–1945* (Lawrence, Kans.: University Press of Kansas, 1992), 73–74.

5. J. Alfred Burden, letter to author.

6. Harrington, *Yankee Samurai,* 109.

7. Mamoru Noji, letter to author.

8. Carroll V. Clines, *Attack on Yamamoto* (New York: Orion Books, 1990), 1.

9. Harold Fudenna, interview by Walter Tanaka.

10. Interview by author with Yukio Kawamoto.

Chapter 6: The Struggle Against Odds

1. Report of the Commission on Wartime Relocation and Internment of Civilians, *Personal Justice Denied* (Washington, D.C.: Government Printing Office, 1982), 189.

2. Ted Tsukiyama, *Honolulu Star-Bulletin,* December 7, 1978.

3. Bill Hosokawa, *Nisei: The Quiet Americans* (New York: William Morrow, 1969), 365–66.

4. Daniel K. Inouye with Lawrence Elliot, *Journey to Washington* (Englewood Cliffs, N.J.: Prentice-Hall, 1967), 53.

5. Ibid., 82, 86.

6. Ibid., 85.

7. Eric Saul, speech, Honolulu, March 24, 1984.

8. *Americans of Japanese Ancestry and the U.S. Constitution* (San Francisco: National Japanese American Historical Society, 1987), 54.

9. John Tsukano, *Bridge of Love* (Honolulu: Hawaii Hosts, 1985), 122.

10. Forrest C. Pogue, *George C. Marshall: Organizer of Victory* (New York: Viking Press, 1963), 147.

11. John H. Hougen, *History of the Famous 34th Division* (Nashville, Tenn.: Battery Press, 1949), pages are unnumbered.

12. 100th Battalion Journal, 16.

13. Hougen, *34th Division.*

Chapter 7: The Mountains of Italy

1. Associated Press, World War II (New York: Henry Holt & Company, 1989), 177.

2. John Ellis, *Cassino: The Hollow Victory* (New York: McGraw-Hill, 1984), 111.

3. Chester Tanaka, *Go For Broke* (Richmond, Calif.: Go For Broke, Inc., 1982), 28.

4. *Puka Puka Parade,* May–June 1989 (Honolulu: 100th Infantry Battalion Veterans Club), 50.

5. U.S. Army, "Salerno to Rome," Official History of the 100th Infantry Battalion (Separate), 2 September 1943 to 11 June 1944, Box 21085, Folder INBN, 100-0.3 (23473), National Archives Branch Depository, Suitland, Md.

6. Dates of the Volturno River crossings are based on the 100th Infantry Battalion journal and on *Chronology,* published by the Center of Military History, U.S. Army.

7. *Puka Puka Parade,* May-June 1982, 21.

8. Arnold Hiura, *The Hawaii Herald,* June 10, 1992.

9. Eric Sevareid, *Not So Wild a Dream* (New York: Atheneum, 1976), 366.

10. *Puka Puka Parade,* May–June 1982, 32.

11. Ibid., 32–35.

12. Ben Tamashiro provided information about "Turtle."

Chapter 8: The Purple Heart Battalion of Cassino

1. Fred Majdalany, *The Battle of Cassino* (Boston: Houghton Mifflin, 1957), 100.

2. Ellis, *Cassino,* xiv.

3. Otto Friedrich, "Monte Cassino: A Story of Deaths and Resurrection," *Smithsonian* magazine, 1987, 128.

4. Hougen, *34th Division.*

5. Majdalany, *Battle of Cassino,* 90.

6. Ellis, *Cassino,* 52.

7. Ibid., 62.

8. 100th Battalion Journal, 38.

9. Ibid., 39.

10. Ibid., 40.

11. Charlie Nishimura, personal communication.

12. Young Oak Kim, speech to 100th Battalion veterans reunion, Honolulu, July 3, 1982.

13. Arnold Hiura, *The Hawaii Herald,* June 19, 1992.

14. Kim, speech to 100th veterans.

15. *Puka Puka Parade,* April–June 1983, 10.

16. 100th Battalion Journal, 43.

17. *Honolulu Star-Bulletin,* February 29, 1944.

18. Ibid., February 24, 1944.

19. Martin Blumenson, *U.S. Army in World War II: Salerno to Cassino* (Washington, D.C.: Center of Military History, U.S. Army, 1969), 405–6.

20. Mark Clark, *Calculated Risk* (New York: Harper & Brothers, 1950), 323.

21. Ibid., 319.

22. U.S. Army, Mediterranean Theatre of Operations, Information Section, *The Story of the 442nd Combat Team* (Washington, D.C.: U.S. Government Printing Office, 1945), 13.

23. Majdalany, *Battle of Cassino,* 99.

24. 100th Battalion Journal, 46.

Chapter 9: Secret Warriors in Burma

1. Charlton Ogburn, Jr., *The Marauders* (New York: Harper & Brothers, 1959), 27.

2. Tad Ichinokuchi, *John Aiso and the M.I.S.* (Los Angeles: MIS Club of Southern California, 1988), 86–87.

3. Ibid., 87.

4. Richard S. Oguro, *Senpai Gumi* (privately published, 1990), 88.

5. Ibid., 89.

6. *Merrill's Marauders* (Washington, D.C.: Military Intelligence Division, U.S. War Department, 1945), 39–40.

7. Ogburn, *The Marauders,* 197.

8. *Merrill's Marauders,* 76.

9. Harrington, *Yankee Samurai,* 194.

10. Oguro, *Senpai Gumi,* 92–93.

11. John Costello, *The Pacific War 1941–1945* (New York: Rawson, Wade, 1981), 469.

12. Ogburn, *The Marauders,* 258.

13. Oguro, *Senpai Gumi,* 94.

14. Ogburn, *The Marauders,* 258.

15. Oguro, *Senpai Gumi,* 95–96.

16. Ogburn, *The Marauders,* 205–6.

17. Ichinokuchi, *John Aiso,* 196.

18. Oguro, *Senpai Gumi,* 87.

19. Ichinokuchi, *John Aiso,* 94.

20. Ibid., 197.

21. Ibid.

22. Harrington, *Yankee Samurai,* 357.

23. Ichinokuchi, *John Aiso,* 195.

Chapter 10: Anzio to Rome—and Beyond

1. U.S. Army, "History of the 100th," 48.

2. Martin Blumenson, *Mark Clark* (New York: Congdon & Weed, 1984), 391.

3. Associated Press, *World War II,* 191.

4. 100th Battalion Journal, 51–53.

5. Ernest F. Fisher, Jr., *U.S. Army in World War II: Cassino to the Alps* (Washington, D.C.: Center of Military History, U.S. Army, 1977), 179.

6. Associated Press, *World War II,* 14.

7. *Puka Puka Parade,* May–June 1982, 41.

8. *The Pacific War and Peace* (San Francisco: MIS Association of Northern California, 1991), 69.

9. Hougen, *34th Division.*

10. *100th Battalion 50th Anniversary booklet* (Honolulu: 100th Infantry Battalion Veterans Club, 1992), 129.

11. Orville Shirey, *Americans* (Washington, D.C.: Infantry Journal Press, 1946), 37.

12. Tanaka, *Go For Broke,* 168–69.

13. Report of the Commission on Wartime Relocation and Internment of Civilians, *Personal Justice Denied,* 260.

14. Shirey, *Americans,* 36–40.

15. *Puka Puka Parade,* May–June 1981, 5–6.

16. Ibid., July–August 1982, 8.

17. Blumenson, *Mark Clark,* 228.

Chapter 11: An Ocean Red with Blood

1. Associated Press, *World War II,* 196.

2. Costello, *The Pacific War,* 451.

3. Harrington, *Yankee Samurai,* 209–10; interviews by author.

4. Ibid.

5. Harrington, *Yankee Samurai,* 183.

6. Costello, *The Pacific War,* 484.

7. Carl W. Hoffman, *Saipan: The Beginning of the End* (Washington, D.C.: Historical Division, Headquarters, U.S. Marine Corps, 1950), 245.

8. Harrington, *Yankee Samurai,* 211.

9. Ibid., 212.

10. Ibid., 211.

Chapter 12: Forests of Death

1. Frank Gervasi, *The Violent Decade* (New York: W. W. Norton, 1989), 602.

2. U.S. Army, *The Seventh United States Army in France and Germany, 1944–1945* (Washington, D.C.: Government Printing Office, 1946), 363.

3. Ibid.

4. Shirey, *Americans,* 58.

5. Ibid.

6. Ibid.

7. Tsukano, *Bridge of Love,* 229, 237.

8. Ibid., 231–33.

9. Ibid., 246–48.

10. Ibid., 252.

11. *100th Battalion 50th Anniversary booklet,* 179.

12. Chris T. Shigenaga-Massey, "The Rescue of the Lost Battalion," *Honolulu* magazine, November 1985, 156.

13. Interview by author.

14. Ibid.

15. Shigenaga-Massey, "Rescue," 153.

16. Interview by author.

17. As quoted in Shigenaga-Massey, "Rescue," 153.

18. U.S. Army, "442nd Infantry Journal, 29 October 1944," Box 21253, Folder INRG-442-0.7 (23457), National Archives Branch Depository, Suitland, Md.

19. Billy Taylor, letter to author.

20. Chester Tanaka, letter to author.

21. *Honolulu Star-Bulletin,* December 10, 1987.

22. Tsukano, *Bridge of Love,* 268.

23. Interview by author.

24. *Congressional Record,* March 9, 1945.

25. Tanaka, *Go For Broke,* 103.

26. Tsukano, *Bridge of Love,* 268.

27. Kim, speech to 100th veterans.

Chapter 13: The Philippines Recaptured

1. *Beachhead News,* November 12, 1944, reprinted in the *Congressional Record,* March 9, 1945.

2. Costello, *The Pacific War,* 516.

3. *The Pacific War and Peace* (San Francisco: MIS Association of Northern California, 1991), 44.

4. Harrington, *Yankee Samurai,* 240–41.

5. Ibid., 247.

6. Oguro, *Senpai Gumi,* 88.

7. Notes prepared by Mrs. McKeown and loaned to author by Homer Hachiya.

8. Harrington, *Yankee Samurai,* 255.

9. Ibid.

10. Costello, *The Pacific War,* 521.

11. Harrington, *Yankee Samurai,* 170–71.

12. Ichinokuchi, *John Aiso,* 95.

13. Drea, *MacArthur's Ultra,* 130–31.

14. Sakakida letter to author.

15. Sakakida letter to Ted Tsukiyama.

16. Ichinokuchi, *John Aiso,* 125.

17. Ibid., 126.

18. Ibid.

19. Report of the Commission on Wartime Relocation and Internment of Civilians, *Personal Justice Denied,* 233–34.

Chapter 14: Caves of Hell
1. Associated Press, *World War II,* 271.
2. Bill D. Ross, *Iwo Jima: Legacy of Valor* (New York: Vanguard, 1985), 19.
3. Robert Sherrod, *On to Westward* (New York: Duell, Sloan & Pearce, 1945), 193.
4. Associated Press, *World War II,* 271.
5. Harrington, *Yankee Samurai,* 280.
6. Ibid., 175.
7. Ibid., 355.
8. Ross, *Iwo Jima,* 231.
9. Ichinokuchi, *John Aiso,* 197.
10. Ibid.
11. Harrington, *Yankee Samurai,* 277.
12. Costello, *The Pacific War,* 547.
13. Harrington, *Yankee Samurai,* 277.
14. Costello, *The Pacific War,* 545.
15. *The MIS Album* (Nashville, Tenn.: Battery Press, 1946), 115.
16. Harrington, *Yankee Samurai,* 282.
17. Ibid., 277.
18. Associated Press, *World War II,* 275.
19. Costello, *The Pacific War,* 547.

Chapter 15: The Champagne Campaign
1. Tanaka, *Go For Broke,* 111.
2. Ibid., 97.

Chapter 16: Germany and the Death Camps
1. Martin Gilbert, *The Second World War* (New York: Henry Holt, 1989), 657.
2. Robert H. Abzug, *Inside the Vicious Heart* (New York: Oxford University Press, 1985), 61.
3. Tanaka, *Go For Broke,* 117.
4. Tsukano, *Bridge of Love,* 389.
5. Daniel Valk, letter to author, March 7, 1991.

Chapter 17: Victory in Europe
1. *Puka Puka Parade,* May–June 1981, 6.
2. Tsukano, *Bridge of Love,* 217.

3. Ibid., 293.
4. Shirey, *Americans,* 83.
5. Ibid., 85.
6. Ibid., 97.

Chapter 18: Okinawa: Gateway to Japan
1. Costello, *The Pacific War,* 554.
2. Gilbert, *The Second World War,* 656–57.
3. Robert Leckie, *Delivered from Evil* (New York: Harper & Row, 1987), 877.
4. Tom Ige, *Boy from Kahaluu* (Honolulu: Kin Cho Jin Kai, 1989), 79.
5. Ibid., 74–75.
6. Ichinokuchi, *John Aiso,* 81.
7. Harrington, *Yankee Samurai,* 307.
8. Ige, *Boy from Kahaluu,* 80–81.
9. Karleen Chinen, "The Military Intelligence Service," *The Hawaii Herald,* July 2, 1993, 1, 10; Takejiro Higa, "Unforgettable Encounters: Battle of Okinawa" in *Secret Valor,* ed. Ted Tsukiyama (Honolulu: Military Intelligence Service Veterans of Hawaii, 1993), 101–102.
10. Harrington, *Yankee Samurai,* 309.
11. Ige, *Boy from Kahaluu,* 95.
12. *The Pacific War and Peace,* 56.
13. Ichinokuchi, *John Aiso,* 133.
14. Ibid., 132–33.
15. Harrington, *Yankee Samurai,* 329.
16. Ibid., 345.
17. Gilbert, *The Second World War,* 700.
18. Harrington, *Yankee Samurai,* 309.
19. Costello, *The Pacific War,* 578.
20. Ichinokuchi, *John Aiso,* 195.
21. Harrington, *Yankee Samurai,* 176–77.
22. Ibid., 357.
23. Gilbert, *The Second World War,* 452, 594.

Chapter 19: Pearl Harbor Avenged
1. Deborah Schapley, "Nuclear Weapons History: Japan's Wartime Bomb Projects Revealed," *Science* 199 (1978), 152–57.
2. Harrington, *Yankee Samurai,* 351.

3. Ibid., 353.

4. Ibid., 350.

5. *The Pacific War and Peace*, 72–80.

Chapter 20: Echoes from the Past

1. Irons, *Justice At War*, viii–ix.

2. Ibid., 210.

3. Ibid., note 56, Chapter 8.

4. Ibid., 211.

5. Harrington, *Yankee Samurai*, 307.

6. Report of the Commission on Wartime Relocation and Internment of Civilians, *Personal Justice Denied*, 259–60.

7. Inouye, *Journey to Washington*, 208.

8. *Pacific Citizen*, July 21 and August 11, 1945.

9. *High Angle* (weekly publication of 522nd Field Artillery Battalion), June 16, 1943, 3.

10. Bill Mauldin, *Back Home* (New York: W. Sloane Associates, 1947), 164–66.

11. Tanaka, *Go For Broke*, 171.

12. Inouye, *Journey to Washington*, 277.

13. Ralph G. Martin, *The New Republic* 115, (1946): 814–16.

14. Tsukano, *Bridge of Love*, 349.

Appendix

1. *Americans of Japanese Ancestry*, 68.

2. *The MIS Album*, 104–5.

SELECTED BIBLIOGRAPHY

Abzug, Robert H. *Inside the Vicious Heart.* New York: Oxford University Press, 1985.

Agawa, Hiroyuki. *The Reluctant Admiral.* Tokyo and New York: Kodansha International, 1979.

Allen, Gwenfread. *Hawaii's War Years, 1941–1945.* Honolulu: University of Hawaii, 1950.

Americans of Japanese Ancestry and the U.S. Constitution. San Francisco: National Japanese American Historical Society, 1987.

Associated Press. *World War II.* New York: Henry Holt, 1989.

Blumenson, Martin. *Mark Clark.* New York: Congdon & Weed, 1984.

_____. *U.S. Army in World War II: Salerno to Cassino.* Washington, D.C.: Center of Military History, U.S. Army, 1969.

Clark, Mark. *Calculated Risk.* New York: Harper & Brothers, 1950.

Costello, John. *The Pacific War, 1941–1945.* New York: Rawson, Wade, 1981.

Drea, Edward J. *MacArthur's Ultra: Codebreaking and the War Against Japan, 1942–1945.* Lawrence, Kans.: University Press of Kansas, 1992.

Ellis, John. *Cassino: The Hollow Victory.* New York: McGraw-Hill, 1984.

Fisher, Ernest F., Jr. *U.S. Army in World War II: Cassino to the Alps.* Washington, D.C.: Center of Military History, U.S. Army, 1977.

Frank, Richard B. *Guadalcanal.* New York: Random House, 1990.

Gervasi, Frank. *The Violent Decade.* New York: W. W. Norton, 1989.

Gilbert, Martin. *The Second World War.* New York: Henry Holt, 1989.

Griffith, Samuel B., II. *The Battle for Guadalcanal.* Philadelphia: Lippincott, 1963.

Harrington, Joseph D. *Yankee Samurai: The Secret Role of Nisei in America's Pacific Victory.* Detroit: Harlo Press, 1979.

Hoffman, Carl W. *Saipan: The Beginning of the End.* Washington, D.C.: Historical Division, Headquarters, U.S. Marine Corps, 1950.

Hosokawa, Bill. *Nisei: The Quiet Americans.* New York: William Morrow, 1969.

Hougen, John H. *History of the Famous 34th Division.* Nashville, Tenn.: Battery Press, 1949.

Hoyt, Edwin P. *Japan's War.* New York: McGraw-Hill, 1986.

Ichinokuchi, Tad. *John Aiso and the M.I.S.* Los Angeles: MIS Club of Southern California, 1988.

Ige, Tom. *Boy from Kahaluu.* Honolulu: Kin Cho Jin Kai, 1989.

Inouye, Daniel K., with Lawrence Elliot. *Journey to Washington.* Englewood Cliffs, N.J.: Prentice–Hall, 1967.

Irons, Peter. *Justice At War.* New York: Oxford University Press, 1983.

Layton, Edward T. *And I Was There.* New York: William Morrow, 1985.

Leckie, Robert. *Delivered from Evil.* New York: Harper & Row, 1987.

Majdalany, Fred. *The Battle of Cassino.* Boston: Houghton Mifflin, 1957.

Mauldin, Bill. *Back Home.* New York: W. Sloane Associates, 1947.

Merrill's Marauders (February–May 1944). Washington, D.C.: Military Intelligence Division, U.S. War Department, 1945. Box 169, Project 745074, National Archives, Suitland, Md.

Morison, Samuel Elliot. *The Two-Ocean War.* New York: Little Brown, 1963.

Murphy, Robert. *Diplomat Among Warriors.* Garden City: Doubleday, 1964.

Murphy, Thomas D. *Ambassadors in Arms.* Honolulu: University of Hawaii, 1955.

Ogburn, Charlton, Jr. *The Marauders.* New York: Harper & Brothers, 1959.

Oguro, Richard S. *Senpai Gumi.* Privately published, 1990.

Okihiro, Gary Y. *Cane Fires.* Philadelphia: Temple University Press, 1991.

100th Battalion 50th Anniversary booklet. Honolulu: 100th Infantry Battalion Veterans Club, 1992.

Pacific Citizen. Los Angeles: Japanese American Citizens' League.

The Pacific War and Peace. San Francisco: MIS Association of Northern California, 1991.

Pogue, Forrest C. *George C. Marshall: Organizer of Victory.* New York: Viking Press, 1963.

Puka Puka Parade. Honolulu: 100th Infantry Battalion Veterans Club, periodical.

Remembrances. Honolulu: 100th Infantry Battalion, 1992.

Ross, Bill D. *Iwo Jima: Legacy of Valor.* New York: Vanguard, 1985.

Schmidt, Dietmar. *Pastor Niemoellor.* London: Oldhams Press, 1959.

Sevareid, Eric. *Not So Wild a Dream.* New York: Atheneum, 1976.

Sherrod, Robert. *On to Westward.* New York: Duell, Sloan & Pearce, 1945.

Shigenaga-Massey, Chris T. "The Rescue of the Lost Battalion," Honolulu: *Honolulu* magazine 20, no. 5 (November 1985): 100–156.

Shirey, Orville. *Americans.* Washington, D.C.: Infantry Journal Press, 1946.

Tanaka, Chester. *Go For Broke.* Richmond, Calif.: Go For Broke, Inc., 1982.

The MIS Album. Nashville, Tenn.: Battery Press, 1946.

Tsukano, John. *Bridge of Love.* Honolulu: Hawaii Hosts, 1985.

Tsukiyama, Ted, ed. *Secret Valor.* Honolulu: Military Intelligence Service Veterans of Hawaii, 1993.

U.S. Army, "442nd Infantry Journal, October 1944." Box 21253, Folder INRG-442-0.7 (23457), National Archives, Suitland, Md.

U.S. Army, "Salerno to Rome," Official History of the 100th Infantry Battalion (Separate), 2 September 1943 to 11 June 1944, Box 21085, Folder INBN-100-0.3 (23473), National Archives Branch Depository, Suitland, Md.

U.S. Army, Mediterranean Theatre of Operations, Information Section. *The Story of the 442nd Combat Team.* Washington, D.C.: U.S. Government Printing Office, 1945.

U.S. Army, *The Seventh United States Army in France and Germany, 1944–1945.* Washington, D.C.: Government Printing Office, 1946.

U.S. Report of the Commission on Wartime Relocation and Internment of Civilians. *Personal Justice Denied.* Washington, D.C.: Government Printing Office, 1982.

Willoughby, Charles A., and John Chamberlain. *MacArthur, 1941–1951.* New York: McGraw-Hill, 1954.

INDEX